LONG SUFFERING

THEATER: THEORY/TEXT/PERFORMANCE

Series Editors: David Krasner, Rebecca Schneider, and Harvey Young
Founding Editor: Enoch Brater

Recent Titles:

Long Suffering

AMERICAN ENDURANCE ART

AS PROPHETIC WITNESS

Karen Gonzalez Rice

UNIVERSITY OF MICHIGAN PRESS

Ann Arbor

Published in the United States of America by the
University of Michigan Press
Manufactured in the United States of America
♾ Printed on acid-free paper

2019   2018   2017   2016   4   3   2   1

A CIP catalog record for this book is available from the British Library.

Library of Congress Cataloging-in-Publication Data

Names: Gonzalez Rice, Karen, author.
Title: Long suffering : American endurance art as prophetic witness / Karen
    Gonzalez Rice.
Description: Ann Arbor : University of Michigan Press, 2016. | Series: Theater:
    theory/text/performance | Includes bibliographical references and index.
Identifiers: LCCN 2016020070| ISBN 9780472073245 (hardback) | ISBN
    9780472053247 (paperback) | ISBN 9780472122332 (e-book)
Subjects: LCSH: Performance art—Themes, motives. | Arts, American—21st
    century—Themes, motives. | Art and religion—United States—History—21st
    century. | BISAC: PERFORMING ARTS / Theater / History & Criticism.
Classification: LCC NX456.5.P38 G85   2016 | DDC 700—dc23
LC record available at https://lccn.loc.gov/2016020070

Acknowledgments

Ron Athey, John Duncan, and Linda Montano have been remarkably generous in sharing with me their life stories, artworks, and archives. This book carries the traces of my time with each artist: cataloging books in Linda's hundred-degree attic, sharing a meal with John at a sidewalk café in Bologna, and drinking a cup of tea at the kitchen table in Ron's Silverlake home. I also thank Kristine Stiles for providing invaluable guidance and criticism. David Morgan, Rick Powell, and Tom Tweed offered crucial observations and lively discussions. Esther Gabara, Pat Leighten, Mark Antliff, and Caroline Bruzelius also contributed important insights.

Versions of my thoughts on these artists have been previously published. An early section of chapter 2, "Linda Montano and the Tensions of Monasticism," was included in *Beyond Belief: Theoaesthetics or Just Old-Time Religion?*, edited by Ronald R. Bernier (Eugene, OR: Wipf and Stock, Pickwick Publications, 2010), used by permission of Wipf and Stock Publishers (www.wipfandstock.com). Selections from my interview with Ron Athey appeared as "An Infection of Theology: An Annotated Interview with Ron Athey" in the online publication *E-misférica* 12, no. 2 (Winter 2016), used by permission of the Hemispheric Institute of Performance and Politics. Chapter 4 includes material from "'No Pictures': Blind Date and Abject Masculinity," *Performance Research* 19, no. 1 (June 2014), incorporated here with the permission of Taylor & Francis (www.tandfonline.com), and from "Cocking the Trigger: Explicit Male Performance and Its Consequences" in *Scenes of the Obscene: Representations of Obscenity in Art, Middle Ages to Today*, edited by Kassandra Nakas and Jessica Ullrich (Weimar: Verlag und Datenbank für Geisteswissenschaften, 2014) and used by permission of VDG Weimar. I am grateful to these editors and publishers, including Rina Arya, Ron Bernier, Nicholas Chare, Kassandra Nakas, Ann Pellegrini, and Jessica Ullrich, and to Rebecca Schneider, David Krasner, LeAnn Fields, and several anonymous readers for their thoughtful suggestions.

In addition, I extend my thanks to Tehching Hsieh, Bob Orsi, John Corrigan, and Frida Berrigan for brief but influential exchanges. Audience members at the National Gallery of Art, College Art Association, Association of Art Historians, Association of Historians of Christianity in the History of Art, and colleagues in the Connecticut College Department of Art History and Architectural Studies and in the Duke University Department of Art, Art History and Visual Studies participated in vigorous and helpful dialogues about my project.

The research and publication of this book have been generously supported by Connecticut College, particularly the Sue & Eugene Mercy Jr. Professorship, the Judith Tindal Opatrny '72 Junior Faculty Fellows Fund, the Dean of the Faculty, and the Department of Art History and Architectural Studies; and by Duke University's Franklin Hope Institute, Graduate School, and the Department of Art, Art History and Visual Studies. Anitra Grisales, Catie S. Anderson, Anique Ashraf, and Dakota Peschel assisted in the preparation of the manuscript. To everyone mentioned here and to those unnamed: thank you.

Contents

ONE

The Arc of the Moral Universe
Bends toward Justice

Endurance artists suffer. They practice self-discipline by testing their bodies' physical and psychic capacities, performing long-term actions, or submitting to pain or hardship. These performance strategies set the conditions for open-ended, ethically charged encounters between artists and audiences. From Chris Burden's *Shoot* (1971), in which the artist was shot, to Marina Abramović's *The Artist Is Present* (2010), a three-month-long action in which the artist lived publicly and maintained eye contact with a stream of individual audience members, endurance actions animate the most powerful and controversial artworks of the past fifty years.

Endurance art intensifies the defining characteristics of performance art, a post–World War II, post-Holocaust, post-atomic-bomb medium that presents the artist's body as a material of art. Performance artists offer their own bodies as artworks, refiguring traditional distinctions among artists, artworks, and audiences. The artist's body becomes the object of the viewer's contemplative gaze; at the same time, the artist remains the active agent of art making. In this way, performance art maintains the subject-to-object relation characteristic of traditional media such as painting and sculpture while simultaneously positing a subject-to-subject encounter. Art historian Kristine Stiles has elaborated the ethical nature of this dynamic interplay in performance art: "Performance posits an interpersonal visual aesthetic that asserts human exigency and agency at the center of the lived conditions of being."[1] Endurance art pushes these existential concerns to extremes. The artworks discussed in this book take place at the limits of the personal and the interpersonal, straining social relations and challenging definitions of art and of ethics. Linda Montano spent one year tied by an eight-foot rope to artist Tehching Hsieh in *Art/Life One Year Performance 1983–1984* (1983–84). In *4 Scenes in a Harsh Life* (1993–97), Ron Athey cut into a colleague's back and used paper towels to create blood prints from the wounds, igniting national debates over public arts funding. In *Blind Date* (1980), surely one of the most reviled artworks of the twentieth century, John Duncan

Fig. 1. Tehching Hsieh, Linda Montano, *Art/Life One Year Performance 1983–1984*. (Photograph by Tehching Hsieh, Linda Montano. Copyright © 1984 Tehching Hsieh, Linda Montano. New York.)

had sex with a corpse. These deeply troubling artworks clarify the stakes of endurance art: nothing less than survival itself.

Endurance art metonymically enacts survival through the practice of self-discipline. In response to profound suffering and marking the proximity of death, endurance artists set intentions, make decisions, train, form habits, and repeat actions. As bodily manifestations of irresolvable tensions—conflicting desires, competing needs, incompatible intentions, external pressures, unjust conditions—disciplined actions acknowledge the multiplicity of the self and visualize the marks of cultural authority and institutional power on the body. In *Long Suffering*, I insist on the reality of physical, psychological, existential, and other forms of suffering performed in endurance art actions.[2] In diverse endurance artworks ranging from Carolee Schneeman's *Up To And Including Her Limits* (1973–76) to Tracey Rose's *Span II* (1997) and from Sherman Fleming's *Something Akin to Living* (1979) to Kris Grey's *sub(Merge)* (2012), strategies of discipline signal endurance artists' attempts to visualize, legitimize, and testify to the conditions of suffering. Through self-restraint, repetitive work, self-denial, vulnerability, small- and large-scale risk taking, and other disciplines, endurance artists contemplate and confront death, but they are intensely aware of the limits of body and mind. Though profoundly difficult, and sometimes potentially dangerous, endurance art can be distinguished from suicidal actions. Thích Quảng Đức's tragic self-immolation in 1963 externalized suffering and demanded social justice—both important elements of endurance art actions—but at the cost of his life.[3] Endurance artworks retreat from that precipice, staving off death by setting the conditions for survival. The disciplined hardship an artist undergoes in these intense, painful actions testifies to the dramatic and persistent affect of trauma, which defies language and challenges knowledge itself. The endurance artist's performance of suffering and survival offers public testimony—nonlegalistic but nonetheless authentic—presented in good faith. As Jacques Derrida has observed, "Testimony does not consist in an experience of knowledge. Its act is not reduced to informing, teaching, making known."[4] Rather, its function is interrelational. Testimonies to the experience of trauma assume—and require—the encounter with witnessing audiences, present and future, absent or imagined. Through the intersubjectivity of testimony, endurance art constitutes witnessing publics, bringing together communities whose relations are as yet undetermined. Whether in person or through documentation, this encounter connects viewers in the moment of witness through the action of witnessing.

Audiences witnessing an endurance action enter an ethical zone of extremes. Foregrounding the enduring body, endurance art taxes viewers' visual and ethical stamina. Variously confrontational, painful, and monotonous to observe, endurance art presents a situation in which *something is wrong*.[5] The artist's testimony seems to demand a response, but endurance art catches observers in an aporic challenge, a double bind. Due to the interiority and isolation of traumatic experience, reparation is impossible. No reaction can provide succor or satisfaction; every offered response is always already inadequate. Rather than demanding specific action, the endurance artist's open-ended testimony invites ethical reflection, responsiveness, and responsibility.[6] In these subject-to-subject encounters, the extremity of endurance forces viewers to confront their own complicity in these acts and to consider their own bodily, emotional, and moral reactions and decisions. For example, during *Tompkins Square Crawl* (1991), as endurance artist William Pope.L crawled in the gutter wearing a suit, an outraged onlooker challenged him, prompting a productive conversation.[7] While witnessing Alejandra Herrera's *Domestic Labor* at the ANTI Performance Festival in Finland in September 2012, I and other observers were preoccupied with urgent questions. In this outdoor performance, the artist repeatedly plunged naked into icy water, and we wondered, Should I give my coat to this naked, shivering artist? Can I turn my eyes away? Endurance art asks witnessing audiences to stay with these uncertainties, to hold the tensions of performance in mind, and to respond with Derrida's notion of "the ultimate compassion . . . to be . . . the subject of the other, subject to the other."[8] Endurance art challenges audiences (in the moment and beyond it) to witness *without knowing how to respond*. The resulting inner conflicts and personal processes of decision making constitute the ethical habitus of contemplating endurance art. For audiences and artists, the open-endedness of these encounters resists redemptive or heroic resolutions; their ethical effects remain ambiguous.

Despite its aspiration to testimony in good faith, and perhaps due to the open-ended nature of its exchange, the pathos of endurance art often engenders confusion, horror, repugnance, derision, or fear.[9] These responses are bound up in concerns about human agency in the face of pathos and pathology. If these actions are grounded in pathology, how are they art? If endurance strategies react to trauma, are they simply compulsive rather than ethical? These important questions echo Aristotle's juxtaposition of ethos and pathos—a distinction between moral action and suffering, ethics and pathology, reason and passion—underlying western discourses of human agency. Endurance art radically collapses these familiar dichotomies. Through the mechanism of performance, the endurance artist presents the suffering body as both art-making subject (artist) and art object (artwork). The irresolvable tension between these roles fundamentally opposes the Aristotelian split between agentive subject and passive object. In the face of physical and psychic extremity, the endurance artist simultaneously embodies ethos and pathos, death and survival, vulnerability and discipline, victimhood and heroic agency. Both pathology *and* art, endurance actions respond to trauma *and* constitute ethical relations. This ethical project becomes particularly important in light of the persistent violence and oppression that constitute many individuals' experiences of the contemporary world. Trauma and pathology are foundational human experiences; as the writer Joyce Carol Oates has observed, "It seems disingenuous to ask a writer why she, or he, is writing about a violent subject when the world and history are filled with violence."[10] Endurance artists critically intervene in the moral universe by responding to suffering with opportunities for interrelational acts of testimony and witnessing—the preconditions for responsibility and, perhaps, social justice.

In endurance art, particularly in the United States, religions shape *how*, *what*, and *why* artists endure. Disciplined thoughts and actions, bodily practices, habits of thought, ritual patterns, and visual and verbal rhetorics of religions profoundly inflect the forms and meanings of the ethically charged encounter in endurance art. At first glance, this claim may appear strange. How can religious institutions and traditions influence avant-garde contemporary artists whose performances of trauma and survival seem to exceed the boundaries of conventional morality? Yet endurance artists work within, against, and through the historically contingent moral fields, discursive norms, social forms, and values established through the bodily inflected, meaning-making practices of religions. Though not in any absolute or original relation with ethics, religions are one powerful way in which communities, cultures, and nations construct and live their ethics.[11] For endurance artists, religious practices rehearse survival, model endurance, and offer modes for analyzing and judging the moral worth of actions. The forms and meanings of the artworks discussed in this book find their foundations in artists' early experiences of religion, from Montano's service as a novice at Maryknoll convent to Athey's virtuosity at Pentecostal healing revivals, and Duncan's meditation on Calvinist doctrines of human evil. These and other endurance artists frequently report deeply ambivalent or outright oppositional relationships to religion; their actions may fundamentally reimagine or seriously criticize the content of their religious traditions. Yet, even to its opponents and critics, religion supplies the terms and forms for serious dialogue about ethical life and justice.

SANCTIFY YOUR DISSENT

Sometimes oppositional and consistently calling for justice, strategies of endurance art in the United States participate in deep traditions of American prophetic religious discourse. With roots in interpretations of the Hebrew Bible that emphasize political and social justice, the American prophetic tradition since the eighteenth century has provided the means and justification for adopting oppositional political stances.[12] Political theorist George Shulman has identified prophets in this tradition as those who "testify to what they see and stand against it."[13] Witness, in this way, doubly consists of an encounter (observing) and the act of taking a stand (testifying). Since the 1980s, faith-based political stands of this kind usually have been associated with the Religious Right and political conservatism. However, religious responses to oppression, violence, and trauma also have driven the most influential radical liberal reform movements in American history. This historical imbrication of the prophetic tradition with radicalism in America has been well documented, especially as it has been mobilized and inflected across diverse American religious communities.[14] In the nineteenth century, the prophetic tradition produced such tenets of American radicalism as abolitionism and vegetarianism. In contemporary politics, this lineage endures with faith-based liberal activism in the New Sanctuary movement, prison reform, the Occupy movement, identity politics, civil rights issues from gay marriage to undocumented immigration, and in endurance art.

The strategies of survival, presence, and discipline that endurance artists deploy derive from American reformers in the prophetic traditions. Like war resisters, disarmament activists, and temperance agitators, endurance artists protest political and social trauma by connecting the cosmic with the deeply personal.[15] Using religious forms particular to their own histories and experiences, they testify to the persistent experience of trauma and create communities of witnessing audiences.[16] By performing survival, endurance artists echo reformers who prepared themselves to withstand violence in resisting public norms, in the words of Rev. Martin Luther King, Jr., "to accept suffering without retaliation, to accept blows from the opponent without striking back."[17] And finally, like nineteenth-century suffragettes and Salvation Army bell ringers, endurance artists demand an ethical response.

In the 1960s, King famously proclaimed, "The arc of the moral universe is long, but it bends toward justice."[18] His words echoed those of nineteenth-century abolitionist and Unitarian minister Theodore Parker, who described his vision of social justice in a sermon of 1853: "I do not pretend to understand the moral universe, the arc is a long one, the eye reaches but little ways. I cannot calculate the curve and complete the figure by experience of sight; I can divine it by conscience. But from what I see I am sure it bends toward justice."[19] Parker and King protested the lived realities of slavery and its legacies by connecting the act of surviving trauma to an empathetic, faith-based, moral act of visual projection. At the same time, they condemned cultural norms that obscured widespread complicity in perpetuating injustice, reserving special ire for religious communities whose complacency occluded moral responsibility; both Parker and King generated important texts in response to pastors who opposed them. Strategies of prophetic witness acknowledge more than one lever for moving the arc, more than one point of persuasion. This tradition of political discourse recognizes diverse possibilities for political action, from direct action and policy-oriented protest to consciousness-raising and simply holding space in which further political action can flower in the future.[20] Public memory of King has emphasized his legacy of legal reform, but years before his direct efforts to catalyze policy changes his prophetic witness to African American suffering raised moral consciousness and laid the ethical groundwork for civil rights.[21] This formulation of justice as religious rather than legalistic is, like testimony, interrelational, a "bending toward."

Recognizing the relationship between endurance art and the American prophetic tradition brings into focus the devastating political critiques embedded in these performances. Endurance artists testify to real conditions of life, building the moral foundations for future change. Their self-disciplined actions hold space, raising moral consciousness around matters of common concern to address overlapping vectors of identity and injustice. For example, in 1979–80 Mierle Laderman Ukeles shook hands with each of the 8,500 sanitation workers in New York City; she wrote, "I call the performance TOUCH SANITATION, a maintenance ritual act, celebrating daily survival. To each man I said, 'Thank you for keeping New York City alive.'"[22] In a series of performances titled *My Calling (Card) #1* (1986–90), Adrian Piper distributed cards calling attention to racist, sexist behavior that occurred in her presence.[23] Endurance artists' political claims, their acts of bearing witness, critically inform the meaning of their testimonies and sharpen their ethical demands. In this way, endurance art in the United States contributes to the ongoing hard work of social justice by bending the arc of the moral universe and looking beyond the horizon. *Long Suffering* theorizes endurance art as a contemporary iteration of progressive American prophetic witnessing. In the traumatic origins, theological content, and ethical demands of their artworks, endurance artists carry on the work that religiously motivated American reformers have been doing since the eighteenth century. In this book, I explore how endurance artists Linda Montano, Ron Athey, and John Duncan have inherited and inhabited the practices of American prophetic traditions. Many American endurance artists could have been discussed in *Long Suffering*—Chris Burden, Guillermo Gómez Peña, James Luna, Paul McCarthy, Ana Mendieta, William Pope.L, and Barbara T. Smith, to name just a few—but the endurance artworks of Montano, Athey, and Duncan provide particularly instructive iterations of prophetic witness. I maintain a narrow focus on these three artists to allow space for substantial, in-depth, multidisciplinary analysis of the interaction of religions and trauma in their work.

The visual forms and ethical content of Montano's, Athey's, and Duncan's performances draw on the intellectual, aesthetic, and bodily traditions of their religious backgrounds and on intensely sense-based modes of traumatic representation. Their artworks are rooted in the bodily worship practices and the visual, aural, and theological conditions of their childhood religious faiths: Catholic, Pentecostal, and Calvinist, respectively. In limiting my investigations to these American Christian traditions, I seek to clarify the place of endurance art in the lineage of prophetic witnessing in the United States, which historically has correlated directly, but not exclusively, with Christianity. Born between the 1940s and the 1960s, this transgenerational set of artists represents a range of Christian traditions in the United States: the liturgical rituals and daily disciplines of Montano's Catholicism; Athey's improvisational, charismatic Pentecostal healing revivals; and mainstream Protestantism in the form of Duncan's Calvinist Presbyterianism. These artists' current relationships with these religious institutions range from bitter rejection (Duncan) to daily devotional practice (Montano), but all three acknowledge and insist on the importance of religion in their work. At the same time, each of these artists struggles with the persistent affect of trauma. Montano, Duncan, and Athey have experienced the extremity of overwhelming life experiences. As survivors of a diverse set of traumas, from domestic violence to sexual assault, these artists face the daily difficulties of posttraumatic affect. Their artworks directly testify to their endurance of the psychic threat of traumatic events. Their performances index the continued, intrusive presence of trauma with the visual marks of various posttraumatic responses, including dissociation, nonsuicidal self-injury, and cyclical revictimization. Through endurance, these artists condemn the social conditions that generate trauma; with the visual languages of their theological traditions, they sanctify their dissent.

Little existing scholarship or criticism attends to these concerns. Of the three artists discussed in this book, only Montano has received substantial critical attention, especially from feminist art historians.[24] Until recently, few scholars or critics had written serious accounts of Athey's work, while Duncan's art has been thoroughly neglected.[25] Neither religions nor trauma figure prominently in scholarly discussions of these artists' performances. When art historians and critics have mentioned these subjects, they have employed the religious and traumatic terminologies without historical specificity. As a result, even the most important scholarship on these artists has neglected, inadequately explored, misunderstood, or subsumed the interconnection of religions and trauma into other considerations of identity.[26] Other discussions have sensationalized these endurance performances by focusing on their violence, nonnormative sexuality, distressing content, or even eccentric humor.[27] *Long Suffering* counters these discourses by analyzing the visual forms of these artists' performance works in relation to their biographies, religious histories, and intellectual and theological foundations and by identifying the overarching prophetic sources of their practices. While rooted in traditional art historical methodologies, my research dialogues with art history, religious studies, American studies, and trauma studies. In recognition of the multidisciplinary ambitions of the book, and assuming an art historical audience familiar with the scholarship of contemporary art in general and performance art in particular, here I focus on briefly clarifying the terms and relevant debates in religious studies and in psychology and psychiatry, which inform my approach to trauma studies.

RECUPERATING RELIGION

Despite a tradition of attention to religious iconography, religious practice, and religious representation in the scholarship of art historians from Giorgio Vasari and Erwin Panofsky to Roberta Gilchrist, religion is a touchy subject for contemporary art historians.[28] Many cosmopolitan academics, including contemporary art historians, manifest a deeply entrenched distrust of religions—a pervasive attitude that is rooted in the academy's long-standing commitment to secular modernity. Mid-twentieth-century formulations of the secularization thesis predicted that modernization had initiated the privatization, marginalization, and eventual decline of religions.[29] In this view, religion is a singular, static, and institutionally bound phenomenon that is separable from other aspects of life.[30] This formulation of religions relegates them to the realm of the personal, circumscribing religious practices from and rendering them irrelevant to intellectual activity.[31] These ideas can be traced to Enlightenment-based definitions of religion as personal belief and opinion, which deemphasize it as a meaningful subject of representation or public discourse. At the same time, recent and ongoing political tensions and acts of political violence have highlighted the relationship between religious practice and conservative political ideologies, both domestically and abroad. From a secularization-thesis point of view, these developments may appear both puzzling and threatening to the democratic public sphere.

Critics of the secularization thesis, including sociologist José Casanova and religious studies scholar Mark C. Taylor, have argued that turn-of-the-century history—from the US culture wars in the 1980s to tensions in the Middle East—have revealed the inadequacy of the secularization thesis to describe or understand the role of religion in the twentieth and twenty-first centuries.[32] Yet, for many contemporary academics, especially those influenced by Marxism, believers' passionate attachments to religious experience, religious ideology, or related moral values or ethical codes all signal an embarrassing earnestness, naïveté, or antimaterialism.[33] Individuals' and communities' religious commitments seem to conflict with attitudes of critical distance in academic circles, particularly in the contemporary art world. Faced with religious content in contemporary art, many invoke Freud's late-career characterization of religion as illusion or Marx's aphorism that religion is "the opium of the people."[34] Applied to such topics as race or sexuality, these simplistic and essentializing premises would be untenable, yet they continue to figure prominently in academic discourses. Since 9/11, these tendencies have intensified. In scholarly and public discourses, many theorists and commentators make assumptions about the meanings and implications of religious extremism—and religious devotion—with little or no explanation or research.[35] Further, in the field of contemporary art history, attention to religions unsettles disciplinary boundaries. Art historian David Morgan has observed that the multidisciplinary skills necessary for interpreting religion in works of contemporary art "far excee[d] the narrower and more defensible boundaries of formalist art criticism, knowledge of artists and their works," and other art historical competencies.[36] By delineating disciplinary boundaries that exclude religion, art historians reinforce these areas of expertise. In the process, important artists, histories, and visual discourses have been overlooked, misunderstood, or subsumed.

Long Suffering intervenes in these prevailing attitudes to recuperate religion as a crucial area of contemporary art historical concern. I follow current theorizations in religious studies to emphasize the historical, theological, material, and psychological contexts of artists' spiritual biographies. This view moves beyond symbolism and iconography to encompass broad aspects of lived religion, including emotional, social, cultural, structural, material, and mental practices.[37] I also highlight the importance of theology in identifying religious practice as a rigorous, intellectual endeavor with serious and enduring consequences in these artists' aesthetic practices. Although I engage with theology in history, I follow most religious studies scholars in refraining from doing theology or biblical exegesis. My attention to historical particularity and subjectivity counters generalizing tendencies in attitudes toward religions in art history and performance studies. Similarly, while most art historical and performance studies scholarship locates endurance art within cosmopolitan, transnational dialogues, my American studies perspective brings a nuanced view of the way religions have shaped American intellectual history and culture. The embodied and intellectual practices of American prophetic witness are necessarily deeply local and informed by national mythologies, embodied regional histories, particular congregational practices, and rhythms of family life. As a result, my theory of prophetic witness is historically specific to American endurance art. Issues of religions, trauma, and dissent do resonate with global endurance actions, for example, by the Viennese Action artists, Orlan, Regina José Galindo, Teresa Murak, Zhang Huan, and others, but their subjective, regional, and historical circumstances inflect their gestures differently.[38]

Studied together, the performances of Athey, Montano, and Duncan suggest a network of relations among art and religions linked by and manifested in endurance. Religion has functioned typologically in these artists' pieces, signing, mimicking, echoing, speaking, manifesting, protesting, healing, suffering, and testifying to religious experience while simultaneously confronting the loss and pain of persistent trauma. Athey, Montano, and Duncan diverge in life experiences, religious affiliations, and aesthetics, but each has used the visual languages and theological content of specific American Christian traditions to grapple with traumatic experiences in their performances. For Athey, Montano, and Duncan, their childhood religious traditions—including church organizational structures, Sunday school strategies, assumptions about human nature, child-rearing practices, and cultures of authority in these particular Christian communities—deeply imprinted their religious experiences as well as the forms and content of their artwork.

Long Suffering explores these artists' specific experiences of religions in relation to the ambiguous and shifting dynamics of their families and communities, the particular settings of a pre–Vatican II Maryknoll convent in upstate New York (Montano), 1970s tent revival meetings in Southern California (Athey), and post–World War II era reflections on human evil at a family church in Wichita, Kansas (Duncan). At the same time, rather than purely expressing a single Christian denomination, all three artists have appropriated and mixed western and nonwestern religious imagery, forms, and content. Always a hallmark of American religious practice, this type of religious improvisation reflects the changing status of religious institutions in the American Cold War context, when shifts in economic expectations, social norms, and cultural values placed religious denominations in the United States under stress.[39] As a result, these artists were exposed to multiple and contradictory religious, cultural, and countercultural influences that, in combination with their primary church affiliations, shaped their religious sensibilities. For example, after her time in a Catholic convent,

Montano lived in a Zen monastery and later traveled to India to work with a guru. While I do call attention to the complexities of these artists' religious participation, each chapter remains focused on their primary Christian affiliations in order to clarify prophetic witness in their work. Their enduring habits of faith, across faith traditions, are visualized in their endurance performance sufferings and their embodied means of highlighting and agitating against injustice. This crucial influence suggests that questions of religions remain critical for the interpretation of contemporary art beyond endurance art. Just as medieval, Renaissance, and Baroque art historians routinely excavate the religious meanings, contexts, and implications of their objects of study, contemporary art historians must take seriously artists' religious commitments and the historical religious discourses in which art practices are embedded.

VISUALIZING TRAUMA

Psychoanalysis has provided the theoretical framework for most examinations of visual expressions of trauma, including endurance art. This approach has yielded important work such as Kathy O'Dell's *Contract with the Skin*.[40] However, I am troubled by the "phantasy" at the root of psychoanalytic views of trauma. Freud located trauma in the mind, in the imagined fulfillment or frustration of unconscious desires, as he argued, "Neurotic symptoms were not related directly to actual events but to wishful phantasies."[41] I am concerned that in following Freud, psychoanalytic approaches to trauma studies undermine the real experiences of trauma survivors by, for example, figuring trauma as metaphor. Endurance artists work in the medium of endurance art—an art form that both presents and re-presents the lived effects of trauma—precisely because metaphor is inadequate in communicating trauma's impact. Challenged by the materiality of suffering in endurance art, I insist on the subjective reality of trauma and the posttraumatic experience. To this end, my work draws on contemporary clinical psychology and psychiatry, disciplines that recognize trauma as originating in lived experience.

In *Long Suffering*, I reimagine trauma studies in dialogue with psychology and psychiatry. What questions might trauma studies address if rooted in history, in lived experience, rather than phantasy?[42] Humanities scholars may express reservations about the perceived inflexibility of scientific knowledge and question its relevance in the context of the humanities and the arts. However, this view overlooks the agility, creativity, and subjectivity fundamental to contemporary scientific inquiry, as well as the ongoing disciplinary revision that takes place through debates within scientific communities. As the daughter of a research psychologist, I respond to psychology and psychiatry as creative, generative disciplines. Clinical studies, new research on neuropsychopharmacology and behavior, and debates about revisions of classifications in the most recent *Diagnostic and Statistical Manual of Mental Disorders* (*DSM*) fuel my critical theory imagination. Just as psychoanalysis has served as a productive and suggestive source for many scholars, I use paradigms of psychology and psychiatry as sources for my critical work. From Robert Jay Lifton and Judith Herman to James Chu, researchers and mental health professionals have theorized the complexities of trauma and created postmodern recovery models that are critical of institutions and the *DSM*. While I have consulted with mental health professionals in the course of my research, my implementation of their ideas diverges from traditional uses of psychology and psychiatry. I am neither a psychologist nor a psychiatrist, and my work does not intend to diagnose or address treatment issues, nor does it seek to contribute to dialogues about mental health in psychology or psychiatry. Further, rather than drawing on science as a claim to authority, I assume that the scientific research discussed in this book will change; in fact, it is a tenet of scientific inquiry that this knowledge *will* undergo revision and refutation. Taking seriously the ongoing insights of these disciplines opens new possibilities for making sense of the challenges of endurance art.

The theological claims and radical moral demands of endurance art visualize and embody profound suffering. For psychiatrist Robert J. Lifton, the survivor of trauma "has come into contact with death in some bodily or psychic fashion and has remained alive."[43] These encounters with death may include sudden catastrophes such as rape, accidents, or natural disasters; long-term abuses such as captivity, domestic violence, or incest; social settings such as homophobia, the legacy of slavery, or political persecution; and many other situations. While living within and through traumatic events, survivors may feel that they have stepped aside, that this violation or violence is happening to someone else. During traumatic events, chemical processes at work in the brain may alter or block normal processes of memory creation.[44] Trauma distorts the integrative means of building memory, which rely on verbalization and symbolic association. Instead, the brain registers trauma through the senses. Traumatic memory, then, is highly resistant to language and narration; it rests, rather, in bodily sense perceptions.

Psychologist Nanette C. Auerhahn and psychiatrist Dori Laub, post-

Holocaust specialists, have argued that trauma takes place "with no experiencing 'I.'"[45] Deferring experience in this way allows for psychic survival, but it also splits the self and creates a void, an experiential knowledge that cannot be fully integrated into the narrative of one's whole self, cannot be accessed through normal channels of memory, and thus must remain obscure even to oneself.[46] Survivors may experience a wide range of traumatic affects, including vivid, intrusive, and fragmentary images or memories; feelings of disintegration of one's identity; and a sense of drastic disconnection from the self. Survivors may turn their rage and anger on themselves in attempts to relieve unbearable feelings through nonsuicidal self-injury, or they may repeat their traumatic experiences in their behavior by taking risks or victimizing themselves or others. Intrusion, dissociation, reenactment, and other posttraumatic responses may be frequent or rare, immediate or delayed, temporary or prolonged, or may not manifest at all. The *DSM*—a document used by insurers as well as clinicians—lists some of these responses as stand-alone conditions; others are collected and together considered symptoms of post-traumatic stress disorder (PTSD). While research on PTSD has informed my work, in *Long Suffering* I avoid the language of PTSD because it indicates a particular diagnosis, a specific billable code in the *DSM*, and because it consists of a quite broad set of symptoms, affects, and behaviors. Instead, I privilege research relevant to each artist's narratives and actions: particular contexts of trauma, such as sexual assault and domestic violence; and specific posttraumatic responses, including dissociation (Montano), nonsuicidal self-injury (Athey), and cyclical victimization (Duncan). My discussion of these responses is by no means exhaustive; other behaviors and affects—intrusion and hypervigilance, for example—may resonate with the performances of other endurance artists. *Long Suffering* addresses those responses that contribute most to witnessing the expression of trauma in the endurance actions of Montano, Athey, and Duncan.

As expressions of traumatized subjectivities, representations of trauma in images and actions themselves carry the markers of the behaviors and symptoms of traumatic subjectivities.[47] As a result, endurance artists' expressions of posttraumatic behaviors such as dissociation and reenactment function not only as symptoms or presentations of trauma but as traumatic representations. The complexity of these ideas, as well as overlapping language in the context of performance art, requires making careful distinctions among the related concepts of representation, presentation, and representation. Art historian Kristine Stiles has identified both representation and presentation as important operations of the medium of performance art: "As representation, performance remains an aesthetic object of contemplation. But as presentation, performance exhibits actual subjects who associate with viewers in a subject-to-subject relationship."[48] As a performance artist, then, one both mimetically *represents*—exists as an art object—and actively and interactively *presents*—enacts—oneself as an art-making subject. These two concepts function concurrently in performance art, which exists "simultaneously [as] a presentation and a representation, presented and represented in real time. . . . Performance art both *is* and is a representation *of*, life itself."[49] In the context of posttraumatic discourses, artists may re-present their experiences as art; re-presentation connotes the conscious or unconscious visual repetition of traumatic content.

Although biography has been criticized as contributing to the construction of a canon in art history, these artists have insisted on autobiography as a critical element of their work, and *Long Suffering* relies on their autobiographical interviews, written texts, art objects, and performances. I spoke with Montano, Athey, and Duncan about their lives and artworks at their homes and studios. In our discussions—documented in audio recordings and written notes—and e-mail correspondence continuing to the present, these artists have actively shared their personal narratives, often volunteering sensitive information about their lives and work. Aware that my research would be published, they intentionally contributed to the creation of a historical archive about themselves and their art. Their courageous commitment to the public dissemination of this information highlights their perception of its importance to the legacy of their endurance art. At the same time, the precarity of traumatic memory complicates my use of artists' narratives as key sources. In response, *Long Suffering* deliberately foregrounds survivors' verbal, visual, and performative accounts of their lives, privileging their own subjective experiences of trauma. Rather than discerning the particular historical accuracy of these artists' autobiographical narratives, I consider their testimonies not as fact but as representation. Athey has described performing endurance art and narrating autobiography as simultaneous activities crucial to his praxis: "I decided [I would be] sincerely telling my biography to make sense of why I was making the work. I decided to continue doing that even though I saw people not wanting to be known as an HIV-positive artist, not wanting to be known as an 'I'm telling my story' artist."[50] In telling endurance artists' stories, *Long Suffering* also limns my own autobiography. As the only child of a trauma survivor, since childhood I have enacted the role of witness to traumatic narratives: visual, verbal, and somatic; direct and indirect; conscious and unconscious. In this book, then, I attend to the needs of survivors, and I continue to perform as listener and witness to the lived reality, everyday implications, search for moral meaning, and calls for justice embedded in representations of trauma.

DO WE LOOK, OR DO WE LOOK AWAY?

The artworks discussed in *Long Suffering* demand an ethical response. Athey, Montano, and Duncan present extreme, sometimes abject actions that initially may appear inexplicable, even disgusting. When survivors represent trauma, verbally or in images or actions, their expressions may register with others as hyperbole. Not only do traumatic experiences exist so far outside the realm of ordinary experience that they seem disconnected from reality, but actually speaking about, showing, or admitting trauma can be a transgressive act. As such, representations of trauma often seem to inspire shock, fear, and even disgust among witnesses to traumatic testimony. As psychologist Ann Scott has observed, "Something unthinkable is seen to have been thought; and, because it is seen as the unthinkable, its expression in words is met with aggression."[51] As profoundly visceral markers of suffering, endurance artists' performances frequently encounter this type of aggressive rejection. Viewers may dismiss these artists and their work as sensationalizing, attention seeking, and perverse. The very vividness of traumatic representation suggests spectacle, and in an age of Photoshop, green screens, and YouTube stunts, audiences may approach these performances with skepticism, considering traumatic testimony intentionally exaggerated and overstated. At the same time, many readers, particularly those who have experienced traumatic events, may find the performances described and reproduced in this book to be extremely disturbing. These endurance actions may invoke discomfort, shock, disbelief, and fear, generating a powerful urge to look away. How do we, as viewers of these artworks and readers of this text, respond to these challenging representations? In the face of profound suffering, and aware of the desire not to see, what are our responsibilities? Do we look, or do we look away?

The chapters in this book present artworks that generate this tension between looking and looking away, addressing the work of Montano, Athey, and Duncan in this sequence—out of chronological order—to define a spectrum of religious practices, traumatic encounters, and prophetic conditions. Chapters progress from the intense but accessible actions of Montano to Athey's challenging performances and finally to Duncan's violent transgressions, the most difficult, distancing artworks of the book. The trajectory of *Long Suffering* also maps differences in artists' engagement with religions, from the deep childhood devotion of both Montano and Athey to Duncan's more mainstream, less invested approach to his religious training. In this way, the book considers the impact of religions on American artists in straightforward but unusual examples, as well as in a less direct but more typical correlation.

Linda Montano (b. 1942) has embraced the physicality of religious practices in her endurance actions. By adopting strict self-disciplines rooted in Catholic monasticism, she has measured her performing body against convent standards. These daily disciplines are the subject of chapter 2, "Linda Montano, Performance Art Saint." In her youth, Montano lived for two years as a pre–Vatican II novice in a Maryknoll Catholic convent. The daily rituals, strict disciplines, and ascetic practices of convent life have marked the visual strategies and ethical claims of her art to the present. She consistently has presented herself in the guise of a nun, from *Sitting: Dead Chicken, Live Angel* (1971), in which she swathed herself in flowing robes and sat silently in a chair on the street for three hours a day for three days, to *Linda Mary Montano Celebrates Mother Teresa's Birthday* (2010), in which she dressed in the blue-bordered robes of Mother Teresa's order and offered blessings and prayers to passersby at the Empire State Building, again three hours a day for three days. In these and other endurance actions, Montano has cultivated public asceticism with a very specific goal: sainthood. Both appropriating and abstracting the visual language of the convent, Montano's monastic disciplines have invested her art practice with prophetic meaning. Preoccupied with monastic actions as a means of attaining sainthood, Montano's endurances persistently have drawn attention to the gendered nature of suffering in Catholicism. She has observed that female saints, in particular, achieved spiritual recognition through mutilation and assault. For Montano, the promise of a heavenly reward for the endurance of suffering resonated with her early experience of sexual assault. By inhabiting the gendered figure of the nun, Montano has performed prophetic witness to female victimhood and survival. Whether performed directly by wearing a nun's habit or referenced abstractly in habitual actions, Montano's iconography of female monasticism simultaneously embodies transformation and oppression, encounter and isolation, victimhood and justice. Her monastic endurances perform survival daily, manifesting her posttraumatic subjectivity—the passivity of victimhood—in the powerful agency of prophetic witness.

Ron Athey (b. 1961) was raised as a Pentecostal child prodigy in a violent, abusive household, and his endurance art actions have modeled survival in the context of religious and traumatic extremes. Chapter 3, "The Faith Healings of Ron Athey," explores prophetic witness in three performances collectively titled the *Torture Trilogy* (1992–97), which fused the physicality of Pentecostal spirituality with the enduring wounds of domestic violence and multigenerational incest. Across the trajectory of the three performances, a series of loosely connected vignettes, akin to tableaux vivants in their vividness, presented his early spiritual virtuosity and abusive family life, his adolescent drug use and suicide attempts, his HIV-positive diagnosis and search for wholeness and healing, and his experience of caring for and mourning the deaths of loved ones with AIDS. Throughout the series, actions of cutting, bloodletting, and the release of bodily fluids corresponded to Athey's posttraumatic experience of nonsuicidal self-injury and to his lifelong search for healing. Suffused with the accoutrements and imagery of sadomasochism, heroin addiction, and tattooing and piercing, Athey's wounding actions also directly incorporated the uniquely embodied practices of faith healing that he observed at the Pentecostal healing revivals of his youth. Overflowing blood, for example, mimicked and intensified the Pentecostal practice of the baptism in the spirit. In a powerful appropriation of the prophetic religious form of revival, Athey drew on the spiritual showmanship of particular ministers active in the Pentecostal healing revival movement in 1960s and 1970s Southern California, including A. A. Allen and Kathryn Kuhlman. Throughout the *Torture Trilogy*, Athey took on the persona and responsibilities of a healing evangelist. He used the visual and verbal rhetoric of religious revival to share his own narratives of loss, foster new communities of care, and create his own healing rituals. He mobilized prophetic Pentecostal discourses of healing to remind audiences of communal responsibilities and to model relational forms of justice based on public testimony. This chapter also explores the evolution of Athey's demands on witnessing audiences in his later endurance actions, such as *Incorruptible Flesh (Dissociative Sparkle)* (2006).

In striking contrast to Montano's disciplines and Athey's healing revivals, John Duncan (b. 1953) has infused his performance actions with violence, ferocity, and disorder. In chapter 4, "John Duncan's Confrontational Aesthetics," I examine how Duncan's performances visualize the violent consequences of male sexual aggression. Mimicking fiery Calvinist rhetorical strategies, Duncan's confrontational actions challenge the perpetration of dangerous stereotypes of masculinity. In *Blind Date* (1980), one of the most infamous and disturbing performances of the twentieth century, Duncan visualized male sexuality as violence and death: he had sex with a female corpse, and then received a vasectomy. Like Montano's, Duncan's

Fig. 2. Ron Athey and Company, "The Holy Woman," *4 Scenes in a Harsh Life* (1995), Museo Ex-Teresa, Mexico City. (Photograph by Monica Naranjo. Courtesy of Ron Athey.)

art practice has been profoundly influenced by sexual trauma. As a male survivor of sexual abuse, Duncan experienced the contradictions of masculinity, manifested in the gendered dynamics of violence and victimhood in his endurance artworks. This chapter explores how Duncan participated in feminist art circles in 1970s Southern California and how feminist art practices shaped his devastating critique of gender socialization. Parallel to Athey, the moral force of Duncan's performance actions relies on the prophetic traditions of his religious upbringing. Raised as a fundamentalist Calvinist Presbyterian, but with little interest in the subtleties of theology or religious practice, Duncan nevertheless aggressively tests the theological paradoxes of Calvinism. His performances engage midcentury Sunday school tenets of Calvinist theology such as total depravity, which assumes a universal human propensity to evil, and mainstream Calvinist rhetorical

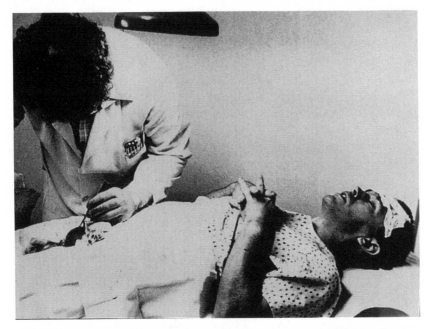

Fig. 3. John Duncan, *Blind Date* (1980). (Photograph by Paul McCarthy. Copyright © 1980 John Duncan.)

strategies such as the jeremiad, a preaching style that locates evil in the moral decay of contemporary life and prophetically reimagines the future. Like the hellfire and brimstone of eighteenth-century Calvinist preacher Jonathan Edwards, a key figure for midcentury Calvinists, Duncan rages against the dystopic present and its violent consequences. In his difficult endurance actions, his harsh condemnations demand moral justice while simultaneously transgressing moral boundaries.

The epilogue, "Endurance at the Corner of State and Bank," explores the three-decades-long peace vigil of my friend Veterans for Peace activist Cal Robertson in order to situate endurance art in continuing traditions of prophetic witness. At a busy corner in downtown New London, Connecticut, Robertson holds his gruesome antiwar sign in view of a naval submarine base and nuclear submarine factory, but his action exists at the intersection of trauma, religion, and social justice. American endurance artists participate in deep historical traditions of trauma- and religious-based dissent, like Robertson's vigil, and their work must be considered within broad historical contexts beyond the currents of art history and performance studies.

When confronted with Robertson's gruesome signs, or with Duncan's furious condemnations, do we look, or do we look away? Psychologist Bessel A. van der Kolk has advised, "When dealing with individuals who have lived in a psychotic environment and whose reality was beyond the scope of the ordinary life and expectable environment, the therapist must be prepared to deal with extraordinary events, extraordinary ideas, and extraordinary feelings and responses on his or her own part."[52] Of course, neither I nor my readers are mental health professionals, yet the artworks elaborated in this book transform us into witnesses by confronting us with the extraordinary. The presentation, representation, and re-presentation of trauma in these performances sharply amplify the subject-to-subject relationship established in performance art. These endurance artworks demand our attention to a central challenge of trauma, what Auerhahn and Laub have described as "the paradoxical yoking of the compulsions to remember and to know trauma with the equally urgent needs to forget and not to know it."[53] Witnessing testimonies of trauma catches audiences—and readers—in artists' contradictory attempts to both display and hide the wounds of trauma. Viewers replicate this traumatic knowing and not knowing by alternately looking and looking away from the painful subjects and forms of these artworks. I ask readers to endure this oscillation: to look, to look away when necessary, and to look again. Through discomfort and empathic pain, endurance art connects our experiences as witnesses to artists' experiences as trauma survivors. This form of human encounter reiterates the productive tensions central to radical action in American prophetic traditions. As King observed, "There is a type of constructive, nonviolent tension which is necessary for growth. . . . Injustice must be exposed, with all the tension its exposure creates, to the light of human conscience and the air of national opinion before it can be cured."[54] As witnesses, we endure endurance art, unable, like the nineteenth-century abolitionist Theodore Parker, to "complete the figure by experience of sight." Rather, it is through presence and encounter, through uncertainty and tension, that we may participate in the important work of bending the arc toward justice.

TWO | Linda Montano,
Performance Art Saint

In an early action, *Happiness Piece* (1973), endurance artist Linda Montano photographed herself smiling every day. Describing the motivation for this performance action, she wrote, "I wanted the habit of happiness to be available to me so I disciplined myself to smile everyday."[1] This simple piece called attention to Montano's lifelong performance commitments: the discipline of a daily vow; the cultivation of an outward appearance that, in turn, fostered inner conditions; and her quiet dedication to endurance in the face of persistent suffering. In quotidian art actions like *Happiness Piece* and other endurance artworks continuing to the present, the artist has measured her existence against monastic standards. In her youth, Montano lived for two years as a pre–Vatican II novice in a Maryknoll Catholic convent, where she dwelled in collaboration with her fellow nuns and in isolation from everyone else. Her intense experiences in the convent—its daily rituals, strict disciplines, ascetic practices, and missionary zeal—have marked the visual strategies and ethical claims of her art to the present. Through the medium of endurance art, Montano has replicated the asceticism of monastic life, appropriating the visual language of the convent, practicing sainthood, and investing her art practice with prophetic meaning.

Montano has written, "My primary concern in most events was to become a presence (Catholic saint) via self imposed disciplines."[2] As a child, obsessed with sainthood and yearning for a spiritual calling, Montano noticed that achieving holiness seemed to demand violence: "[T]he only way to be good was to be crucified or have breasts cut off."[3] Female saints, in particular, achieved spiritual recognition through mutilation and assault. For Montano, the promise of a heavenly reward for enduring suffering resonated with the early traumatic experience of sexual assault. In her endurance artworks, she has performed prophetic witness to female victimhood and survival by inhabiting the gendered figure of the nun. As a theologically charged embodiment of sexual purity, the nun has become the

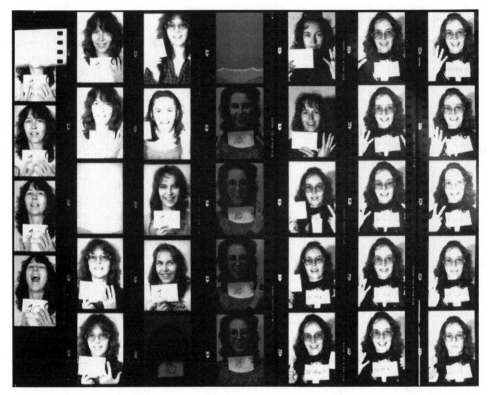

Fig. 4. Linda Montano, *Happiness Piece* (1973). (Photograph by Linda Montano. Copyright © 1973 Linda Montano.)

most persistent, flexible, and multivalent sign in Montano's visual vocabulary. Whether wearing a nun's habit or referencing it abstractly in habitual actions (as in *Happiness Piece*), Montano has incorporated the iconography of female monasticism in her work to simultaneously embody transformation and oppression, encounter and dissociation, victimhood and justice. Preoccupied with monastic discipline as a means of attaining sainthood, Montano has worked to manifest her posttraumatic subjectivity—the passivity of victimhood—in the powerful agency of prophetic witness.

Montano's attention to prophetic monasticism echoed deep traditions of Catholic activism rooted in centuries of multivalent dissent and advocacy. When Montano decided to enter convent life, she chose to join the Maryknoll order, which she has described as "probably the most forward thinking, liberal, human/activist yet Christo-centered and ecumenical religious order ever founded."[4] From its founding at the beginning of the twentieth century to the present day, the Maryknoll order's progressive approach to missionary work has consistently aligned Maryknoll nuns with indigenous and marginalized peoples on issues of social justice. Catholic monasticism also played an important role in radical American prophetic traditions in the twentieth century.[5] In the 1930s, Dorothy Day agitated for labor activism in her publication *Catholic Worker*, and her houses of hospitality built nondenominational intentional communities in the tradition of Jane Addams's Hull House.[6] Her inclusive approach to monasticism continues to inspire spiritual communities working for social justice, including the twenty-first-century New Monasticism movement.[7] During the Depression, Chicago priests were early participants in Saul Alinsky's model of community organizing, a relational, cross-cultural approach to progressive reform modeled in the present by Barack Obama's early career and his grassroots 2008 presidential campaign. At midcentury, southern nuns were important and visible facilitators of civil rights activism.[8] In the 1960s, Catholic priests (and brothers) Phillip and Daniel Berrigan staged antiwar demonstrations and engaged in well-publicized acts of civil disobedience while wearing their vestments; they later founded the Plowshares Movement to advocate nuclear disarmament.[9] Montano's endurance actions have contributed to this trajectory of Catholic prophetic witness and activism at the same time that her work has participated in other important cultural dialogues, including histories of feminism, feminist art, and feminist sexualities.

Montano has framed her art practice consistently in terms of monasticism, explicitly taking on nuns' personas and enacting monastic rituals in her endurances. Rather than *monasticism*, Montano has preferred the term *convent life*, which highlights the gendered nature of her experience.[10] While recognizing the centrality of gender in this context, I follow medievalist art historians and religious studies scholars in using the more flexible term *monasticism*, which can refer to either male or female religious communities. In this way, this chapter situates Montano's experience within the long history of aesthetic activities of religious communities from late antiquity to the present. Further, Montano's monastic background is not limited to Catholicism: between 1970 and 1998, she committed herself to the study and practice of eastern religious traditions, including Zen Buddhism and Hinduism.[11] Her enduring interest in eastern religious traditions began in the early 1970s with the diligent study of yoga at a San Francisco ashram. In 1981 she and then partner Pauline Oliveros moved to the Zen Mountain Monastery in Mt. Tremper, New York, where they lived for two years.[12] In the 1990s, she furthered her study of Hinduism to become a *sanyasi*, and she traveled to India in 1997. In 1998, when she returned to her hometown to care for her ailing father, Montano also returned to the religion of her youth. She has remained strictly devoted to Catholicism to the present day: "I practice Roman Catholicism now because I feel I'm imprinted. . . . But now I have enough skill to divide, to take out of the meal the things I can't eat and still be true to those incredible sacramental mysteries."[13] Since her rededication, her endurance artworks have included pilgrimages to Catholic holy sites in Europe, the United States, and Latin America (2006); prayer pieces such as *A Silent Three-Hour Prayer Retreat inside St. Patrick's Cathedral* (2007); and reenactments of the lives of Catholic female saints and famous women religious, as in *Teresa of Avila* (2007) and *Linda Mary Montano Celebrates Mother Teresa's Birthday* (2010).

While Montano's complex spiritual journey reflected the cross-cultural, individualistic character of American religious experience in the late twentieth century, this chapter focuses on the specifically Catholic resonances of Montano's endurance art actions. Many religious traditions have impacted her art practice, but her Maryknoll convent experience was foundational. Montano has consistently verbalized her endurance art commitments in Catholic language, actions, and metaphors: "I literally took the smells of church, the sights of church, the sounds of church, and almost, as if speaking another language, translated those into my work."[14] Critical analyses of Montano's work have mentioned her interest in and connection to Catholicism without exploring the specific origins and particular implications of this religious investment.[15] This chapter attends to the formation of Montano's prophetic, monastic vision of sainthood, tracing in her endurance art the lived experience of Catholicism as it coincided with the visual markers of dissociation as a posttraumatic response to sexual assault.[16] Montano's monastic disciplines instantiated the figure of the nun to perform a uniquely Catholic form of prophetic witness beyond convent walls.

BECOMING SISTER ROSE AUGUSTINE

Montano directly connected her personal religious experiences to her endurance actions in a set of two vivid lists.

LIST 1: CATHOLIC MEMORIES

the smell of high quality incense
the inflexibility of doctrine

the dedication of vow-taking nuns
the talking saint statues
the patriarchal exclusivity
the Tiffany stained-glass windows
the fasting before Communion, Fridays, and Lent
the stories of statues crying blood
the sounds of small bells at Communion
the sounds of the large Angelus bells
the fear of dropping the host
the poetry of the Latin Mass
the ritually-tailored vestments
the possibility of purgatory
the daily examen of conscience
the mystery of Transubstantiation
the ecstatic surrender to creed
the nun's/priest's unavailable celibacy
the obedience
the stories of miracles, martyrdoms, missionaries, curing of leprosy
the offering up (to God) anger, rage, trauma
the repetition of trance-inducing rosaries
the Stations of the Cross, the Stations of the Cross
the relief and humiliation of weekly confession
the prayer beads and holy cards
the May Day hymn singing and rosary at Lourdes shrine
the belonging the belonging the belonging
the promise of heavenly reward

LIST 2: A FEW OF THOSE MEMORIES AS ART

wearing blindfolds for a week (penance)
creation of Chicken Whiteface Woman (trying to be statue)
anorexia videos (holy anorexia)
three-hour acupuncture performances (crucifixion)
riding bikes on Brooklyn Bridge tied by a rope to Tehching Hsieh
    (miracle of walking on water)
fourteen years of living art (imitation of priest's vestments)[17]

These rich, provocative juxtapositions illustrated the lived realities of daily
religious practice in both lay and monastic communities, and they revealed
the depth of Montano's intellectual, emotional, and sensorial debt to Ca-

tholicism. Born in 1942 in Saugerties, New York, to second-generation Italian immigrants, Montano was educated in Catholic schools in her childhood, attended church with her family, and from an early age, she has said, she "wanted to be a saint."[18] She has observed, "My total consuming passionate focus was religion. I was a saint. I prayed constantly, continuously. . . . I looked at statues until they moved or talked. I visited nuns on off-hours. I was a religiomaniac."[19] Like many Catholic women at the time, Montano chafed at the gendered barriers to full participation in the spiritual and institutional life of the Catholic Church. Despite these tensions — and motivated by a traumatic sexual experience in adolescence — in 1960 Montano entered the Maryknoll convent in Ossining, New York, as a postulate, taking the name Sister Rose Augustine. She described this experience, lovingly, as an "incredibly rich time," but she became anorexic and was asked to leave the order in 1962.[20]

> At twenty I entered a convent, "enduring" two years as a Catholic nun, living in silence those two years except for one hour a day when we all talked together in recreation. I loved the community and dedication to a higher good and absolutely pure goal, but I left anorexic, having lost nearly 50 pounds in six months, high as a kite on endorphins.[21]

For Montano, living in a disciplined community fulfilled a deep desire for collaborative work toward the incarnation of a progressive vision. Yet her reliance on an ecstatic, self-denying high in the midst of this work points to the complicated role of monasticism in Montano's traumatic subjectivity. At the same time, her convent trajectory traced broader trends related to Catholic women religious at midcentury.

Montano entered the Maryknoll convent in 1960 at a time when the population of women religious was approaching its height in the United States.[22] Convents were successfully recruiting new nuns, but they were unable to retain them; increasingly, young women like Montano left their orders before taking their final vows.[23] While older nuns were content with traditional, private spiritual actions, many novices yearned for shared religious experiences.[24] Responding, in part, to the cultural shifts that generated these desires, in the early 1960s the Second Ecumenical Council of the Vatican (Vatican II) instituted revolutionary changes in Catholic practice, including lay participation and the use of the vernacular rather than Latin in conducting the Mass. Vatican II had a profound impact on the lives of women religious in terms of participation, democracy, and laity interactions. However, long before the 1960s, centuries-old convent traditions, rules, and attitudes were already changing. Vatican II addressed and codified the Church's response to questions that had been contested for decades.[25] The activities of the Maryknoll sisters in particular helped to incite this shift. Founded in 1911 by Mary Josephine Rogers (Mother Mary Joseph), this American order was devoted to missionary work. Montano entered the convent in 1960 expecting to change the world, to "go to Africa and cure leprosy, or to China and do something similarly dramatic."[26] In addition to this missionary focus, the Maryknoll order established a cloister in 1932 to support sisters interested in pursuing contemplative lives.[27] For Mother Mary Joseph, isolation and encounter were complementary activities within the order. She wrote that "a missioner must be a contemplative in action."[28] She described Maryknoll nuns' responsibilities as follows: "Sisters shall be encouraged to undertake direct catechetical and evangelical work and for that purpose will expect to go from station to station for visitations comparable to those of the priests."[29] This concept of missionary action, known as the direct apostolate, represented a significant shift from conventional practice and marked the progressive character of the Maryknoll order from its inception. Maryknoll sisters in China were the first nuns to receive permission to evangelize rather than simply providing social services to indigenous peoples. With these new priorities, restrictions on nuns were relaxed: the sisters wore modified habits so they could ride bicycles, and rather than returning to the cloister each evening they could live with families in remote villages.[30] This flexible, highly successful approach drew large numbers of postulants in the United States and globally. By 1960—even before the changes instigated by Vatican II—the Maryknoll order was sending more missionary sisters overseas than any other Catholic organization.[31]

Montano was profoundly influenced by the activities and structures of daily life in the Maryknoll convent. Prior to Vatican II, Catholic convent communities, including liberal orders like Maryknoll, were distinguished from lay or secular communities by three key features: discipline, collaboration (as a commitment to living in community), and the integration of life and prayer.[32] In particular, female monasticism was characterized by an almost complete lack of privacy. While outsiders generally perceive monasticism as an experience of isolation and seclusion, these women lived in constant community. Communal living in dormitories, uniform dress—for novices, a modified form of the habit—and a routinized daily schedule separated novices from their communities of origin in order to constantly reinforce a sense of religious identity and belonging to the convent community.[33] Obedience to superiors was crucial, a basic discipline highlighted in nuns' vows. All aspects of life were open to the approval or disapproval of the convent leadership. For example, nuns and novices were allowed to leave the physical space of the convent only with permission, and then only in the company of another nun.[34] In this way, a scaffold of social support organized interactions with the outside world, representing and asserting the convent community's beliefs and practices against any outside pressures. Thus the communities created within convents were socially as well as architecturally cloistered.

In this experience of living in community, discipline emerges as a central challenge. In the form of the vow, discipline presents itself as a question of will: one must constantly choose to fulfill it. The novice must cultivate this discipline through an extreme willingness to collaborate—to stretch her self-perception by identifying wholly with the community. Discipline thus becomes intimately linked to collaboration and intersubjective encounter. At the same time, collaboration clashes with the notion of a contemplative life. Meditation and prayer isolate members of the convent community from the outside world but not from each other; the negotiations of living in community are central to the experience of convent life. In addition, missionary work, as an alternative collaborative project, challenges this insider dynamic by calling for sustained, active engagement with outsider others. Devotion to missionary work and commitment to the contemplative life require different, though equally extreme, forms of collaboration. Coming out of her convent experience, Montano internalized these two forms of encounter. Her artwork throughout her career has consistently encompassed both contemplative and missionary impulses, beginning with her earliest endurance actions, performed less than ten years after leaving the Maryknoll convent. In a series of performances titled *Lying: Dead Chicken, Live Angel* (1971, 1972) and *Sitting: Dead Chicken, Live Angel* (1971), she swathed her nude body in transparent, gauzy white robes. Wearing a wimple and a set of large wings made of plastic bags and chicken feathers, Montano laid on a table or sat in a chair for several hours in various public locations in Rochester, New York, and San Francisco, California. Through complete silence and stillness, Montano cultivated her own inner, contemplative space, but her public performance of monastic contemplation punctuated the urban landscape with a prophetic presence. She observed, "I was getting the kind of attention that I used to give to nuns, priests, saints, statues, crucifixes, etc. I had reversed religion for myself."[35] In this way, beginning with her earliest performances, Montano has posited endurance art as a fundamentally ethical encounter, an exchange of attention charged with religious significance.

Montano's artworks from this period merged and replaced saints and nuns with chickens, as indicated in their titles, which include *Lying: Dead Chicken, Live Angel* (1971); *Sitting: Dead Chicken, Live Angel* (1971); *Lying: Dead Chicken, Live Angel* (1972); *Chicken Dance: The Streets of San Francisco* (1972); and *Chicken Dance* (1974). Chickens had entered Montano's visual vocabulary during her graduate work in sculpture at the University of Wisconsin–Madison.[36] Embarrassed by the explicitly religious content of her work, including the large-scale, car-parts assemblage *Crucifixion* (1964), she began to exhibit chickens: "I found that live chickens best expressed my internal-external state."[37] For Montano, the nervous, erratic behaviors of chickens manifested inner anxieties and outer restlessness; she also punned on the notion of "being a chicken," pointing to deeply held fears and repressed desires. She soon recognized that these placeholders for religious subjects took on their own religious significance. "The chickens began to be Catholic saints," she observed.[38] Finally, Montano herself took the place of the chickens, which in turn had stood in for religious subjects. These "chicken woman" performances, in addition to those listed above, included *The Screaming Nun* (1975) and others presented between 1971 and 1976. In these endurance actions—her first performance pieces—Montano set herself apart, disciplined herself from agitated chickenhood into stillness, and offered herself as an object of devotion. She was practicing sainthood.

THE TENSIONS OF MONASTICISM

Living in disciplined, intentional community is hard work, and in the monastic context multivalent pressures demand a series of ongoing, productive negotiations among its members, particularly new additions. These negotiations may be more or less contradictory, more or less conflictual, and more or less resolvable, but they always involve commitment, extension, and expansion of the self and the community. After she left convent life, Montano's representations of monasticism revealed the transformative possibilities and prophetic potential of living in community even as she lived outside it. In her collaborative performance with endurance artist Tehching Hsieh, *Art/Life One Year Performance 1983–1984* (1983–84), Montano struggled to come to terms with the fundamental tensions of monasticism: the vow and its visual marker, the habit; collaboration; and, finally, suffering. *Art/Life One Year Performance 1983–1984* took place in Manhattan

Fig. 5. Linda Montano, *The Screaming Nun* (1975). (Photograph by Mitchell Payne. Copyright © 1975 Linda Montano.)

between 1983 and 1984. As a collaboration between two artists, the piece drew on themes from both Hsieh's and Montano's past work. Hsieh had been presenting ascetic, long-term performances in New York since 1978, including living in a cage for one year (1978–79), punching a time card every hour for one year (1980–81), and living outdoors for one year (1981–82).[39] Montano was attracted by the rigor of Hsieh's work. In order to collaborate with him, she left the Zen monastery where she had lived with Pauline Oliveros for two years: "I was living in a Zen Center in upstate New York and during a trip to the city I saw one of Tehching's posters and literally heard a voice in my head that said, 'Do a one-year piece with him.'"[40] In another account of her decision to collaborate with Hsieh, Montano described her decision as vocational, indicating, in the Weberian sense of *Beruf,* an occupational calling of divine origin.[41] Montano has said, "Although I would have preferred to have stayed in the monastery, I knew that my calling was to be a fringe, outsider artist."[42] Montano's desire for secluded contemplation in the intimate Mt. Tremper community—one form of monastic collaboration—conflicted with her desire for more unbounded, unpredictable processes of encounter, like those of missionary work. The title of the piece illustrated the influence of each artist's investments; the lack of punctuation deliberately equalized their contributions.[43] *One Year Performance* repeated the title that Hsieh used for all of his endurance actions between 1978 and 1986.[44] *Art/Life* directly referred to Montano's small business and long-running performance piece *Art/Life Counseling.* Begun in 1980, these therapeutic, interactive performances collaged aspects of her study of yoga, palm and tarot card reading, karate, visualization exercises, and other techniques.[45] In addition, *Art/Life* referenced previous collaborative pieces in which Montano had attempted to blur the boundary between art and life. These included *Handcuff* (1973), a three-day collaboration with Tom Marioni in which the artists remained handcuffed to one another for three days, and several works performed with Oliveros in 1975, including *Living with Pauline Oliveros in the Desert for Ten Days.* In these endurances, Oliveros and Montano declared that "everything we did would be considered art," collapsing the distinction between art and everyday life.[46]

Art/Life One Year Performance 1983–1984 established a set of promises or assertions that bound Montano and Hsieh. In the form of a signed contract, their vow stipulated that the artists would remain tied together with an eight-foot rope for one year, without touching. The full contract, dated July 4, 1983, and signed by both artists, read:

We, Linda Montano and Tehching Hsieh, plan to do a one-year performance. We will stay together for one year and never be alone. We
will be in the same room at the same time, when we are inside. We
will be tied together at waist with an 8 foot rope. We will never touch
each other during the year. The performance will begin on July 4,
1983 at 6 P.M. and continue until July 4, 1984 at 6 P.M.[47]

When indoors, Hsieh and Montano would remain together in the same
room. In effect, this vow created a monastic community of two. In literally
tying the two artists together, the eight-foot rope connecting Hsieh and
Montano functioned as a metonym of the vow itself, and it visually marked
the vow. In this sense, the rope became both vow and habit. As the means
by which the two artists were connected, the rope both enforced and materialized their vow to remain tied together. Echoing Buddhist and some
Christian monastic practices, both Montano and Hsieh shaved their heads
the day before the piece began and did not cut their hair throughout the
year. (Hsieh has observed that "this gesture is not related to religious practice" but rather illustrated the passage of time.)[48] The use of the rope as
abstracted habit in *Art/Life One Year Performance 1983–1984* also recalled
Montano's practice of wearing a modified nun's habit in her chicken
woman pieces and in endurance artworks to the present. In addition, the
rope mimicked the convent practice of leaving the cloister with at least one
other nun: the rope materially enforced their discipline, constantly and
mutually bringing them into the presence of one another. Further, the rope
differentiated Montano and Hsieh from onlookers, confronting everyone
in their presence with the physicality of the vow. In an interview conducted
during this piece, Montano described the discipline of the vow as a kind of
separation of the will from both the mind and the body: "Once you give the
mind a command, then you watch the body carry out the process."[49] Here
Montano identified at least three aspects of the self—mind, body, and
will—an observational attitude echoed in the extensive documentation of
Art/Life One Year Performance 1983–1984. The artists photographed their
daily activities and recorded all conversations. Any deviation from the
rules (e.g., accidental touching) was rigorously documented. Montano
came to believe that this extensive documentation failed to adequately cap-
ture the piece: "It seems that the primary document is the change inside the
performer and the audience. The results are felt and cannot always be photographed or expressed."[50] Instead, the "results"—the potentially transformative outcomes of the piece—were embodied in the artists' radical encounters with one another and their audiences.

Art/Life One Year Performance 1983–1984 required an extreme degree of intimacy and trust. As in the convent (or a cage), the two were absolutely restricted from privacy. Each action, comment, and gesture could be observed by the other. In addition, any decision required extensive discussion. Each day, Montano and Hsieh spent approximately five hours at desks, back to back. They used this time to make decisions about their daily activities: "We think about what we want to do and then we talk until we come to a consensus. So it takes many hours of sitting before we can do one thing."[51] In this way, negotiation became a central activity of the performance. Montano became interested in documenting the inevitable conflicts that took place between them, many of which arose in relation to different gender expectations. In particular, Hsieh, a carpenter, refused to allow Montano to help him with his carpentry jobs, which angered her.[52] For Montano this tension was an integral aspect of the piece, a working out of the problems of living in community. Hsieh, on the other hand, was concerned with more abstract formal and symbolic meanings and did not support personal, social, or political interpretations, as in his observation that shaved heads visualized the passage of time.

Over time the artists began to vent their anger over their different theoretical points of view, as well as over daily trivialities. Conflicts arose over what and where to eat, how and when to contact friends and art critics, and how to manage the demands of their jobs (Hsieh's carpentry work and Montano's teaching). Montano explained, "If we fought, then we would look ahead to what the other might want, and then take away that privilege."[53] Eventually, she said, "yanking [became] a chief mode of expressing anger."[54] The artists recorded these conflicts in images of crumpled paper marked with the word *fight* and in photographs of themselves in the act of yanking. The artists documented yanking on November 25, 1983, and March 17, 1984; the word *fight* appears in photographs from January 28, 1984, January 29, 1984, and March 21, 1984. Hsieh refused my request to publish these particular photographs, indicating that these non-"neutral" images from the piece "can only be presented as part of the whole year-long photo documents."[55] His reluctance concerning these specific images underscores his more conceptual investment in the piece. The violence of yanking spoke to the difficulty of the vow and the difficulty of the commitment to living in community. As Hsieh said, "We become each other's cage."[56] Montano framed the experience in terms of cultivating humility through the painful and problematic discipline of collaboration: "By staying tied to Tehching Hsieh in his *Art/Life One Year Performance 1983–1984*, I died a little every day, learning humility and collaboration."[57] For Montano the stakes of this endurance artwork went beyond suffering and self-inflicted hardship to survival itself. Completing the piece without losing herself became her priority. Conflict management thus equaled survival: "For survival we have to work things out."[58] While the language of death and survival may seem hyperbolic in this context, the experience of this piece radically destabilized Montano's identity. One day she encountered a policeman on the street and considered banging her head into a glass window to draw his attention so he would come to her aid.[59] This endurance piece tested the limits of Montano's ability to withstand extreme vulnerability; but it was also an investment, a project related to the mitigation of long-term fears and anxieties. For Montano discipline through collaboration served as preparation for future hardship: "I do hard work in case life gets hard. Then I will be ready."[60] In this way, Montano's public asceticism communicated an apocalyptic, prophetic sensibility.

While tied to Hsieh, Montano conceived a plan for her next performance, *7 Years of Living Art* (1984–91): "It was to be an 'art job' imposed on me, for me, for seven years. An 'art vow.'"[61] In this long-term piece, Montano continued her experiments in combining art and life activities. She established a set of prescriptions that structured her life on an annual, monthly, and daily basis: each year of the piece corresponded to one of the seven Hindu chakras and was associated with one color and one of seven personas. Montano drew on seven personas that she had created in an early video work, *Learning to Talk* (1977). In this video performance, Montano had experimented with role-playing and developed a set of personas, including a sexy Frenchwoman, a country western singer, and the character of a nun with her Maryknoll name, Sister Rose Augustine.[62] In *7 Years of Living Art*, Montano explicitly engaged with Hindu symbolism, but she also referred to Catholic metaphors of the seven sacraments, the seven sorrows, and others. The structure of the piece itself echoed structures of monastic encounter: Montano designated three sets of commitments: inner, outer, and others. Daily vows, or inner commitments, included wearing only clothing of the year's color, spending at least three hours in a room of that color, listening to one tone for seven hours each day, and speaking in an accent associated with the persona of the year.[63] Here, as in *Art/Life One Year Performance 1983–1984*, Montano created a set of multivalent habits. Mimicking the nun's uniquely identifiable garb, she visually marked the vow with her colored clothing, and she assumed a set of repetitive daily practices—habits—that shaped her speech and mannerisms. In this way, Montano transformed contemplative convent behaviors into art actions. During *7 Years of Living Art*, these physical, behavioral activities constituted

Montano's inner work. However, in her continuation of the piece, *Another 7 Years of Living Art* (1991–98), she redefined these rules: clothing colors and listening to a single sound became outer rather than inner commitments, and she defined her inner work as increasing her attention to spiritual matters. This echoed the graduation of postulate to novice, or novice to nun, when habits of speech, dress, and schedule are maintained but deemphasized in favor of more abstract, interior forms of spiritual commitment.

As part of the outer commitments of *7 Years of Living Art*, Montano held monthly, public, one-on-one art/life counseling sessions at the New Museum, where she met individually with strangers for discussion and tarot, palm, and psychic readings. In addition, each year she hosted one or more artist collaborators ("others") in her home for sixteen days; for several years, these collaborators were Annie Sprinkle and Veronica Vera.[64] As such, the piece incorporated both seclusion—in the cloister of the one-color room and the daily inner disciplines—and its outer and other complements, missionary work. In particular, Montano's uniquely Maryknoll approach to collaboration in the confessional space of the New Museum consultations and her in-home workshops echoed the direct apostolate, the missionary practice of directly engaging with individuals around spiritual issues. Montano wrote that through these seven-year commitments, she learned to "die daily to prepare for final retirement."[65] This symbolic language echoed the spiritual writings of nuns such as St. Marguerite Marie Alacoque, but her explicit preoccupation with the habit of death and dying also signaled Montano's traumatic subjectivity.[66] For Montano monastic discipline, self-denial, and sainthood coincided with the suffering female body.

ERASING THE PAST

In 1977 performance artist Suzanne Lacy invited Montano to perform at the Woman's Building in Los Angeles. Montano remembered, "I think they were having a circus. . . . It was upstairs, and festive."[67] Deliberately locating her body on the margins of this lively social event, Montano performed *Erasing the Past* on the floor in the Woman's Building basement. She covered her face and lower body with a sheet, echoing the gauzy habitlike garment of her chicken woman pieces, but left her belly and breasts bare: "I laid for three hours in an empty room, my torso exposed, seven acupuncture needles in my conception vessel. I intended to forget the past."[68] Montano described her adolescent experience of sexual assault briefly in "Love

Sex: The Ecstatic Writings of Linda M. Montano," an unpublished manu-script of erotic texts: "At sixteen my world collapsed when I was betrayed sexually."[69] Montano's spare statement lacked specifics, and she has re-sisted further discussion of this event, but she has identified trauma as foundational for her endurance art practice: "Much of my work is about . . . mending the past."[70] Psychologist Judith Lewis Herman has defined "any physical contact that had to be kept secret" as traumatic for children and adolescents, and psychiatrist Anna C. Salter has observed that adolescent sexual trauma is "always emotionally violent and marked by destruction of trust and betrayal of intimacy."[71] Rather than speculating about the details of this event, this chapter foregrounds the artist's subjective experience of sexual trauma as visualized in her discourse of endurance art. In this way, attending to Herman's charge that "the victim herself may be the most reli-able judge of the long-term effects of her experience," I seek to deliberately interrupt the biographical coherence of this text, disrupt my own narrative voice, signal the instability of traumatic experience, and preserve the ambi-guity and contradiction of Montano's presentations and representations of traumatic content.[72]

In *Erasing the Past*, Montano described herself as "isolated, silent, face-less and feeling somewhat foolish."[73] Alone and distanced from the boister-ous party, she marked the invisible but powerful presence of her traumatic past and visually manifested the dissociation central to her posttraumatic experience of sexual trauma. As a routine mental activity, dissociation al-lows the temporary fragmentation of the self; for example, when arriving at work, one may not remember the particulars of driving there.[74] This brain function, when it occurs in the midst of trauma, may help victims survive by distancing or detaching from overwhelming affect. Survivors may feel that they were floating above or beside their bodies, witnessing traumatic events that seemed to be happening to someone else. However, some can continue to experience bouts of dissociation that disrupt the con-tinuity of the self. Well beyond the traumatic moment, they may feel the intrusion of numbness, distance, or detachment from their bodies, from strong emotions, or from upsetting memories. Dissociated behaviors are diverse and their impact far-reaching: dissociation can prevent the integra-tion of trauma into survivors' internal self-narratives, resulting in a tension between knowing and not knowing. As psychologist Nanette C. Auerhahn and psychiatrist Dori Laub have observed, this doubleness reflects a post-traumatic, "paradoxical yoking of the compulsions to remember and to know trauma with the equally urgent needs to forget and not to know it."[75] Dissociation, as a mechanism of not knowing, separates survivors from

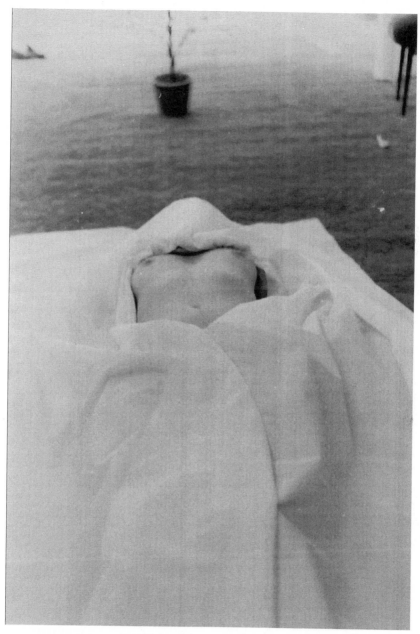

Fig. 6. Linda Montano, *Erasing the Past* (1977). (Photograph by
Woman's Building staff. Copyright © 1977 Linda Montano.)

their own life experiences and isolates them from others. Compounding this sense of difference from others, the experience of sexual assault may be surrounded by silence motivated by family pressures, feelings of shame, or fear of stigma.[76] According to psychologists Leslie Lebowitz and Susan Roth, this secrecy can result in "a discrepancy between one's inner and outer experience of self, thereby promoting alienation," generating a sense of difference between self and body, and exacerbating the survivor's fragmented identity.[77] In *Erasing the Past*, Montano performed dissociation physically. Rather than participate in the circus of human activity at the Woman's Building, she situated herself on the margins. She lay silent and alone, aurally and physically marking her sense of difference. Swathed in the gauzy habit of her chicken woman persona, she obscured her face but laid bare her breasts and belly. Sexualizing and depersonalizing her identity, Montano eradicated her facial features and unveiled her torso, echoing sculptures made as art therapy by survivors whose sexual trauma coincided with the development of eating disorders. One survivor depicted herself "as an 11-year-old lying on her back with enormous manacles over her arms and legs. . . . Her genital region was exposed and vulnerable, and no features were imprinted on her face."[78] *Erasing the Past* presented a female figure similarly evacuated of identity, covered in the white robes of a novice nun. Manifested in the draped robes and figure of the nun, the affect of sexual trauma pervaded the visual structures and content of *Erasing the Past* and other endurance artworks. Charged with religious and sexual meaning, the nun's recurring presence, both explicit and implied, visualized the centrality of Catholicism to Montano's traumatic subjectivity and her prophetic witness to female victimhood.

Montano's posttraumatic response to sexual assault took on a uniquely religious character. Religion had served as her retreat since childhood: "I became an escape artist at a very early age. Religion was a way to transform, transcribe, and move beyond, on the sensual, visual, conceptual level, my predicament as a woman, as a child in Saugerties, New York."[79] She has explicitly identified her sexual trauma and its psychic damage with Catholicism: "I was deflowered and depowered by the Church."[80] This powerful indictment directly associated her assault with Catholic patriarchal structures that degraded female agency and participation.[81] Yet, in her adolescence, immersion in Catholic life provided a radical opportunity to break with the past: after her sexual assault, Montano, always a devout child, decided to enter the convent.[82] In "Love Sex," Montano situated her decision to become a nun in the context of her sexual assault: "To escape further into 'purity' and away from shame, I entered a convent at nineteen and stayed there for two years, basking in celibacy."[83] The passage continues, "The life was utopian: time was devoted to silence (we talked only one hour a day), a study of scriptures and singing in an echo-chambered chapel with 150 other nuns while wearing a costume right out of the middle ages." Montano narrated her retreat into monasticism—the first of many attempts to erase the past—specifically in terms of sexual purity. She noted that sexuality, in the form of "a crush on another nun," invaded this safe place near the end of her time there.[84] This understanding of the sexual purity of convent life derived not only from the traditional Benedictine vow of chastity but from popular midcentury Catholic children's literature. Maryknoll publications such as *Bernie Becomes a Nun* (1956), which were avidly consumed by Montano and other Catholic young women preparing to take the veil, described convent discipline in terms of moral and physical cleanliness.[85] Montano remembered this book and the Maryknoll magazine (as well as the relative geographic proximity of the convent to her hometown) as major influences on her decision to join the Maryknoll order.[86] At the same time, Montano's search for a space free of threatening sexuality echoed the actions of many survivors of rape and sexual assault, who may avoid sexual encounters and practice abstinence for many years.[87] As a Maryknoll novice, following standard novitiate procedure, she discarded the name Linda Montano and was rechristened Sister Rose Augustine. Though processed through institutional means, this gesture furthered her already dissociated subjectivity. It reinforced her fragmented identity by positing a pure, undamaged persona that she has since described as the "Holy Girl," visualized in the nun personas adopted in endurance actions from her earliest chicken woman performances to her most recent art actions.[88] As the imagined, alternate self—the whole self as opposed to the fragmented, traumatized self—the Holy Girl existed outside of, before, or beyond her sexual assault. In particular, Montano consistently has identified her Holy Girl persona with childhood, reflecting her desire, common to survivors of early sexual trauma, for a purified, innocent youth.

Monastic asceticism presented Montano with an opportunity to regain a sense of agency by asserting control over her body. The structure and bodily surveillance of convent life and the convent's goal of creating an undifferentiated community of nuns appealed to her: "It was totally to my liking and extremely structured."[89] Montano described the uniformity of her daily regimen as a novice.

Up at 4:00 or 5:00 AM—thirty women slept in one room with little curtains for cubicles, sort of like hospital curtain cubicles separating us. Army barrack lockers were used for our clothes. Everyone wore the same undergarment, nightgowns I guess they were called. . . . We would all get up together, close our curtains together, put on our hats together . . . put our eyes down, go to the bathroom, never look. Then go down, meditate together, go to Mass, breakfast, change to work clothes, work for three hours, lunch, go to school for four hours (theology), supper, and then an hour of talking. . . . So there were rules based on daily living. Life was: letter writing (receiving mail once a week), one hour of talking a day, silence, prayer, a lot of coming into the main chapel, sitting, facing 700 nuns on one side and 700 nuns on the other.[90]

Montano compared the similarity and simultaneity of novices' appearances, gestures, and activities to the visual spectacle and choreography of *Alice in Wonderland* and *The Sound of Music*.[91] Despite their aesthetic appeal, these practices minimized, alienated, and subsumed individual identity by insisting on novices' uniformity. The strict regimes of convent organization focused novices' attention on managing and hiding their bodies. They were expected, she said, to "put our eyes down, go to the bathroom, never look."[92] In this way, monastic asceticism replicated and furthered Montano's dissociation. While not inherently pathological, convent values coincided with Montano's trauma reaction. In response to the fragmenting experience of dissociation, many survivors of sexual trauma may implement regimes of self-denial and self-monitoring or become deeply concerned with perfection or cleanliness. As attempts to regain a sense of ownership and control over a violated body, these dissociative behaviors nevertheless block the integration of trauma and the restoration of agency by obscuring the relationship between past and present, mind and body, trauma and self.[93] Convent life facilitated Montano's split sense of identity and feelings of estrangement. The organization of pre–Vatican II convent life deliberately suppressed individualism, isolated individuals from past experiences, and demanded the selfless surrender of individual identity.[94] By specifically positing a new, pure identity, enforcing a highly supervised, regulated daily life, and providing institutionally sanctioned access to self-deprivation, the convent exacerbated Montano's posttraumatic dissociation. By allowing her to take refuge in the illusory perfection of her Holy Girl persona, monastic routines repressed and postponed her confrontation with trauma. Many young women found convent life at midcentury to be dissatisfying and stressful, but for Montano the untenable contradictions of living with a suppressed, split identity led to the development of anorexia in the second year of her novitiate. Montano named her condition anorexia nervosa, although she was not diagnosed at the time of her illness: "I . . . left [the convent] with anorexia or a situation like anorexia. I'm not sure if it was full-fledged 'Karen Carpenter anorexia.'"[95]

Bodily discipline, and particularly fasting, has played a key role in Catholic religious practice for centuries. Teresa of Avila, a sixteenth-century saint Montano has long admired, wrote, "[T]he first thing that we have to do, and that at once, is to rid ourselves of love for this body of ours."[96] Historian Caroline Walker Bynum has documented medieval women's extensive uses of food, the symbolism surrounding eating, and the central role of fasting in their daily Catholic practices, as well as how food practices offered possibilities for the expression of gendered dissent.[97] In the mid-twentieth century, fasting remained a traditional form of asceticism for Catholics and was practiced regularly by both monastic and lay communities. References to food suffused Montano's memories of Catholic practice: "the fasting before Communion, Fridays, and Lent . . . the mystery of Transubstantiation."[98] These elements of lived religion directed her attention to rigorous, ascetic, food-related Catholic practices. Anthropologist and nun Patricia Curran has argued that in pre–Vatican II convents in the twentieth century, "the rituals of convent dining were cultural performances that attempted to reestablish the fundamental facts and values of religious congregations—the ascendance of grace over nature, of mind over body, of the common good over individual interest."[99] At the same time, convent authorities struggled with the tension between bodily renunciation and the vigorous activity required for nuns' participation in manual labor.[100] Food regimes in pre–Vatican II convent dining halls manifested this tension with a variety of strictures that promoted nuns' discomfort. Curran noted, "To avoid making food into a God substitute, a number of controls were built into the ascetic system. One ate whatever one was served, in posturally uncomfortable positions, as quickly as possible."[101] Novices and committed nuns alike were expected to respond with indifference to the timing, content, and portion size of meals. Refectories' spatial organization and seating arrangements barred intimacy and "recreation" (conversation). Prostrations and other physical penances often took place during meals.[102] Montano remembered that gruesome stories of saints and martyrs were often read aloud while the novices ate.[103] She described the extreme self-consciousness that she felt at these times: "[My] attention was usually on *myself* or all of the above [penance, food, neighbor, reading] . . . because [I was so] 'uncomfortable.'"[104] She and other novices were required to maintain "custody of the eyes," meaning they were not allowed to make eye contact or observe one another in the act of eating.[105] Mealtimes were a time of distancing, isolation, and assisted dissociation.

Montano has described the origin of her anorexia in various ways. In 2009 she said, "I gagged on powdered sugar on a cookie in the dining hall and this 'started' my anorexia."[106] In her video *Anorexia Nervosa* (1981), in which she discusses her struggle with the illness, Montano described how she and another nun began dieting. Regardless of its origins, in the context of this convent culture, Montano's self-imposed fasting soon drew the attention of her superiors. In a letter dated July 6, 1962, Sister Paul Miriam informed Montano's parents that their daughter would leave the order.

> Yesterday Sister could not promise to eat normally, not because of physical reasons, but because she could not make up her mind to do it. . . . [I]t is the general consensus of opinion here that Sister Rose Augustine is out of place in religious life. . . . We also feel that this non-eating program is an expression of the resistance—even perhaps sub-conscious—"a square peg in a round hole." At any rate she and we are aware that it could be unwise for her to continue any longer in the novitiate.[107]

Sister Paul Miriam's letter framed Montano's illness in terms of agency: she refused to "make up her mind" to eat. Her body disciplines served as a form of dissent from convent authority. Montano said, "We had daily confession with one nun. . . . I was not confessing that I wasn't eating normal amounts of food. . . . So I was playing this incredible control game with myself and with them."[108] Marked by her silence during confession, Montano registered her opposition somatically rather than verbally. She elaborated on these nonverbal power issues: "The situation there was difficult for me to swallow, and so my body reacted. I'm referring to a situation of being nonverbal in an institution that had a lot of structure, demands, and pressure—things for me to respond to. I did not give my full consent, or did not know how to give my full consent, or how to question whether or not I was giving my full consent."[109] Even twenty years after her experience, Montano insisted that she enjoyed assuming control over her body: "I liked controlling my food intake, I liked watching what I was eating and not eating, and hiding it. . . . I liked the challenge of making myself do something, controlling my body."[110] Montano has acknowledged that she continues to struggle with ascetic attitudes toward food.[111]

Montano's concern with agency and control recalled the fundamental violation of sexual assault described by Lebowitz and Roth: "The defining characteristic of sexual trauma is the elimination of the victim's choice and the obliteration of her agency."[112] Psychiatrist Ann Kearney-Cooke has suggested that "abusive sexual experiences, as well as the feeling of powerlessness which result from them, can be important contributing factors in the development of an eating disorder."[113] Anorexia nervosa, bulimia, and other eating disorders are common responses to sexual trauma because they can physically manifest the dissociation, violation of bodily integrity, and disintegration of self induced by traumatic experience. Montano addressed the nature of this somatic communication in her video artwork *Anorexia Nervosa* (1981), in which five women, including Montano, discuss their eating disorders: "My basic problem was being nonverbal. . . . I didn't know what I was feeling. . . . I had no way to verbalize what I was feeling. . . . [M]y body started to talk for me because no words were coming out of my mouth."[114] In this way, Montano suggested, the dissociated memory of sexual trauma found its voice in the marginalization and diminishment of her body.

Montano's association of disordered eating with somatic communication responded to foundational research on anorexia conducted by psychiatrist Hilde Bruch in the 1970s and 1980s. Bruch identified conflicts of identity, selfhood, and autonomy as the most important factors in the development of anorexia.[115] Although she contributed this analysis to the definition of *anorexia* in the *DSM-III* (1980), neither the final publication nor its updated versions, the *DSM-IV* (2002) and the *DSM-5* (2013), adopted this understanding of the nature of disordered eating. Some practitioners have suggested that the manual's emphasis on body image obscures patients' underlying motivations related to identity and agency. Psychologist R. A. Gordon, for example, has argued that the *DSM*'s focus on body image without regard to issues of autonomy was a product of the 1970s cultural setting and does not reflect the reality of women's experiences.[116] On the other hand, sociologist Paula Saukko has explored the underlying assumptions of Bruch's analysis and suggested that Bruch's focus on autonomy was predicated on post–World War II American values of personal freedom and masculinity.[117] While Bruch did not directly study the role of sexual trauma and eating disorders, current research suggests the relevance of her views on agency for sexually traumatized populations.[118]

Montano herself knew and admired Bruch's work, and in the 1980s she sent Bruch her video *Anorexia Nervosa* and her book *Art and Everyday Life*.[119] Bruch argued that anorexics tend to hold certain beliefs about themselves. She observed that they consider themselves to be—and usually are seen by others as—high-achieving "good girls" who feel "eternally preoccupied with the image they create in the eyes of others, always questioning whether they are worthy of respect," and have grandiose aspirations that are difficult if not impossible to dislodge.[120] For Montano these qualities coalesced in her preoccupation with sainthood. In Catholic theology, a saint is an individual recognized by the Catholic Church for exceptional devotion. Through extreme devotional acts, saints become subjects of devotion themselves. They usually achieve this elevated spiritual status by mimicking Christ's virtues, including charity, care of the sick, asceticism, and especially physical suffering. Montano's lifelong fervor to become a saint has persisted since childhood. Speaking in the third person of her childhood self—itself a linguistic act of dissociation—she wrote:

> Little Linda became interested in one thing—being a saint. She tried different ways of doing that. . . . She attended every First Friday Mass, Stations of the Cross, and even entered the convent because the persona that most inspired her was that of a "Holy Girl." Her constant question was how can I be one? How can I get close to God? How can I be just like Jesus?[121]

Montano's impulse to assume the mantle of sainthood, to authenticate her Holy Girl persona, combined her trauma reaction with her emotional and intellectual investment in Catholicism. Her commitment to asceticism reflected her dual impulses to discipline herself to "be just like Jesus" and to discipline the frightening memories of trauma. As such Montano's conception of sainthood centered on suffering: "When I was seven years old, I wanted to be a saint and I thought that I had to suffer like Jesus. That became the plot and story line for my entire life quest."[122] These aspirations, which she has pursued in strict regimes of suffering in her endurance art actions to the present, were profoundly shaped by Catholic perceptions of suffering in midcentury America.

ENDURANCE AND THE PURSUIT OF SAINTHOOD

St. Augustine framed suffering as "tests of virtue"; for centuries before and since, Catholic theologians have debated the role and meanings of suffering.[123] Religious studies scholars Robert A. Orsi and Paula M. Kane have identified a uniquely American, post–World War II attitude toward suffering. Influenced by the Catholic Church's increased emphasis on the interiority of religious experience, American Catholics at midcentury equated

the endurance of pain—physical pain—with saintliness. Devotional literature argued that only the spiritually accomplished could mimic Jesus by
successfully enduring pain with cheerful acceptance, even indifference.[124]
Orsi argued that this sanctification of pain emphasized difference and
made ill people "into inhuman others whose inner lives were radically unlike everyone else's, and ultimately unrecognizable. First it made them into
others—and then devotional culture celebrated them for this otherness and
difference, which was called holiness."[125] Holiness was defined in direct
relation to the experience of pain. This cultural focus on suffering, which
Orsi called a "darkly erotic aesthetic of pain," nurtured Montano's desires
to become a saint.[126]

Orsi has suggested that ideas about suffering accompanied socioeco-
nomic shifts in Catholic communities after World War II. As second-
generation Catholic immigrants moved away from ethnic enclaves to pursue financial and social advancement, traditional values of self-denial and
sacrifice came into conflict with middle-class materialist ambitions.[127]
Montano's childhood memories reflected this cultural situation. The grand-
daughter of "stately silent and dignified Italian grandparents," Montano
has noted that she grew up in an "outsider family," the only Italians in their
small, upstate New York community.[128] Her father's parents were "non-
English speaking from Campobasso, both devout, silent, hardworking."[129]
Her father, Henry Montano, a successful shoe salesman, articulated his
generation's conflicting set of values in an interview with his daughter. In
response to a question about his business acumen, he said, "Any time that
I had after work, I was home with the family. I was never in bars, or dancing. I was always home. It was business and family, nothing in between."[130]
Here Mr. Montano deflected attention from his business success, instead
highlighting the activities that his commitments excluded. For Orsi discourses of sacrifice and suffering mediated this type of discomfort with
material success: "The children of immigrants, in transition from one way
of life into another, constructed for themselves an ethos that proclaimed
pain (not hard work, ambition, or a desire for success) as a road to the
greatest achievement (which was sanctity, not a bigger apartment, a new
car, or a good job)."[131] The rhetoric of sacrifice could alleviate both men's
and women's anxieties over postwar prosperity—as it did for Mr. Montano, for example. However, physical pain carried a particular gendered
connotation. Kane has observed that the ethos of pain in twentieth-century
Catholicism coincided with gender expectations. The passive acceptance of
suffering was a female phenomenon: the "ideal of extreme suffering [was]
the true expression of the feminine."[132] Discourses of suffering allowed

women to talk about their pain and provided a framework of meaning for their experiences. However, Kane has cautioned against interpreting narratives of suffering from this era as empowering. Instead, she suggested, "Self-inflicted bodily suffering, even if interpreted as a rebellious act by women seeking salvation, is not a universally emancipating gesture, particularly inside a patriarchal system like the Catholic Church."[133]

Montano's endurance art practice has pivoted on this notion of suffering as both gendered and culturally powerful. She articulated the direct connections among femininity, pain, and prophetic witness in her cartoon *Visualization #1* (1982). In this series of provocative self-portraits, Montano grappled with suffering in the context of gender and sexuality. She penned these images at a crucial moment in her biography, twenty years after her convent struggles with anorexia, one year into her two-year stay at the Zen Mountain Monastery, and just before her collaboration with Hsieh in *Art/ Life One Year Performance 1983–1984*. In the 1970s, before joining the Zen Mountain Monastery, Montano had lived for a decade in California, where she became a key figure in the rich West Coast performance art scene. She moved to San Francisco in 1972 with her husband, Mitchell Payne, a photographer and former Presbyterian seminarian whom she married in 1971. In California, Montano performed extensively. She collaborated with Tom Marioni, presented work at the Woman's Building in Los Angeles, and participated in *Close Radio*, a performance art radio program hosted by Chris Burden and John Duncan.[134] As she became involved with California feminist art circles, Montano began to consider the fluidity of gender and sexuality; she has explained that "what distinguishes a lesbian from a nonlesbian was a big issue for me in San Francisco."[135] These questions came to the fore in 1975, when she met composer Pauline Oliveros. Montano separated from her husband and joined Oliveros in San Diego, where she created her first video artworks, including *Learning to Talk* (1977), in which she experimented with seven different female personas, from sexy Frenchwoman to pious nun. In 1977 Payne died in an accidental shooting. Montano documented her grief in *Mitchell's Death* (1979), one of her best-known works. *Visualization #1* documents Montano's response to this accumulation of weighty life transitions. While this and other artworks included or referred to sexually explicit content and explored the fluidity of gender identity and sexuality, the presence of this material complicates but does not contradict its Catholic forms and influences.

Montano's series of drawings began with an upward-gazing nun, followed by a sketch of a powerful, androgynous practitioner of karate. The aggressive stance of this figure mirrored the poses that Montano and Olive-

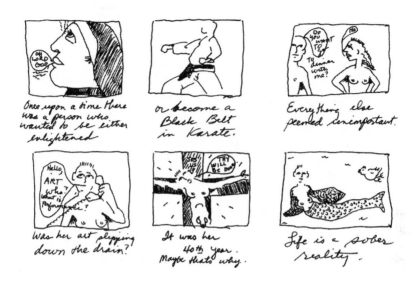

Fig. 7. Linda Montano, *Visualization #1* (1982). (Copyright © 1982 Linda Montano)

ros assumed in their collaborative performance *Learning to Pay Attention* (1979), in which they slowly performed synchronized karate movements.[136] Next, Montano sketched herself naked from the waist up, with unshaven armpits and buzz-cut hair, characteristics that identified her with 1980s lesbian culture. In the second-to-last frame, this short-haired, breasted figure has been nailed to a cross, a large penis visible between her legs. Finally, in the last frame, the artist appeared as a mermaid, with a fishlike tail and winglike arms. *Visualization #1* represented the internal negotiations among Montano's Holy Girl urges; her transgender, lesbian identity; the demands of artistic productivity; and other competing impulses. She depicted herself as both Jesus and nun, male and female, human and otherworldly. Montano's self-portrait as Christ reinforced her preoccupation with sainthood. It echoed the medieval devotional practice of *imitatio Christi*, in which believers imagine themselves suffering alongside or in place of Christ, and it reiterated the visions of many female saints (usually nuns) who imagined themselves on the cross.[137] Montano's vision of herself as Christ incorporated breasts as well as a penis, visualizing the transgender dynamics of women's experiences of *imitatio Christi*. She has described herself as "envious of the priests" and their access to ritual mysteries while also noting that she identified with Christ in the absence of female religious leaders: "The crucifix was so potent and so right there, and there were no women on the altar giving any other message."[138] In addition, Montano's conflation of gender in the figure of Christ registered her ambivalence about the relationship among femininity, sexuality, and holiness: "the only way to be good was to be crucified or have breasts cut off."[139] Female suffering and female holiness were thus equated with the mutilation and assault of the female body. In this way, Montano's transgendered image presented a sharp critique of Catholic patriarchy, its gender-exclusive policies, and its violent consequences. Further, Montano's drawing of herself as Christ visualized her psychological pain—resulting from the conflicting demands of her desires, fears, and dreams—as physical pain. The devotional literature of Montano's childhood admonished Catholics that the gruesome physical pain of Jesus's crucifixion and the saints' martyrdoms trumped any other form of suffering. Compared to these excruciating and very common Catholic images of the suffering of Christ and the saints, psychological suffering was particularly scorned.[140] Just as Montano's identification with Christ in *Visualization #1* legitimized her suffering, abstaining from eating in the convent refigured the psychic pain of sexual trauma into physical form, marking her suffering as morally valuable and worthy of attention from her community. In addition, by physically manifesting her psychological distress, Montano connected herself to the long tradition of women who achieved sainthood—and prophetic authority—by enduring physical suffering in imitation of Christ.

The medium of endurance art resonated with two aspects of Montano's understanding of suffering and sainthood. First, she connected both suffering and performance art with the endurance of pain: "When I was introduced to art soon after [leaving the convent], I immediately found a way to transfer religious fervor and my predilection for penance and suffering into my work . . . as performance art."[141] In addition, Montano has crucially linked both suffering and performance to purity. Both responding to posttraumatic affect and drawing on convent imagery, she sought purity in the medium of endurance art: "I didn't want to make more things . . . the invisible, sculpting the invisible, seemed less polluting."[142] Rather than producing objects, strategies of endurance allowed her to explore internal states, daily life, and the ethical negotiations of collaboration, interaction, and encounter as art. Montano has most frequently, and most powerfully, presented these concepts in her recurring iconography of the nun, a theologically charged embodiment of sexual purity and monastic discipline. Akin to her Holy Girl persona, her nun performances marked her concern with female suffering, expressed her posttraumatic feelings of difference from others, and presented her dual desires to display and hide the wound of trauma, both to transcend or escape the pain of trauma and to garner spiritual acclaim for her suffering and survival. In this way, Montano's monastic approach to endurance action can be understood as both an artistic strategy and a moral imperative. Psychiatrist Robert J. Lifton observed that posttraumatic responses can challenge the meaning of the traumatic event for the survivor and initiate reflection on moral questions.[143] As such, Montano's quest for sainthood signifies the posttraumatic longing for the restoration of bodily integrity, purity, and justice.

PERFORMING SISTER ROSE AUGUSTINE

The recurring iconography of the nun in Montano's endurance art clarified the moral value of her suffering and tracked changes in her attitude toward suffering over time. From her first performance works to her most recent actions, Montano has consistently presented herself as a nun. Just a few of the pieces in which she performed in nun's garments, modified a habit, and/or included photographs of herself as a novice are *Lying: Dead Chicken, Live Angel* (1971), *Sitting: Dead Chicken, Live Angel* (1971), *Lying: Dead Chicken, Live Angel* (1972), *Chicken Dance: The Streets of San Francisco* (1972), *Chicken Dance* (1974), *The Screaming Nun* (1975), *Learning to Talk/Living in Mandeville, UCSD, for Five Days as Five Different People* (1977), *Learning to Talk* (1978), *Listening to the 80s: Inside/Outside* (1980), *The Nun's Fairy Tale* (1981), *On Death and Dying* (1982), *Seven Spiritual Lives of Linda M. Montano* (1996, in which a photograph of herself as a novice hovered over a famous photograph of Mother Mary Joseph, the founder of the Maryknoll order), *Teresa of Avila* (2007), and *Linda Mary Montano: I Dreamed I Was Mother Teresa* (2009). Whether explicitly wearing convent garments or more abstractly bearing the marks of her vows, Montano's monasticism both embodied and challenged midcentury American Catholic notions of suffering and sainthood.

In Montano's first performance actions—her chicken woman pieces, created only a few years after she left the novitiate—Montano assumed her convent persona, Sister Rose Augustine. Dressed in gauzy white gowns that echoed traditional novices' garments, she "present[ed herself] as a symbolic religious, a nun-chicken in disguise."[144] Naked beneath the transparent fabric and weighed down by wings made of clear garbage bags stuffed with feathers, the artist remained as motionless as possible throughout these performances: "I tried to imitate the statues by becoming a saint via art: dressed in white, sitting still, white on my face."[145] In attempting to turn into a statue, Montano objectified herself. She has explicitly connected this distancing with death: "I felt somewhat vulnerable lying there, not talking, eyes closed, not really dead, object-like."[146] Montano's chicken woman actions pivoted on the presentation of her live body as if dead. Her white, waxy skin; closed eyes; silent, inert body; and the filmy curtains and otherworldly staging of the works recall a funeral or wake.[147] In this dramatic imagery, Montano's use of the figure of the nun approximated death. Underscored by the eroticism of her nudity beneath her habitlike garment, her actions enacted the psychic death of self that she experienced as a result of sexual trauma. She has referred to these performances as her "early lying in state images" and as a series of "death simulations."[148] Her performance of *Lying* in 1972 was alternately titled *Don't Be a Chicken Last Rites While Lying in My Own Shell*, merging fear, isolation, and death in the figure of the nun.[149] Subsequent works continued to layer the nun with images of death, as in the video *On Death and Dying* (1982), in which three nuns played poker accompanied by an audio track in which an elderly nurse described the physical deterioration of dying bodies.

Death also characterized the artist-audience relationship that Montano actively worked to create in her "lying in state" performances. She performed these works in public, anticipating a devotional form of audience encounter. Her attempt to become a statue resulted in a totally silent, impassive, and restrained relation to members of her audience. She hoped to cultivate the admiration and regard of strangers: "[I asked] audiences to watch me endure. Give me attention, witness my long-term commitment. . . . Their presence was like a bath of recognition and approval."[150] Montano's language resonated with theories of witnessing developed by psychiatrist Dori Laub, who argued that "there is, in each survivor, an imperative need to *tell* and thus to come to *know* one's story."[151] However, by its nature, he argued, traumatic experience "cannot be fully captured in *thought, memory,* and *speech*."[152] By performing as a statue in the garments of a nun, Montano's early endurance actions sought empathetic witnesses to her suffering. However, as Auerhahn and Laub noted, "[T]estimonies are not monologues; they cannot take place in solitude."[153] The attitude and demeanor of Montano's nun/saint statue did garner attention, but presenting herself as an object of devotion also rendered her mute, limiting her body's actions, stifling her voice, and curtailing encounters with audiences. The rigidity of Montano's presentation of the nun began to crumble in *The Screaming Nun* (1975), a turning point in her presentation and representation of trauma in the figure of the nun.[154] As Montano describes the work, "I dressed as a nun, danced, screamed, and heard confession at Embarcadero Plaza. . . . [A friend] said that I screamed uncontrollably and that the sound echoed throughout the entire space. I don't remember doing this."[155] Photographic documentation of the performance shows the artist wearing the white habit of a novice; rather than a gauzy interpretation of a habit, as in her earlier chicken woman pieces, these robes hewed more closely to a novice's authentic garb. While earlier performances presented a still body and pristine garments, in *The Screaming Nun* suppressed energy imbued her pose. Her hands seemed to grasp her rosary convulsively; her lower lip seemed to tremble. Most strikingly, Montano appeared disheveled, her habit spotted with dirt and creased with wrinkles, marked by her movements in the world. Here the restrained, immobile statue of previous works was replaced with an angry, straining woman. In *The Screaming Nun*, Montano vocalized her psychic wounds in art for the first time. Rather than attempting to awaken strangers' regard and empathy with the pre–Vatican II ideal of her beautiful, impassive endurance of pain, Montano screamed her rage and anger to passersby. This somatic expression marked the beginning of a series of endurance actions that literally gave voice to her psychological suffering.

ABSTRACTING THE HABIT

After this performance, Montano's work began to suggest a new understanding of suffering, marked by a looser, less literal appropriation of her nun persona. Instead of the garments and outward characteristics of the nun or the physical challenge of remaining as still as a statue, she subjected herself to intense psychological disciplines. Her concern with discipline was already present in her earliest work, as in the chicken woman performances and *Happiness Piece*. By the late 1970s, however, her work increasingly began to suggest the seeds of a new approach, as in one of her best-known video works, *Mitchell's Death* (1978). Montano created this piece in response to the sudden death of Mitchell Payne, her estranged husband, who was killed by his cousin in an accidental shooting. The death initially was considered a suicide, but in a therapy session a month later Payne's cousin recovered the memory of the shooting.[156] Montano mourned Payne in a series of performance events: *A Tribute to Mitchell Payne, March 31, 1944–August 19, 1977* (1977), *Z . . . A Dream, Just after Mitchell Died* (1977), *A Tribute to Mitchell Payne* (1978), and *Mitchell's Death* (1978). She produced a video, also titled *Mitchell's Death*, as an accompaniment to the last of these performances. In this much-exhibited video, Montano documented her grief by inserting acupuncture needles into her face while chanting a detailed narrative of the events of the days immediately following Payne's death. The monotone she used for this narrative recalled the recitation of Mass, novenas, and other aural aspects of Catholic daily life: "[C]hanting singsong was a device I used to make a churchlike experience out of horror."[157] In this and later endurances, Montano drew on a more varied set of religious and visual traditions rather than relying on nun's garb and direct convent imagery. She later joked, "As Shakespeare, Annie Sprinkle, and others have said, 'Dresseth liketh undt nuneth, duth noteth undt sainteth maketh!'"[158] This process of abstraction continued in *Art/Life One Year Performance 1983–1984*, in which Montano developed a more flexible model for addressing the tensions of monasticism in her work. She established new ways of representing the key elements of monastic life—including the vow, the habit, collaboration, and suffering—in terms of a series of long-term commitments to specific behaviors and attitudes.

Montano continued to develop and evolve these new monastic modes of endurance in her next work, *7 Years of Living Art* (1984–91), which radically collapsed her art and her life. She structured her daily life according to a series of "inner," "outer," and "other" vows: she organized each year around one of the seven Hindu chakras, which she associated with a persona, a color, and a tone. These associations dictated her inner commitments: the color of her clothing, her hand gestures, her accent, her behavior with others. "Outer" disciplines were performed monthly at the New Museum, where she offered confessional art/life counseling sessions to passersby. Each year, to fulfill her "others" commitment, she invited an artist to collaborate in her home for sixteen days. In its combination of interiority and collaborative encounter, this work replicated the monastic environment's dynamic between contemplation and missionary work. However, in the midst of the intense, daily demands of this piece, Montano's attitude toward suffering changed. She learned some flexibility within the vow: "[I was] so disciplined, so difficult on myself that after the third year . . . all the disciplines fell away and it became a fashion statement."[159] She no longer assumed accents in speaking, but she did continue to wear single-colored clothing, practice some interior commitments, and conduct her New Museum work and collaborative workshops. In *Another 7 Years of Living Art* (1991–98), she continued to fine-tune her attention to the long-term sustainability of her performance vows. She fulfilled her others commitment—annual visits to the United Nations' Chagall Chapel in New York—by "sit[ting there] physically or astrally."[160] With these releases, Montano marked her new, more flexible understanding of suffering. Rather than seeking and passively enduring pain, she presented suffering as a more neutral, experiential process. By dropping the less successful vows of *7 Years of Living Art* and working to manage her commitments over the years, Montano allowed herself the authority to shape her own experiences. Unlike the dissociative stillness of her early actions, *7 Years of Living Art* and *Another 7 Years of Living Art* implemented discipline and self-control in a gentler fashion. While this increased sense of agency seemed to mitigate some aspects of Montano's dissociative traumatic subjectivity, *7 Years of Living Art* also reinforced her continued investment in purity. As the work progressed, Montano declared, "[M]y priority now is to be attentive, natural and pure enough in heart to walk in the snow and enjoy it."[161]

The continued evolution in her attitude toward suffering is registered in two letters that Montano wrote to Italian performance artist Franko B, an endurance artist who, like Ron Athey, has used bloodletting and other self-harming actions in his work. In 1982, she was captivated by the grandiosity and Catholic aesthetic of his painful performances.

> Having returned from your Italy, I have a deeper understanding of you and your work: What more is left for an Italian artist to do, given that daily cultural diet of baroque, bizarre beauty that you saw growing up in Italy, day after day? A diet of saints and popes and majestic giants! What more could you do than to make yourself a bleeding, breathing breath-taking *LIVING SCULPTURE*—and more shocking—one as brilliant as the blood-drained mighty marbles that dwarf consciousness? Franko, you responded with reality, with real blood, with stillness, with luminous flesh, with pulsation. We applaud and gasp in silence in the "eternal" presence of your life/art.[162]

By comparing his body to the still, "blood-drained mighty marbles" of Italian sculpture, Montano linked Franko B's work to her early chicken woman performances, in which she objectified her own body in attempting to become a statue. Twenty-four years later, at age sixty-four, she wrote:

> Franko, my friend, I must say I had to leave your performance I saw in Scotland. The medical imagery and references to illness and hospitals were just too much for me. Plus it made me worry for you. Now that I'm 64, I worry about infections and damage to the body, about misuse of this house for the soul. Please listen to me: I am dis-

gusted by my own use of art props and actions that brought gasps and silence to my "audiences" and I don't want you to reach my age and say "what was I doing?" So listen to Aunt Linda: do the opposite for a while. Feed hungry puppies or rock AIDS babies, but please, please love your body, temple of holy spirit.[163]

In this letter, Montano repudiated the self-deprecating forms of suffering that she herself had endured in her early performance actions. By returning to Franko B's work in this way, Montano enacted the paired actions of looking and looking away that I advocate for readers of *Long Suffering*: she allowed for changes in her perspective over time, opened herself to the painful, personal impact of traumatic representation, and responded to the artist as a subject with an invitation to empathic, ethical dialogue. At the same time, her concern for Franko B's physical and psychological being revealed a fundamental re-conception of endurance and discipline in her work. Montano's artistic praxis has depended on the dedicated implementation of self-discipline from its origins in her chicken woman pieces. In the early 1980s, she defined her art in terms of asceticism: "Discipline is my style."[164] In 2002 she qualified this commitment: "Self-discipline can never become self-punishment or it will backfire."[165] She elaborated on this sentiment in the video *Teresa of Avila* (2007). In the character of St. Teresa, she said, "Do not make the mistake that I did of mortifying yourself inappropriately with too many penances so that you can feel special. . . . Do not make the mistakes I made of designing your own penances and mortifications."[166]

Since the turn of the century, Montano's asceticism has become more mindful, though no less difficult; she has continued to pursue sainthood with her art/life disciplines. However, in her twenty-first-century endurance art Montano has assumed a position of spiritual authority. In taking on the personas of famous nun-saints, including St. Teresa of Avila and Mother Teresa, she has affirmed her own spiritual status: "Now, I feel I am a nun—the real nun, the kind of nun I would have been—because I integrated art and religion."[167] In 2010 she performed a three-day event entitled *Linda Mary Montano Celebrates Mother Teresa's Birthday* (2010) on the streets of New York City. Due to a painful medical condition that led to the deterioration of her posture, she noticed that her stooping walk resembled Mother Teresa's gait, and she decided to impersonate her in a public space. Three hours a day for three days, wearing the blue-bordered habit of Mother Teresa's order and surrounded by an entourage of female security guards in black suits and slicked-back hair, Montano prayed with onlookers in front of the Empire State Building, offering "a word, a blessing, a hug, a hope."[168] In these and other works, Montano has actively incarnated sainthood for herself. Leading prayers, blessing her audiences, and offering care and compassion to strangers, her actions recall the direct apostolate of her Maryknoll missionary training. Her appropriation of actual saints' personas may appear blasphemous, but few observers objected. Video documentation showed the respect with which most people, deeply touched, approached to request her favor. The image of Montano's Mother Teresa, moving among the crowd and reaching out to her devoted supplicants, contrasted sharply with the still, silent passivity of her earliest chicken woman performances. Rather than supplicating, self-objectifying, or incoherently denouncing, as in past performances, endurance strategies here served to generate dialogue and facilitate meaningful spiritual encounter. At the same time, the presence of security guards complicated this performance. While lending authority and credibility to her impersonation, their subtly transgendered appearances also registered Montano's dissent from institutional Catholic positions on gender and sexuality.[169] Further, these guard figures underscored Montano's abiding concern with vulnerability. Their protective, watchful stances gestured to issues of safety: the potential for violence and the anticipation of suffering. In this way, Montano's endurances continue to signal the weight of her traumatic subjectivity. Though now more authentically performing witness to her own suffering, and generously acting as a witness to the pain of others, Montano has not erased the past. Her late career endurance actions continue to prepare her and others for future hardship, marking her survivor status. Like southern nuns picketing for civil rights and the Berrigan brothers torching draft cards, Montano's public actions enact a uniquely Catholic vision that is both progressive and prophetic, recognizing the reality of violence yet simultaneously honoring the possibility of just human relations by setting the conditions for meaningful encounter. Ethical relations also serve as a touchstone for the endurance art of Ron Athey, whose performances testify to both suffering and communal healing. Parallel to Montano's pursuit of sainthood through Catholic prophetic witness, Athey has sought to heal and be healed in the tradition of Pentecostal healing evangelists. He has appropriated the techniques and spiritual responsibilities of charismatic itinerant revival preachers, just as Montano has performed the nun's persona for herself and others.

| The Faith Healings of Ron Athey

In the final actions of *Martyrs and Saints* (1992–93), performance artist Ron Athey literalized the torture of Jesus and the martyrdom of St. Sebastian in and on his own body. In a scene titled "Surgical Stigmata," his performance collaborators, hands sealed in rubber gloves, carefully pinched and pierced his flesh. They precisely placed thick hypodermic needles, one after another, into his forehead, embedding a cross-hatched crown of thorns. Later, in "Saint Sebastian," while Athey spoke in a low tone, lips moving to form incomprehensible syllables, blood erupted from these wounds as each metal thorn was pulled from his head. Thick rivulets of blood ran down his face and covered his features. As extreme iterations of familiar, violent, religious subjects in western art history, the significance of these and other religious scenes in Athey's performance series *Torture Trilogy* (1992–97) may appear straightforward. Critics and historians have variously interpreted his directly religious language and content as references to the martyrdom of gay men during the AIDS epidemic, ironic gestures toward the role of religious organizations in the 1990s culture wars, or straightforward concessions to a sexual fetish.[1] Yet the religious forms and content of Athey's work cannot be reduced to these circumscribed interpretations. Athey himself has insisted on the sincerity of his appropriation: "I was aware that using Christian images seemed too obvious, but they were the images that I've been affected by my whole lifetime. They are heartfelt. They seem inexhaustible because they are archetypal."[2] The religious resonances of Athey's imagery exceed metaphor, irony, or archetype; instead, the embodied worship practices of Pentecostal faith-healing services have animated his art from his earliest performances. As a young child, Athey regularly attended deliverance services, where he witnessed the chaotic physicality of the baptism in the spirit, the collective experience of uninhibited dancing, convulsing, and vocalizing that for Pentecostals signals divine presence. He observed the visual spectacle of the laying on of hands, watching charismatic itinerant evangelists display the grotesque suffering of ill bodies and orchestrate their miraculous healing. Radically invested in healing as a communal practice, Athey crafted the *Torture Trilogy* as an homage to and reconsideration of the Pentecostal healing revival movement of 1960s and 1970s Southern California.

By grounding his performances in the charismatic, participatory din of religious revival, Athey located his endurance art within deep traditions of American religious expression and social change. His childhood immersion in the healing revival relied on local conditions specific to Southern California, but it also reflected a lineage of revival stretching back to the Great Awakening. Evangelist Billy Graham, one of the best-known revivalists of the twentieth century, articulated the way the effects of these and other revivals have rippled throughout national politics. Preaching in Athey's hometown of Los Angeles in 1949, Graham celebrated the progressive potential of American revival.

> A revival brings tremendous social implications. Do you know what came out of past revivals? The abolishment of slavery came out of revival. The abolishment of child labor came out of revival. When the Wesleys preached in England, people were working 90 hours a week! As a result of that revival, sixty working hours became standard, and our great trade unions were organized. Did you know that the Y.M.C.A., the Salvation Army, most of our charity organizations, slum clearance programs, the Sunday School, Christian reform, and Women's Suffrage are revival results?[3]

From the eighteenth-century fervor of the Great Awakening to the Toronto Blessing of the 1990s, religious revivals in North America have sparked political consciousness by gathering believers into communities outside traditional denominations, transgressing normative practices, exceeding structural boundaries, and generating new social, economic, and political relations. The spiritual impetus of revival can agitate believers, however briefly, to envision different ethical relations between self and other and to practice new ways of being in community. The racial integration that characterized the 1906 Azusa Street revival, which spawned Pentecostalism, is just one example. Although the movement quickly split into white and black denominations—divisions that persist to the present—after the revival, in the spirit of Azusa Street, some healing revival ministers in the 1950s and 1960s deliberately flouted segregation laws during their tent meetings.[4] Pentecostalism has not usually been associated with liberal politics, but in this way religious revival made it possible to acknowledge the injustices of the present and helped foster the conditions for a more progressive future. Like the revivals his performances emulated, Athey's art actions have fostered new communities, drawn attention to communal responsibilities, and posited new ways of being that bore witness to injustice, pain, and survival.

In autobiographical articles, interviews, performance scripts, artist's notes, and other texts and images, Athey has described the formation of his identity in terms of his early experience of Pentecostalism.[5] Raised in a household of Pentecostal believers who regularly attended raucous, spirit-filled revivals, Athey displayed an early affinity for spiritual showmanship. Relatives considered him a Pentecostal child prodigy and expected him to showcase his gifts during public prayer and healing services. At a young age, Athey assumed shared responsibility for the family's spiritual life, allied with his grandmother and aunt, who frequently experienced prophetic visions. Their pronouncements of God's will organized daily life for the household and offered the family, and Athey in particular, a role of cosmological significance, or, as Athey has written, "a life of mystical power and grandiosity."[6] At the same time, Athey's childhood experience of Pentecostalism was severely complicated by emotional abuse, domestic violence, and incest. The extremity of this abusive setting paralleled and contributed to the immediacy of the family's high-stakes religious sensibilities. Athey left the Pentecostal faith as an adolescent, and, burdened with the aftereffects of his traumatic history, he has since survived deep disillusionment, drug use, self-harm, suicide attempts, and an HIV-positive diagnosis. In his performances, particularly the *Torture Trilogy*—which includes *Martyrs and Saints* (1992–93), *4 Scenes in a Harsh Life* (1993–97), and *Deliverance* (1995–97)—Athey has grappled with this troubled history, making sense of the powerful images and ideas of the Pentecostal healing revival in the context of violence and abuse.[7]

The actions performed in the *Torture Trilogy* derived directly from Athey's autobiography. The series posed a question of crucial importance to Athey during the AIDS crisis of the 1990s as he faced the implications of his diagnosis and the deaths of friends and loved ones: "The *Trilogy* started with a question: What is healing?"[8] Throughout the deeply personal narratives of the *Torture Trilogy*, Athey mimicked and transformed Pentecostal faith-healing practices, from embodying the theology of divine presence to impersonating well-known Pentecostal healing evangelists. Across the trajectory of the three performances of the series, a group of loosely connected vignettes, akin to tableaux vivants in their vividness, presented his early spiritual virtuosity and abusive family life, his adolescent drug use and suicide attempts, his HIV-positive diagnosis and search for wholeness and healing, and his experience of caring for and mourning the deaths of loved ones with AIDS. Over years of repeated performances, Athey and his cast honed a sequence of iconic scenes.

Martyrs and Saints opened with a hospital setting in which Athey and others in his company cleaned and performed medical procedures on passive, ill bodies. In subsequent scenes, the hypodermic-needle crown of thorns was inserted into Athey's head and his body was pierced with arrows in a tableau echoing the martyrdom of St. Sebastian. The final image of St. Sebastian reappeared in the introduction to *4 Scenes*: a tattooed, naked figure leaning on a crutch and pierced with real arrows while Athey preached a sermon in the sweeping skirts characteristic of female healing evangelists. This sermon was followed by a strip-club beating and a scene, made famous by controversies over National Endowment for the Arts funding, in which Athey cut into the body of a cast member to create blood prints of the resulting wounds. An intravenous tube filled another man's scrotum with saline solution. Athey then lyrically reenacted his heroin overdose and performed a queer wedding ceremony among three members of the cast. *Deliverance*, the final work in the series, traced three ill men in a desperate search for healing. After circling the space burdened with loads of crutches, they submitted to invasive medical procedures, appealed to icons of several religious traditions, engaged in a carnivalesque sexual interlude, and in the final scene of the *Trilogy* were wrapped in shrouds and buried in mounds of dirt. Infused with the embodied practices of Pentecostal faith healing, these actions became the basic units of Athey's visual language and have continued to appear in later works such as *Incorruptible Flesh (Dissociative Sparkle)* (2006). In this chapter, I argue that the opened, overflowing body visualized in his endurance art is charged with a specifically Pentecostal theology.

OVERFLOWING WITH LIQUID LOVE

The endurances Athey performed throughout the *Torture Trilogy* relied on concepts of divine presence with their origins in early Pentecostalism. Rooted in the emotional American revivalist movements of the late nineteenth century, which sought to incite religious fervor through direct, emotional religious experiences, early Pentecostals rejected the idea of a remote God. Rather than remaining aloof from the world, they argued, God blesses individuals regularly with personal divine experiences called "gifts of the spirit." For Pentecostals, then and now, these charismata manifest physi-

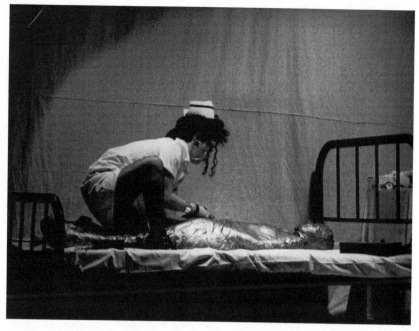

Fig. 8. Ron Athey and Company, "A Nurse's Penance," *Martyrs and Saints* (1992), Lace Contemporary Exhibitions, Los Angeles. (Photograph by Elyse Regehr. Courtesy of Ron Athey.)

cally during worship services in the actions of believers, principally as speaking in tongues (glossolalia), prophesying, and faith healing.[9] Sociologist Margaret Poloma has described the way Pentecostalism locates the miraculous in the everyday.

> Basic to this worldview is the belief that God is active in an ongoing way in the world. It is a worldview that moves beyond the commonly accepted *belief* that God can perform miracles to common *personal* experiences of a divinity that walks and talks on the planet earth. The seemingly paranormal experiences of glossolalia, healing, prophecy, and diverse "miracles" are "supernaturally natural" signs that God is always available, working collaboratively with humans.[10]

The act of receiving the gifts of the spirit—the baptism of the spirit—situates the Holy Spirit within the Pentecostal body. Speaking in tongues occurs within a trancelike state from which the speaker brings forth an ecstatic, wild, and generally unintelligible outpouring of repetitive sounds—as in Athey's repetitive mutterings as his crown of thorns bled at the end of *Martyrs and Saints*. Ostensibly verbal, speaking in tongues expresses the "wonderful nearness of the Spirit, as close as one's own larynx and vocal cords," according to religious historian Harvey Cox.[11] In other words, when one speaks in tongues, the Holy Spirit settles within one's physical body, overflowing into speech. Similarly, prophecy is a public pronouncement, a gift from God to the body, in the vocal cords (speech), mind (dreams), or eyes (visions).[12] In faith healing, central to Athey's experience of the baptism in the spirit, believers place their hands directly on the body of a sick person. For the faithful, this "point of contact" heals ailments by directly transferring Jesus's power from the believer to the sufferer.[13] Faith healer and evangelist Oral Roberts described his first experience of receiving the gift of healing, which came upon him as he preached a sermon titled "If You Need Healing—Do These Things."

> I was just a little over halfway through in this sermon when the anointing of God became so great that I could not stand still. Suddenly, I leaped off the high platform. . . . As if by prearranged signal [the audience] leaped up and stood facing me. . . . I saw at a glance that I would not get to finish my sermon, that the power of the Lord was present to heal and I must act immediately. . . . I started laying hands on them one by one.[14]

Pentecostal services in the 1970s, like those Athey attended as a child, regularly included these and other, even more intensely physical gifts such as dancing in the spirit, singing in the spirit, laughing in the spirit, and being slain in the spirit (swooning).[15] In *4 Scenes in a Harsh Life*, Athey described the visceral, communal experience of baptism in the spirit: "In church I would close my eyes and absorb the rambling vibrations given from the gift of tongues, mixed in with the sounds of foot-stomping, and bodies hitting the floor hard as they went out in the spirit."[16] In this way, the Pentecostal body manifests a deeply material encounter with God. Religious studies scholar Daniel E. Albrecht has observed, "A Pentecostal ideal in worship is to be professing toward a goal of 'radical openness' to God."[17] The baptism in the spirit makes this profound reception of the divine visible to the entire community through the actions of the body. In the cries and calls of those speaking in tongues and prophesying, in the jerks and twitches of those dancing in the spirit, the baptism in the spirit opens believers' bodies, welcoming divine excess and displaying their accessibility to the Holy Spirit. Within a community of Pentecostal believers, the gifts of the spirit serve as evidence of one's communion with God.[18] Controversial among Christians in general and among some Pentecostal denominations, Pentecostal doctrine defines the baptism in the spirit as a necessary marker of salvation: to be certain that one is saved, one *must* physically manifest the baptism in the spirit.[19] Unlike other evangelicals, Pentecostals insist that the baptism in the spirit certifies a believer's salvation.[20] As a result, the communal performance of the baptism in the spirit is charged with profound theological meaning. Publically receiving the gifts of the spirit demonstrates an individual's salvation and marks the spiritual authority of the individual and the community. Physicality and performativity are thus at the heart of Pentecostal worship. Athey's choice of the performance art medium corresponds to the power of this communal embodiment and witness.

Pentecostal theology posits a fluid physical relation among individual bodies, communities, and divine presence. Pentecostals have consistently described these ecstatic experiences in language that visualizes the Holy Spirit as a liquid substance that immerses and invades the body with words like *baptizing, outpouring, filling, falling,* and *coming on.*[21] Early Pentecostal Jenny Moore wrote in 1907 that during the baptism in the spirit "it seemed as if a vessel broke within me and water surged up through my being, which when it reached my mouth came out in a torrent of speech in the languages which God had given me."[22] Roberts spoke of feeling emptied and filled: "I felt something going out of me and something coming into me."[23] Like Georges Bataille's *informe,* the baptism in the spirit creates an excess, a formless divine presence that pours out and spills over in the physical action and rambling vibrations of bodies.[24] Athey's endurances perform this ecstatic saturation and overflow literally, using the liquids of his own body.

Throughout the *Torture Trilogy,* Athey's actions staged the intake and expulsion of bodily effluvia. Liquids penetrate, fill, and overflow, induced by vomiting, urinating, and bloodletting in particular. The scatological nature of these liquids and the violence of their instigation radically depart from traditional Pentecostal practices. However, Athey's liquid actions parallel the basic imagery and experience that Pentecostal believers describe. His performances have exaggerated the particularly fluid character of the physicality already embedded in Pentecostal concepts of the baptism in the spirit, as described in 1923 by evangelist Aimee Semple McPherson: "So conscious was I of the pardoning blood of Jesus that I seemed to feel it flowing over me."[25] Echoing McPherson's immersive experience, Athey's actions in the *Torture Trilogy* paired scenes of *filling up*—bodily penetration, insertion, and invasion—with subsequent actions of *pouring out*. Foreign objects and outside forces repeatedly penetrated and swelled bodies, generating liquid ruptures. The script of *Deliverance* described a representative series of these insertions and releases, which often centered on the anus: "Jewelry is pulled out of my asshole, I have been given an enema, and when I am expelling it I am gagged, causing me to vomit."[26] Bodily fluids leaked from openings in veins, genitals, and other orifices, creating, as art historian Amelia Jones has written, "bodies full of holes."[27] Blood flowed freely, for example, in "Saint Sebastian" (*Martyrs and Saints*), when arrows were buried in and then yanked from skin; in "Suicide" (*4 Scenes in a Harsh Life*), when hypodermic needles traced and pierced the veins of the arm; and in "Rod 'n' Bob: A Post AIDS Boy-Boy Show" (*Deliverance*), when vigorous anal sex with double-headed dildos caused chafing and bleeding. Responding to the Pentecostal call for "radical receptivity," Athey and his performance cast consistently opened bodies by slicing, puncturing, piercing, and penetrating them.[28] These overflowing penetrations and expulsions mimicked the baptism in the spirit by literalizing openness and receptivity in and on the bodies of Athey and his performers.[29]

INTERNAL BLEEDING

Athey's performance interpretations of the baptism in the spirit resonated with the Pentecostal gifts of the spirit, but his actions reflected an extremity that far exceeded traditional Pentecostal worship practices. For Athey the physicality of Pentecostal theology was reinforced and intensified by a traumatic childhood. Raised by their grandmother and Aunt Vena, Athey and his siblings experienced the Pentecostal gifts of the spirit within the framework of a deeply devout and simultaneously severely abusive family. Athey observed direct parallels between the violence of his home life and the ecstatic states of the baptism in the spirit. At revivals and in prayer at home, his grandmother's experience of being filled with the Holy Spirit modeled self-harm: "My fiery, red-haired grandma screamed and pulled her hair; she starved herself and fell face down in the spirit."[30] Fasting, exclaiming loudly, and being slain in the spirit were common prayer activities for Pentecostal women in the 1970s, but the intensity of Athey's grandmother's pursuits normalized self-destructive behaviors and contributed to an atmosphere of unpredictability, fear, and the threat of violence.[31] For Athey's mother Joyce, who was present only when periodically released from mental institutions, the baptism in the spirit coincided with psychotic episodes and attacks of epilepsy. Athey recalled, "My mother was paranoid schizophrenic, manic depressive, and severely epileptic. Her epilepsy voice was almost the same as her other [baptized in the spirit] voice, and her dancing in the spirit would often end on the floor with a seizure. It was neurological, even if [as a child] I believed that it was from the Holy Spirit."[32] In this way, embodied, altered states of consciousness extended far beyond the boundaries of church services. Athey's memories of observing the baptism in the spirit take on new meaning in the context of this violent home life: "In church I would close my eyes and absorb the rambling vibrations given from the gift of tongues, mixed in with the sounds of foot-stomping, and bodies hitting the floor hard as they went out in the spirit."[33] In Athey's childhood experience, the baptism in the spirit accompanied violence, put suffering bodies on display, and located these bodies at the center of family and spiritual life. Athey's endurance actions have testified to his family's extreme embodiment of Pentecostalism and his long-term endurance of the apocalyptic experiences of domestic violence. He has spoken and visualized his traumatic history with courage and painful clarity. Many readers may find his graphic representations deeply disturbing, and some may experience a powerful urge to look away from these spectacles of suffering. Enduring this discomfort, staying with these difficult performances through a sustained process of looking, looking away, and looking again, creates the potential for becoming empathic witnesses to Athey's testimony.

In addition to the heightened physicality of the baptism in the spirit, the Pentecostal metaphor of the liquid infilling and outpouring of the Holy Spirit coincided with sexual abuse in the Athey household. Throughout his childhood, Athey observed an incestuous relationship between his grandmother and his aunt Vena, later extended to include his sister. In response to enigmatic "female problems," Athey's grandmother regularly administered medicinal douches in long, private sessions that took place behind closed doors. Athey explained:

> To say the least, Vena and her mother had a strange relationship, but they shared a bed before I was born, so it never seemed odd to me. . . . What made me suspect the holiness, or even the normalcy of their relationship was the enduring tradition they had of the beta-dine douches. Vena had "female" problems, and for reasons that were not to be questioned, her mother needed to give her a betadine douche once a week. Vena and her mother would go into the bath-

room wearing bathrobes, and disappear for at least an hour. . . . Apparently it took quite a few rinses. . . . Later, when the door finally opened, Vena would walk straight to her bedroom and close the door. My grandma would clean up the bathroom, then meet her in the room.[34]

Athey's sister was spared these weekly douches, but she was forced to endure other procedures, including the invasive application of medicine internally: "LeeAnne would be taken to their bedroom, where she would be made to kneel doggy-style on the bed, rear-end hunched up, head down. First my grandmother would squirt inside of her with the vaginal inserter, then she would mix it in deeper with her finger . . . my sister never talked about it afterwards. Ever."[35] Listening on the other side of the door, Athey served as a firsthand witness to this victimization: "I tried innocently walking in on them in the bathroom, but the door was always locked, and when I pressed my ear against the door, all I could hear was the shower running full blast. . . . Though I was curious, I knew better than to enter their bedroom or get caught listening at the door."[36] Athey's performance actions—his interpretations of filling in and pouring out the baptism in the spirit—visualized the sexualized actions overheard behind the door. His preoccupation with bodily insertions and the expulsion of bodily effluvia directly reenacted this childhood violence. Athey's notes on the "Operating Room" scene in *Martyrs and Saints* echoed his description of events in the household: "Three nurses perform invasive genital procedures simultaneously on three patients."[37] In *4 Scenes in a Harsh Life*, a saline drip hugely enlarged a man's scrotum. And in *Deliverance*, an enema, administered as Athey crouched on hands and knees, revisited the traumatic incest endured by his aunt and sister.[38]

Responding to this violence, Athey observed, "A common metaphor, for us of the emotionally wounded camp, is that we are bleeding inside. Which is a wounds-of-Christ inversion, an interior stigmata."[39] His *Torture Trilogy* manifested these wounds externally through self-inflicted violence. Visualizing what Kristine Stiles has called a "corporeal semiotics of distress," members of Athey's company wounded their own flesh and willingly subjected themselves to painful procedures.[40] The first scene of *4 Scenes in a Harsh Life*, the "Holy Woman," clarified the stakes of these self-injurious actions in Athey's performances. Dressed in the flowing white dress characteristic of female Pentecostal evangelists, Athey preached the following testimony. He described attending, with his grandmother, a three-day

Fig. 9. Ron Athey and Company, "Scene I," *Deliverance* (1997), Eurokaz Festival, Zagreb, Croatia. (Video still. Courtesy of Ron Athey.)

faith-healing service advertised as "Sister Linda and her Miraculous Gift of the Stigmata." When Sister Linda, the itinerant preacher headlining the service, did not reveal her stigmata before the audience, Athey became enraged. He described his response.

> When she still had not bled, I wanted to have a temper tantrum. I thought, "She's a big fat faker." . . . All she had were pictures, cheap snapshots of her blood-stained clothes, as if that were sufficient evidence of a miracle. I didn't want to hear stories of psychic phenomena, I wanted her to bleed. I had gone there with the desire to be anointed in the blood seeping directly from her palms.[41]

Disappointed, Athey turned this rage on himself and his sister.

> I found a brand-new razor blade, and took my li'l sister, Tina, into the backyard. I held her hand in mine, then sliced the tips of all her

fingers on that hand. Instinctively I knew that the clean slices would produce blood, and when it began to flow, Tina started to cry. I knew the cuts didn't hurt, that she was just frightened. I then took the razor to my own hand, to show her how insignificant the wounds were, and to make her stop crying.[42]

Athey positioned this childhood act of self-injury at the center of the *Torture Trilogy*: "This strange children's story gives context for the many angles of bloodletting that occur in the piece. The story ends with my slicing stigmata into my younger sister and myself, my first act of holy defiance."[43] This narrative exposed the networks of spirituality, family, care, and healing at stake in his self-harming performance actions.

For those like Athey who practice nonsuicidal self-injury (NSSI), cutting and other self-harming actions can temporarily alleviate the overwhelming sensations of intense negative emotions, from frustration to despair.[44] Quickly and reliably, self-harming actions can dissipate unbearable feelings, dispel disorder and confusion, and help restore equanimity—at least temporarily.[45] Athey has described the feelings of relief that accompany cutting: "The sight of your own blood, brought forth by your own hand, spells an almost immediate relief, a release to the pressure valve."[46] Despite a sharp increase in self-harming behaviors among children and adolescents from the 1960s to the present, NSSI is not well understood.[47] Long associated with complex PTSD, borderline personality disorder, and dissociative identity disorder, self-injury now appears in the *DSM-5* as a stand-alone condition. Its origins, mechanisms, and treatment are controversial among psychologists and psychiatrists, and recent research has yielded suggestive rather than conclusive findings. However, researchers agree that self-injury usually functions to regulate affect, providing the relief and release that Athey described.[48] Among children and adolescents, persistent self-injury may be a common response to the radical disruption of long-term domestic violence.[49] When caregivers fail to coherently identify and reflect children's feelings, teach effective strategies for managing emotions, or foster secure attachments and connections, children develop their own, often maladapted techniques for coping.[50] Abused children with families—like Athey's—that model impulsive, aggressive behaviors are particularly susceptible to developing self-injurious practices in their efforts to manage emotion.[51] In the absence of adequate techniques for responding to and calming disappointment, depression, anger, and other painful feelings, self-injury can provide a distorted form of care and sense of healing.[52] As psychologist E. David Klonsky has observed, "Some individuals may be better able to care for physical than emotional injuries. Self-injuring, then, may provide a soothing and gratifying opportunity to competently care for oneself by examining, cleaning, bandaging, or otherwise tending to the wound."[53] In this way, the creation of a wound externalizes the interior stigmata, visualizing pain that would otherwise remain hidden and generating the possibility of loving attention and connection, as when Athey held his sister's wounded hand in an attempt to soothe them both.

In *Torture Trilogy*, self-injurious actions occurred within a community of mutually consenting colleagues and friends who gently and tenderly cared for one another's wounded bodies. Athey has noted that at the time of these actions, these performers were ministering to the needs of friends and lovers dying of AIDS; they "were actually living those roles in real life."[54] Acts of cutting may have overshadowed these loving gestures, but quiet caretaking occurred perpetually. For example, in the "Human Printing Press" scene in *4 Scenes*, after Athey carved deep lines into Darryl Carlton's back, he curled his hands protectively around the man's torso. After beating Athey with whips in *Martyrs and Saints*, one cast member (photographer Catherine Opie) helped him to his feet and led him slowly away; she later pulled the hypodermic-needle crown of thorns from his head and tried to smooth the blood from his forehead. In *Deliverance*, during Athey's enema, each of his attendants kept a hand lightly touching his body.[55]

In 1993, at the beginning of the *Torture Trilogy*, Athey insisted on the intentionality of self-injury in his performances: "If you know why you're doing it, you can transcend and work through it. If you deny you're doing it, the problems can perpetuate themselves."[56] In 2007 Athey seemed more ambivalent about the virtues of self-harm and less comfortable justifying it: "There's self-harm you understand and there's self-harm that's going towards destruction."[57] He continued, "I don't think my work is violent. I think I have played with violence, especially in some of those dense scenes [in the *Torture Trilogy*]. Pain isn't necessarily violence."[58] This slippage from a discourse of self-injury to one of pain allowed Athey to argue that critiques of his work in terms of pain (especially as related to inflicting and accepting pain in the context of sadomasochistic sexuality) pivot on culturally constructed notions: "It hurts less to get spanked than it does to get waxed. But somehow just being given pain for beauty is different than being given pain for pleasure, or being given pain for punishment."[59] Athey's self-injurious art actions in the *Torture Trilogy* invoked complex networks of pain, pleasure, desire, and healing.

Cultural psychiatrist Armando Favazza has argued that self-injury is intimately connected to healing because it creates opportunities for tending and self-care. He has identified healing as a direct, if counterintuitive, motivation for acts of self-injury, which in his view seek "to destroy or alter body tissue to foster better health and healing."[60] In this sense, the pursuit of NSSI may evince a deep desire for wholeness. Memoirist Caroline Kettlewell described her experience of cutting in terms of individuation and affirmation.

> When I discovered the razor blade, cutting, if you'll believe me, was my gesture of hope. That first time, when I was twelve, was like some kind of miracle, a revelation. The blade slipped easily, painlessly through my skin. . . . All the chaos, the sound and fury, the uncertainty and confusion and despair—all of it evaporated in an instant, and I was for the moment grounded, coherent, whole. Here is the irreducible self. I drew the line in the sand, marked my body as mine, its flesh and its blood under my command.[61]

The touch of the blade—momentarily and at great cost—unifies the self. For Favazza, the urge to self-injure reveals a deep desire for integrity, an "attempt to foster healing, spirituality, and orderliness."[62] The particular nature of this impulse depends on the specific context of the action. According to Favazza, "Cutting open the skin . . . is an act of self-injury that can be understood only by considering the time, place, and circumstances of its occurrence."[63]

In the "Holy Woman" vignette in *4 Scenes*, Athey presented self-injury within a Pentecostal context. In the scene, he described how his early act of cutting directly responded to his frustration with the false promises of Sister Linda. Further, he recounted this incident while costumed in a long white gown of the style usually worn by female healing evangelists in the 1970s.[64] With these deliberate references, Athey associated self-injury in the *Torture Trilogy* with Pentecostal concepts of healing and with the historical context of mid-twentieth-century Pentecostal healing revivals, in which audiences sought physical, mental, and emotional healing from Pentecostal ministers in the tens of thousands. He has described his grandmother as "a connoisseur of healing services. . . . She believed fervently that she or one of her daughters would experience a miraculous healing. It was never clear to me what exactly needed healing."[65] Driven, like Athey, by an invisible but powerful urge to be healed, his grandmother led the family to seek the help of faith healers like Sister Linda.

FAITH HEALING BEFORE A LIVE AUDIENCE

Sister Linda, touring with her "Miraculous Gift of the Stigmata," was one of many independent Pentecostal preachers who traveled on the healing revival circuit in the 1970s. Sparked in 1947 by the tent meetings of Pentecostal evangelists Franklin Hall, William Branham, Oral Roberts, and others, traveling deliverance ministries fanned across the United States and attracted massive crowds.[66] Pentecostals and many others sought the alleviation of their suffering: the miraculous disappearance of physical pain, the elimination of disease, and the eradication of mental anguish, addiction, and relationship problems. Throughout the 1950s, in tents and auditoriums, churches and hotel ballrooms all over the country, believers lined up before the altar, presenting their suffering bodies and proclaiming their belief in hopes that charismatic ministers would lay hands on them. By 1958, however, in-person attendance at healing revivals had dwindled, and the most successful evangelists, like Oral Roberts, had turned their attention to television. Despite this national downturn, Southern California experienced a particularly intense and prolonged period of revival. Known to Pentecostals as "the cradle of revivals," Los Angeles was uniquely positioned to sustain the healing revival.[67] Believers in Los Angeles had fostered the foundational Pentecostal healing ministries of the early twentieth century, including the Azusa Street revival in 1906 and Aimee Semple McPherson's International Church of the Foursquare Gospel in the 1920s, and the city hosted old-time healing revivals well into the 1970s.[68]

Local enthusiasm for faith healing supported a vast array of Pentecostal deliverance ministries. In and around Los Angeles, scores of itinerant Pentecostal preachers like Sister Linda packed tents for engagements that could last many days. Regularly scheduled miracle services at larger venues, including monthly appearances by Kathryn Kuhlman at the Shrine Auditorium, drew thousands of participants. This density allowed Athey's family to participate in what he has called "an underground Pentecostal church."[69] Rather than affiliating with a single congregation, Athey explained, "We never went to one church for more than a month. We'd go to workshops in the desert [and] special healing services."[70] Throughout his childhood and adolescence, from the 1960s through the late 1970s, he and his grandmother attended tent revivals and storefront Pentecostal churches throughout the Los Angeles area: "[My] Pentecostal grandmother . . . took me to see every charismatic preacher in Southern California during my childhood. . . . My grandmother searched continually for new religious experiences and took us from our home in Pomona to Chino, Ontario, San

Bernardino, San Jacinto, Indio, Lancaster, Rosemead, and to Los Angeles."[71] Athey described the energy of these healing revival events.

> The phrase "never a dull moment" was coined for spirit-filled churches and for the kind of Christianity my grandmother practiced. The apocalypse would be here either today or by next week. . . . Cancers are vomited up and demons are rebuked in the Lord's name. Gifts of the spirit are dealt out, and visions are commonplace. And in most churches, it all happens on a shoestring.[72]

In contrast to the ordered, stable spirit manifestations that took place in more mainstream Pentecostal denominations like the Assemblies of God, the baptism in the spirit as practiced at healing revivals offered participants a space of freedom. Among the diverse communities gathered there, outside the purview of official Pentecostal institutions, believers were vested with more individual authority. Revival ministers encouraged their audiences to express a more exuberant, embodied affect, to more freely experiment with spirituality, and to witness more gripping religious dramas. Athey observed that at "'holy roller' revival meetings [my family] found less rules, less structure, and an entire spirit world to draw off."[73] At the margins, beyond the reach of Pentecostal denominational hierarchies, deliverance ministries provided eccentric, immediate, and powerful worship experiences. Healing evangelist A. A. Allen claimed, "The old time revival service . . . brought men face to face with doom."[74] Rooted in the performance strategies of these old-time healing ministers, Athey attempted to do the same, and thus the legacy of midcentury Pentecostal healing revivals has persisted in his art practice.

The *Torture Trilogy* directly reiterated the structures, aesthetics, and actions of healing evangelists' ministries. Athey observed, "When I started making [the *Torture Trilogy*], . . . I recognized [it] as being akin to these displays in church."[75] His performance actions mimicked the methods of major healing evangelists who were active in Southern California in the 1970s, particularly Kathryn Kuhlman, Velma Jaggers (known as Miss Velma), and A. A. Allen. Thousands flocked to the Shrine Auditorium for the healings that Kuhlman conducted monthly from 1965 to 1975.[76] Miss Velma and her husband, O. L. Jaggers, pastored the Universal World Church, where they constructed a three-dimensional interpretation of the book of Revelation, a Golden Altar "fulgently shimmering, bejeweled, and dazzling."[77] In homage to Kuhlman and Miss Velma, and parallel to Linda Montano's "Holy Girl" persona, in *4 Scenes in a Harsh Life* Athey assumed the character of the

"Holy Woman." Directly invoking the characteristic styles of both preachers, he dressed in a flowing white gown, gestured with elegance and re-
straint, and preached a forceful sermon.[78] Athey has discussed the enduring influence of these women on his art, but the forms and content of the
Torture Trilogy are also closely related to the healing ministry of A. A. Allen,
an itinerant preacher known for his spectacular tent revival meetings.
Based in Arizona, Allen traveled throughout the United States, regularly
pitching his revival tent in Los Angeles. While not mentioned by name in
Athey's writings and reflections, accounts of Allen's services corroborate
the artist's memories of specific healing revival actions, images, and events.
Whether Athey witnessed Allen or the man's many successors, emulators,
and rivals, an exploration of Allen's ebullient performance strategies illu-
minates how the verbal and visual rhetoric of 1970s healing revivals shaped
Athey's art actions. His *Torture Trilogy* performances recalled Allen's tent
meetings in the itinerant preaching style of performance, the rhythm and
layering of actions, his strategic use of bodily effluvia, and the medicalized
display of suffering bodies.

When believers arrived at a healing service, they expected to sing, offer
or observe personal testimonies, listen actively to sermons, and respond to
altar calls by streaming to the stage when ministers called for believers to
be healed or saved.[79] Historian David Edwin Harrell, Jr. has described the
elements that contribute to the atmosphere of a healing revival: "the enthusiasm of the crowd, the excitement of the music, the testimony of those who
have been delivered from sickness, and the presence of the anointed evangelist."[80] Healing evangelists like Allen used these elements to build believers' anticipation of the gifts of the spirit and particularly of divine healing.
As Harrell observed, "The common heartbeat of every service was the
miracle—the hypnotic moment when the Spirit moved to heal the sick and
raise the dead."[81] Evangelists considered the cultivation of the baptism in
the spirit among revival attendees—poured out in perceptible, physical
ways—to be crucial to the success of healing services. LeRoy Jenkins, a
minister mentored by Allen, suggested that healing could not occur without the larger congregation experiencing the baptism in the spirit, but that
"after the Spirit of God comes into the services, you will see people jump
out of wheelchairs."[82] To this end, healing revival ministers encouraged
believers to receive the gifts publicly, and they ensured that these embodied experiences were highly visible to assembled participants. Allen, for
example, broadcast the visceral sounds of glossolalia by bringing his microphone to the lips of women speaking in tongues.[83] At Kuhlman's services, waves of hundreds of believers were slain in the spirit throughout

the auditorium. Describing the spectacle of the baptism in the spirit at these healing events, Athey observed, "You'd go to church and people would be speaking in tongues and hallucinating the walls are on fire and faith healing . . . which, you know, is vaudeville."[84]

The performative aspects of Allen's revival meetings were inflected with the particular demands of itinerant preaching. In contrast to Kuhlman and Miss Velma, who preached regularly at fixed locations in Los Angeles, A. A. Allen traveled throughout the country staging large-scale tent meetings from the early 1950s until his death in 1970. At each city, he pitched his twelve-thousand-person tent outside of town, and like other itinerant preachers he offered services several times a day for days or weeks at a time, with evening events lasting late into the night. Tent revival audiences were looking for miracles. They expected fast-paced, meaningful, and powerful religious experiences, and Allen delivered, night after night, in city after city. Compared to other evangelists of his time, Allen's baptism in the spirit was wilder and more chaotic, his tactics more extreme, and his claims more exaggerated. He regularly asserted that his revivals had raised the dead, for example.[85] Allen's critics—including many Pentecostals—accused him of carnivalesque showmanship, and his ministry was frequently embroiled in lawsuits and investigations. Yet his controversial approach successfully attracted crowds until his death in 1970, well beyond the end of the healing revival in 1958.[86] Allen's assistant, Harold Woodson, described his energy: "Brother Allen is like nobody I've ever seen. He can get a congregation literally climbing the walls. And stop. They all get settled down again. And he'll have 'em right back up there."[87] The challenge of itinerant preaching was to maintain this level of energy and freshness in each service while simultaneously repeating, re-performing, and revising.[88]

As an itinerant artist, Athey constantly performed and revised the *Torture Trilogy* series, attentive to shifts in audience, venue, funding, and other factors. Like the extended, multicity salvation campaigns of Allen and other tent revivalists, the *Torture Trilogy* evolved in relation to the expectations of audiences and the exigencies of the immediate environment. The pace over these five years of performances was grueling. Athey remembered, "Performing 4 *Scenes* in New York was the test. With almost no funding, I was forced to produce five shows in four nights (Saturday we had a late show)."[89] Unique performances of the same work (e.g., multiple performances of *Martyrs and Saints*) differed slightly. Across the *Torture Trilogy*, Athey incorporated different versions of scenes or dropped some scenes altogether, cast more or fewer performers, and changed other production details. Despite these differences, each work of the *Torture Trilogy* usually presented an hour-long series of vignettes that, according to Athey, "unfolded like Stations of the Cross, each scene fluctuating between chaotic action and contrived set-up."[90] Athey first developed these vignettes as a nightclub performer. With repeated performances at venues such as Club Fuck! and the Torture Garden in Los Angeles, he honed every aspect of his actions for maximum impact. As he described this process, "I would get $500 or $1,000 to do a ten-night performance, which would enable me to do it regularly and perfect one scene at a time. It had to be at a clock pitch, louder, faster, and more action packed. It enabled me to be more grandiose, to understand what transmitted to the audience and what didn't."[91] For Athey, this nightclub-based format—short, focused scenes performed in succession—paralleled the rhythm necessary for the survival of deliverance ministries: "Revival meetings are about vaudeville; you show up in a new town and something big better happen the first night or there'll be even less people the next night."[92] Allen's assistant, evangelist Don Stewart, likewise defined the high stakes of establishing an atmosphere of visceral connection at the outset: "If there were one or two outstanding miracles at the beginning of the service, then faith would rise in the audience, and all kinds of things began to happen."[93] Both Allen and Athey responded to this performance pressure by presenting multiple, simultaneous, concentrated actions.

In an article about an Allen service in 1970, a journalist for the *Los Angeles Times* noted the unruly activity: "It is still early in the service and the people have leaped and danced and fallen on the floor and spoken in tongues."[94] The highlight of Allen's revivals, the crowded healing sessions that followed the baptism in the spirit, heightened this chaos with visual and emotional density. Reporting on Allen's seven-day tent meeting in Los Angeles in 1969, *Time* magazine described the tense rhythms of his performance.

> For more than an hour the tension has been building up. Testimonies, gospel songs, pledges, blessings, and more songs—a writhing, Presleyan, shirt-open gospel rock driven home by an organ, drums and piano combo. Women are swaying in the aisles, men clapping and shouting from their seats.
>
> Suddenly, bouncing out of his chair, comes the star. Evangelist A. A. Allen . . . the crowd knows him as "God's Man of Faith and Power," and they also know that something powerful is coming. "We need six strong men to help bring out this stretcher," he shouts.

Half a dozen eager volunteers spring into the wings to bring out an ambulance stretcher carrying a groaning black woman. "This woman was brought into the hospital this morning with third-degree burns over her body," reads an attending nurse. . . .

"This is a sad story," says Allen, in his raspy Ozark baritone. He bends over the victim. "Do you believe God can raise you up?" Weakly, evincing great pain, she answers. "Yes, I do believe." "Raise your hands toward this woman and pray," he commands the crowd. Four thousand arms shoot into the air. . . . As the people pray, Allen lays his hands on the victim. "Heal!" he cries. "Heal her wounds in the name of Jeee-uh-zuss!" Already, the crowd is murmuring "Thank you, Jesus." The woman sits up. "Oh, thank God," she says. The nurse, at Allen's request, trundles her off to check the wounds in the ladies' room. She is back quickly. "There is new skin covering where the burns are," she announces. "It's a miracle."[95]

While this newspaper story resolved the chaotic activity of the event into a linear narrative, for attendees the sensory experience of the service presented an overwhelming, overlapping array of visual narratives. Allen, his assistant ministers, members of the choir, patients, nurses, stretcher carriers, and those shaken with the baptism in the spirit flowed on and around the stage in shifting, chaotic arrangements, while Allen provided a constant rolling monologue of illness and redemption. Another narrative, another suffering body, another nurse, another healing quickly followed.

Athey similarly superimposed actions and narratives in the initial scenes of all three works in the *Torture Trilogy*. In the first scene of *Martyrs and Saints*, attendants drew blood from a seated figure whose mouth, in a tribute to David Wojnarowicz, has been sewn shut, and nurses performed a series of cleansing procedures on unresisting bodies. *4 Scenes in a Harsh Life* opened with an arrow-pierced St. Sebastian trembling while Athey, dressed as the Holy Woman, narrated the difficult story of Sister Linda and anointed audience members with oil. At the beginning of *Deliverance*, a vision of the Buddha hovered above the set, medical professionals buried a figure in dirt, and three men painted gray circled the stage carrying crutches. Reflecting on the density of these vignettes, Athey said, "I felt like I had to lump three pieces together for it to be enough. It's the club thing. People expect something."[96] This attention to the energy of the audience mimicked Allen's manipulation of tension and anticipation to adjust the level of excitement among congregants.

In Allen's revivals, the agitation and simultaneity of the tent-meeting atmosphere was enhanced by the ubiquitous presence of anointing oil. Athey remembered the shining, sticky oil as part of the visual, tactile, and aural spectacle of revival: "All these women with wigs on—because it was the early '70s, like '69—came over with greased-up hands, and they raised the pulse and were shrilling into it."[97] Beginning in 1956, "miracle oil" began pouring from the heads and hands of people attending Allen's revival.[98] In 1967 Allen wrote, "To those who witness the outpouring of the oil, there can be no doubt of the validity of the phenomenon. It appears before your very eyes. Its shining surface reflects the light until it glistens. . . . It appears on hands, on feet, on the face, from the crown of the head!"[99] As liquid manifestations of the baptism in the spirit, these and other bodily excretions played a central role in Allen's ministry. Many participants reported that the mark of the cross, in a liquid resembling blood, appeared on Allen's forehead while he was preaching.[100] Vomiting took place constantly during healing revivals and was particularly common during Allen's tent meetings. In graphic detail, LeRoy Jenkins, one of many young ministers Allen mentored, described a representative incident of vomiting in his own ministry.

> The next night the Lord spoke to me and told me she had a cancer. He told me to have her bring a jar to church and she would spit up the cancer. For three nights she brought that jar in a little old brown paper sack. On the third night God spoke to me and said, "This is her night to be healed." After prayer, she was healed. She spit up a bloody cancer which had long roots on it. She had a terrible time as it almost choked her to death while it was coming up. She has not had any trouble since.[101]

Allen's assistant Stewart remembered the gruesome regularity of these outbursts at Allen's events: "These deliverance sessions were often accompanied by vomiting. It was really very sickening."[102] Athey, too, frequently observed vomiting at healing revival meetings, part of a litany of actions that characterized deliverance ministries for him: "Cancers are vomited up and demons are rebuked in the Lord's name. Gifts of the spirit are dealt out, and visions are commonplace."[103]

Athey's use of bodily fluids, intimately connected to self-injury and to the form of sexual abuse he observed in his childhood home, also directly enacted common scenes from healing revivals. The expulsion of bodily effluvia played a central role in the *Torture Trilogy*. Two parallel scenes—in *Martyrs and Saints* and in *Deliverance*—mimicked the "sickening" spectacle of deliverance ministry healings. In the first vignette of *Martyrs and Saints* ("A Nurse's Penance"), Athey and others, dressed in short nurses' outfits, stripped and washed passive bodies. Athey's performance notes outline the flow of action.

> 3 Bodies Are In the Procession: Already pre-layered w/ seran [*sic*] wrap, then duct tape, very solid mummification. . . . Each nurse cuts her body out and performs one of the following: 1. Cutting with ex-acto blade 2. intensive enema, stainless steel receptacle 3. Piercing and latching Then: 4. Tidy up the body in a lovely rope-bondage job.[104]

Similarly, in the second scene of *Deliverance*, assistants clad in white coats gagged Athey to induce vomiting into a jar. They performed an enema and held him while he squatted and strained over a bowl. For Athey, these explosive actions explored "cleansing rituals and the need to see the filth."[105] In the *Torture Trilogy*, the imperative to heal converged with the urge to see.

Allen and other deliverance ministers staged illness and disability as an unrelenting, medicalized spectacle of suffering. Evangelists invited those seeking healing to the front of revival spaces and highlighted people with visible physical challenges, from open wounds to difficulty walking.[106] An undated photograph shows Allen, in an action image that resonates with stereotypes of evangelists in popular culture, yanking a crutch from the grasp of a stooped man and brandishing it over his head.[107] Medical equipment accompanied many seekers as they lingered at the front of the room, and healing revival stages were littered with curative aids: abandoned crutches, orthopedic shoes, and hearing aids. Some evangelists rented wheelchairs in the hundreds for use by congregants.[108] Reflecting on Allen's healing services, Don Stewart, Allen's successor, observed, "Almost every night in every city, the hospitals would bring out dying patients in ambulances. They would drive up to the tent and wheel people out on stretchers with attendants nearby." He continued, "Some of them were still in their beds with their IVs still hooked up. Doctors and nurses were all over the place with special cases of terminally ill people. It looked tragic and pitiful. There were twisted bodies with grotesque cancers hanging from them."[109] Kuhlman's biographer noted that during her monthly meetings in Los Angeles, "The Shrine Auditorium became a literal outpatient clinic, except this clinic was filled with terminal patients in wheelchairs and hospital beds."[110] Similarly, Athey's performances featured bodies explicitly defined as AIDS afflicted, marked with all the visual indicators and accoutrements of illness and imminent death that were on display at healing revivals. In *Martyrs and Saints*, he fully encased figures in shrouds of duct tape. In *Deliverance*, he shaded skins with sickly gray paint and covered faces with morgue sheets. Littered with these bodies, the *Torture Trilogy* stages could also be described as outpatient clinics. Performers costumed as health care workers (nurses, surgeons, doctors) surrounded these sufferers; with medical precision they alternately executed acts of injury and self-injury and tended to wounds. Rubber gloves, gurneys, wheelchairs, IVs, and crutches suffused the stage.

Athey has posited a direct association between AIDS and the Pentecostal concepts that followed him into adulthood, observing, "This work has always paralleled my HIV infection and what was an infection of theology."[111] Although Athey left the faith as a teenager, Pentecostal notions of brokenness and healing took on renewed significance as he was immersed in the unrelenting grief of caring for the dying, burying loved ones, and living with the then certain death implied by his own diagnosis. He has located his performance art practice in the context of his AIDS-driven search for healing in a lineage than includes diverse divine-healing practices.

> Since becoming HIV-positive, I have drunk water from Lourdes; I have eaten dirt supposedly containing miraculous properties from a church in New Mexico; I briefly attended the healing workshops of Louise Hay and Marianne Williamson. I gazed longingly at the grand services of Miss Velma. Today I stage performances as elaborate, in their own way, as anything the [Universal] World Church puts on.[112]

With this narrative, Athey described a shift from modes of consumption (gazing) to practices of production (staging). In this way, he navigated the complexities of witnessing, from witnessing as an act of observation to witnessing as an act of testifying. In a Christian context, to testify is to speak about one's personal experience of God. Also known as witnessing, this other-directed testimony seeks to strengthen the faith of believers and to convert nonbelievers. Rather than seeking healing by following faith healers, in the *Torture Trilogy* Athey shared his own narrative of loss, built his own communities, and created his own healing rituals. Taking on the responsibilities of a healing evangelist, he generated his own healing revivals and offered testimony in the form of performance art.

REVEREND RON

Athey's mode of spiritual leadership arose from the conditions of his childhood faith: his family's unique approach to Pentecostal practice and the sense of spiritual responsibility that it ingrained in him. Influenced by the teachings of healing revival ministers and restless with received traditions, the matriarchs of Athey's family personalized their Pentecostal beliefs and practices. They elaborated a complex, imaginative religious narrative that situated their family history and their hopes and dreams for the future within an authoritative biblical context. Reflecting on this improvisational attitude toward religious expression, Athey noted, "Pentecostals [have] the ability to prophesy and conjure within your own spirit body. There's a lot of independence in there."[113] For healing evangelist A. A. Allen, other deliverance ministers, and their audiences, this kind of spiritual freedom could only take place outside of recognized Pentecostal denominations in tent revival experiences of the baptism in the spirit.[114] Responding to the air of spiritual autonomy fostered among participants at faith-healing meetings, Athey's grandmother and aunt perpetuated the revival atmosphere at home. Blessed with the gift of prophecy, they often received the baptism in the spirit together until late into the night. Their eclectic religious practice incorporated elements from the healing preachers they encountered in Southern California— including Allen, Kuhlman, Miss Velma, and Franklin Hall (famous for his 1946 book *Atomic Power with God through Prayer and Fasting*)—and from the Pentecostal Latter Rain Movement, which encouraged personal prophecies about everyday life.[115] Family life revolved around one such prophecy: Vena's pronouncement that she would marry Elvis and immaculately conceive the second coming of Christ.[116] Young Ron was charged with the task of establishing a spectacular ministry to pave the way for this miraculous event.

> My grandmother believed I'd been born with "the Calling" on my life. She told me often that blue electricity had crackled all around me at the time of my birth, and that even the doctors had noticed this. According to my grandmother—who claimed the gift of discerning everyone's religious responsibilities—this meant that I was to have a ministry like St. John the Baptist. The second coming of Christ would happen in my lifetime, and soon. I was destined to be not just a minister, but a prophet.[117]

Athey was set apart from other children and trained for this demanding future. He responded to these extraordinary expectations with hard work, garnering praise and attention at home and at the healing revival events he attended throughout his childhood.

> Having the Calling on my life, I was treated differently than my brother and sisters. My religious training included some fairly traditional practices like daily Bible reading . . . and prayer meetings with my aunt and grandmother. But I was gradually led into the more honored gifts. My grandmother arranged for me to spend quiet time in order to seek visions. Late at night, I was taken to healing services, where I eventually received the gift of tongues. I was often the only child there, but I was so sensitive and open, I often cried with rapture.[118]

Athey's grandmother, his aunt, and the women of these revivals strongly encouraged Athey to receive the baptism in the spirit at an early age: "I was anointed and prayed over by screaming women until I received the spirit, whereupon thunderous tongues and wild dancing poured out of me."[119] He has acknowledged his own agency in the midst of this coercive environment, noting that of his siblings he alone participated readily in the family's religious practices: "I was speaking in tongues when I was nine. I just remember that wanting, and figuring out I had to tune into this vibration that had a beat in it."[120] However, with his spiritual skills came profound responsibility. As a child, Athey played a crucial role in maintaining the family's spiritual well-being: "Every time something fucked up happened . . . my grandmother and I would go away to a motel and fast for a few days and just pray. We would come back skinny and crazy."[121] Athey's grandmother relied heavily on his spiritual prowess and, coinciding with the abusive domestic situation, placed him at the center of the family and at the center of Christian theology. While this role was fraught with anticipation and terror, anxiety and victimization, power and certainty, for Athey its urgency and authority generated "a life of mystical power and grandiosity."[122] Critical theorist Michael Warner, who was also raised Pentecostal, described the lasting impact of these gripping ways of thinking: "Religion supplied me with experiences and ideas that I'm still trying to match. . . . The stakes were not just life and death, but eternal life and death."[123] For Athey, raised to take on cosmic responsibilities, healing revivals dramatized these stakes with elaborate spectacles of suffering that paralleled his experience of family life. He observed, "Church played a huge part in trying to soothe my anger and my self-destructive mode."[124] At the same time, the radical urgency of the revival tent was heightened by the apocalyptic experiences of childhood domestic violence and later of the AIDS crisis. Even after he renounced the Pentecostal faith, a sense of spiritual obligation continued to trouble and fuel his performance art. "Why the fucking bloodbath?," he asked of the *Torture Trilogy*. "The shit? The vomit? All performed on a well-lit stage so that, hopefully, no details will be missed. To take a stab at it, using these body functions, assisted by the voice, words, and sound, I'm testifying."[125] At healing revivals, crowd-sourced testimonies preceded the baptism in the spirit. Those who previously had been healed were invited to offer their testimonies, describing their illnesses, detailing their deepest fears and hopes, and sharing proof of their cures. These people publicly reflected on the nearness of death, the relief of redemption, and the joy of restoration on a grand scale. They offered their narratives as a public service to help prepare the congregation to receive the baptism in the spirit, setting the conditions for divine presence and making healing possible.

Among contemporary Pentecostals, shared testimony remains critical for healing. In an ethnography of a late-twentieth-century Pentecostal women's group, religious studies scholar R. Marie Griffith described how women viewed personal testimony as a painful process necessary for supporting the healing of others.

> One woman, whose seventeen-year-old son died of cancer, describes the importance of sharing her pain and being vulnerable with others so that she can willingly suffer with them and even for them, just as Jesus suffers for the faithful: "To not only empathize, but to *share* the hurt of those women God put in my life, I had to retreat from my own point of healing. I had to open my wound far enough to let them see the vulnerability and yet not so much that I got caught in its snare again."[126]

Athey's performance art literalized this delicate procedure of opening the wound. Coinciding with the affect regulation of nonsuicidal self-injury, and twin to the narratives of loss, redemption, suffering, and desire performed in the revival tent, Athey's actions in the *Torture Trilogy* traced the arc of his testimony, a visual and verbal narrative of his search for a healing never fully realized. Like the woman who deliberately retreated from her own healing in order to facilitate the healing of others, Athey has expressed concern about the risks of sharing persistent pain. Distinguishing the public wounds opened in his performance art from private acts of self-injury, Athey has said, "I'm not making art because it's therapeutic. If anything it's the opposite: I'm keeping wounds open all the time, wounds that I could probably have just smoothed over. Showing doesn't have a personal, soothing, therapeutic effect, the way people describe."[127] For Athey the public display of suffering served a purpose related to, but distinct from, the affect regulation of NSSI. In giving his testimony, in witnessing to pain, Athey's ongoing commitment to communal healing limned his deeply ingrained spiritual responsibility.[128]

Healing has featured prominently in Athey's endurance art since *4 Scenes*, when he insisted on its importance: "Most of my pieces deal with actual physical and emotional trauma. What's new in this piece is that every scene has a healing."[129] Since the *Torture Trilogy*, Athey's performance art has recalibrated just how deep to cut, how wide to stretch the wound's edges, how much to reveal, and how much to demand in return. *Incorruptible Flesh (Dissociative Sparkle)* (2006) re-figured the role of the audience and clarified the obligations of witnesses responding to these wounds.[130] Performed alone, this piece was part of a series that included two previous collaborative works, *Incorruptible Flesh* (1996–97) with Lawrence Steger and *Incorruptible Flesh (Perpetual Wound)* (2006–7) with Dominic Johnson. Suspended alone in the middle of an intimate space, strapped to a metal frame with hooks pulling at the skin around his eyes, Athey endured hours of simultaneous penetrations and liquid invasions: a baseball bat penetrated his rectum, saline swelled his scrotum, and an assistant dripped moisture into his dry eyes. He described the scene:

> I displayed myself as a living corpse with a rack, which is a metal bar holding me up, with disco balls trying to keep me hypnotized. . . . People were allowed to touch me. My face was hooked into a table and a baseball bat was in my ass, which was connected to the rack. . . . I couldn't see because my face was pulled too tight. I even had eye drops put in my eyes.[131]

In *Incorruptible Flesh (Dissociative Sparkle)* Athey confronted audience members with an invitation to exceed their usual task of observation. He asked spectators to make a decision: they could choose to don a pair of latex gloves and lubricate his skin with Vaseline. Invoking the interpersonal exchange of energy—the point of contact central to Pentecostal healing—and reversing the authority of the healing evangelist, he invited viewers to lay hands on his body and anoint his skin. As during the baptism in the spirit under the revival tent, individuals stepped forward or stayed back, and these actions made their decisions visible to others.

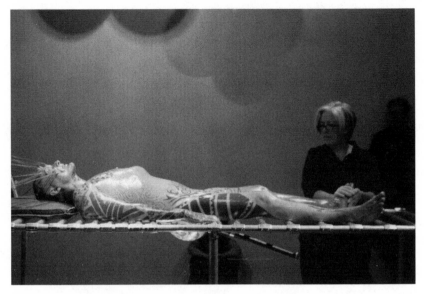

Fig. 10. Ron Athey, *Incorruptible Flesh (Dissociative Sparkle)* (2006), Artist's Space, New York City. (Photograph by Julia Portwood Hipp. Courtesy of Ron Athey.)

I realized two hours into it that the audience was making the piece, not me anymore. . . . I didn't expect everyone to be so gentle. People were actually trying to give me comfort. I was getting sneaked massages or some people would start to touch me . . . and follow the curves, just the way I was laid out. . . . No one made it pervy, and nobody was creeped out because those people wouldn't have come close enough to interact.[132]

Athey charged the audience members with the crucial task of witnessing, asking them doubly to observe his experience and testify to their own. In this way, *Incorruptible Flesh (Dissociative Sparkle)* insisted on the communal character of healing and simultaneously marked its ambiguity.

Athey's funereal portrait invoked the medieval concept of "incorruptible flesh," a miracle that occurred when a corpse (usually that of a saint) failed to decompose.[133] Echoing Linda Montano's still form in *Lying: Dead Chicken, Live Angel* (1971), *Erasing the Past* (1977), and other "lying in state" performances, Athey's prone body in *Incorruptible Flesh (Dissociative Sparkle)* materialized his account of survival as death-in-life.

I've been alive twenty years since the day I thought I was going to die. Twenty years: it's a whole other life. I could have done anything in that time, but half of it I was dying but I wasn't dying. And then the other half, I'm living, but am I just becoming a middle-aged white man, or am I becoming a physical specimen of a monstrous AIDS cocktail body? With those issues, I went back to *Incorruptible Flesh* and gave it the subtitle *Dissociative Sparkle*.[134]

Displaying himself as a living corpse, Athey posed a series of open questions for observers. What healing has been witnessed? What evidence has been offered? What testimony remains? The specter of death lingered in this performance, marking the radical disconnection between the dream of healing—a cure, an uncorrupted self—and the reality of persistent and irresolvable pain, dissociation, and trauma. Death has also haunted the endurance art of John Duncan, who has staged aggressive, confrontational performance interventions directed at others and himself. In contrast to Athey's Pentecostal concern with healing and restoration, Duncan's endurance strategies have been fueled by rage and his dystopic interpretation of Calvinism. While Athey appropriated the charismatic forms and content of 1970s deliverance ministers in service of prophetic wounding and communal healing, Duncan has performed prophetic witness as hellfire-and-brimstone denunciation and fiery moral judgment.

| John Duncan's
Confrontational Aesthetics

Incendiary moral outrage fueled the early works of American performance artist John Duncan. In *Move Forward* (1984), the artist projected collaged film footage of war atrocities and pornography onto a huge paper screen. Accompanied by a shortwave-radio audio composition that incorporated voice recordings of Jonestown leader Jim Jones, Duncan set the flickering screen on fire and used a fire extinguisher to blow its burning remains onto his audience. In an earlier work, *Scare* (1976), the artist knocked at the front door of a male friend's home. When the door opened, a masked Duncan brandished a gun, fired blanks in his friend's face, and ran. The confrontational aesthetics of these artworks prefigured and reiterated the inflammatory tone of Duncan's best-known performance, *Blind Date* (1980). In the central action of this controversial endurance, Duncan had sex with a female corpse. Enacted as a ritualistic self-punishment for the failure of a long-term relationship, *Blind Date* marked Duncan's association of male sexuality with isolation, aggression, and death. The artist's horrific and deeply despairing action tested the limits of his psychological and physical endurance. As an example of endurance art extremes, *Blind Date* holds a unique place in the contemporary performance art canon, mentioned in survey texts and serving as a cautionary tale for young artists.[1] *Long Suffering* offers the only in-depth scholarly analysis of this important performance, theorizing the work in the context of Duncan's 1970s endurance actions, the Calvinist theology of his Presbyterian upbringing, and the enduring posttraumatic affect of childhood sexual abuse.

Throughout his 1970s art practice, and culminating in *Blind Date*, Duncan developed a harsh critique of masculinity rooted in his childhood experiences as a victim of male sexual predation. As a boy, Duncan was sexually victimized by several men in his life, including his father and an elementary school teacher. From his perspective as a male survivor of sexual abuse—the physical and psychological target of aggressive masculinity—Duncan observed firsthand the confluence of violence and sex with authoritarian, patriarchal power. He developed an early deconstruction of masculinity during crucial 1970s encounters with feminist artists in Los Angeles. In conversation with Suzanne Lacy, Cheri Gaulke, Barbara T. Smith, and others, Duncan clarified his understanding of gender constructions, connected his personal experiences with systemic social issues, and practiced strategies of consciousness-raising and confrontation. As a result, the visual rhetoric of feminism suffused his early work. In endurance actions that included *Blind Date* and *If Only We Could Tell You* (1980), Duncan elaborated a devastating assessment of male gender socialization, linking sexualized violence with standards of late-twentieth-century American masculinity that required men to repress their emotions. Yet, while exposing the violence and inhumanity of masculine gender roles, Duncan's art actions simultaneously replicated and reinforced them. *Blind Date* culminated Duncan's extended investigations into the cyclical dynamic between aggressive male sexuality and male victimhood. Intending to offer himself as a negative example of male conditioning, he took on violent behaviors, and he victimized his viewers, frightening his audiences—and himself—with the dangers of violent masculinity.

The moral outrage of Duncan's endurance art participated in long traditions of Calvinist moral denunciation as prophetic witness. His fiery invectives against twentieth-century masculinity and aggression mimicked the hellfire and brimstone of American Calvinist homiletics. Just as the eighteenth-century Calvinist preacher Jonathan Edwards, in his famous sermon "Sinners in the Hands of an Angry God," terrified his congregation in order to dangle them above the yawning abyss of hell, Duncan's actions drew attention to masculine cycles of violence—and implicated him and his audiences in their perpetuation. In addition Duncan's early exposure to neo-orthodox theology, a dominant discourse among post–World War II Presbyterian Calvinists, focused his attention on the doctrine of total depravity. A key tenet of Calvinist theology, this belief in the inherent and ubiquitous evil of all persons coincided with Duncan's experiences of victimization and abuse. In his endurance art, Duncan adapted Calvinist theological, intellectual, visual, and aural traditions of moral activism to figure masculinity as both abject and aggressive, insisting on the contradictions, inconsistencies, and painful discordance of masculine identity.

TOTALLY DEPRAVED

In dramatic contrast to Montano's early monastic commitments and Athey's childhood fascination with Pentecostal healing revivals, Duncan experienced a mainstream religious education. As a child, he attended Grace Presbyterian Church in his hometown of Wichita, Kansas, participated in Sunday school and youth events, and became an official member of the church in order to avoid confrontation with his parents. While Montano and Athey were steeped in esoteric theology from a young age, Duncan attended Sunday school sporadically and formed his own interpretations of Calvinism based on impressions and assumptions, half-heard sermons and half-remembered lessons. During his early teen years, disillusioned with adult hypocrisy and distanced by the intellectual dissonance of what he considered harsh and illogical Calvinist doctrines, Duncan rejected his religious upbringing. As a result of this less rigorous but more conventional religious education, he formed an imperfect understanding of his religious tradition, and his artworks reflect the inconsistencies and incoherencies of lived religion. This chapter embraces Duncan's individual encounter with Calvinism, with all its subjective formations and deformations, and examines how his performances hold disparate transhistorical Calvinist figures and concepts in tension with one another. This approach yields a messier narrative, a less straightforward connection to religious practice than is found in earlier chapters. However, I intentionally address the work of an artist whose religious affiliation has been less extreme and more diffuse than Montano's and Athey's because Duncan's religious history more closely approximates typical contemporary American artists' encounters with religions. In this way, this chapter models how contemporary art historians might extend the project of mapping the complex, uneven geography of religions in American art beyond clear-cut examples.

Although he was neither intellectually attentive to nor emotionally invested in his religious training, Duncan's endurance art nevertheless has visualized deeply ingrained aspects of Calvinist theology and rhetoric since his earliest performances. In works such as the multimedia action *Move Forward* (1984), Duncan directly participated in Calvinist modes of moral discourse. Less than thirty minutes long, *Move Forward* consisted of several distinct but coordinated elements: an uncomfortable environment, a disturbing film projected on a paper screen, a piercingly loud and discordant audio composition, and a fiery performance action. Through this painful sensory experience, *Move Forward* presented a hellish vision of Cold War life that visualized midcentury interpretations of the Calvinist notion of total depravity, a tenet of Calvinist theology that assumes human sinfulness and transgression. Further, as an outraged denunciation of contemporary depravity, *Move Forward* directly appropriated the rhetorical power and denunciatory purpose of the jeremiad, a traditional Calvinist preach-

Fig. 11. John Duncan, *Move Forward* (1984). (Copyright © John Duncan)

ing strategy. Both the concept of total depravity and the form of the jeremiad have undergirded Duncan's endurance actions throughout his career, including *Blind Date*.

Duncan performed *Move Forward* after moving to Japan in the aftermath of *Blind Date*. His art action layered sense experiences in the modernist tradition of artistic appeals to the full range of senses, but the work operated on the extremes of sensory data—from the absence of information to painful overburdening. *Move Forward* took place at the Tokyo art space Plan B, "a basement room with the windows blocked off. There was no light in there at all. It was at night."[2] Audience members arrived to find sheets of blank newsprint suspended from ceiling to floor. These expanses of white paper completely obscured one wall and recalled the performances and installations of Saburo Murakami, who in *Passing Through* (1956) and other actions, propelled himself through a series of paper screens and exhibited their torn remains. At Plan B, beneath the suspended paper, a hard, gritty substance, bright pink, covered the wooden floor.

> The audience walked into a situation. Somebody working at Plan B had gotten a couple of fire extinguishers, ripped them off from a gas station down on the corner. To test them, to make sure they worked,

I fired one and then discovered you couldn't turn it off once you turned it on. So this room was full of pink grit that was sprayed out of this fire extinguisher. People sat in that grit: very abrasive, very uncomfortable.

Duncan's actions intervened in the environment and forced the audience to respond to these contingent circumstances.

Duncan introduced his audio composition into this setting of total darkness and physical discomfort. As he described its impact, it "starts in total darkness; the sound is very loud. In the dark, the soundtrack goes on for ten minutes." In this audio collage, Duncan recorded, layered, crossed, and rearranged the static of Soviet shortwave radio broadcasts to create a wall of droning sound. He initially had experimented with shortwave radio in Los Angeles, where he worked with the L.A. Free Music Society, Throbbing Gristle, and other groups. In Japan he refined his technique in the company of avant-garde musicians such as O'Nancy in French and Hijokaidan.[3] Duncan's approach to shortwave radio composition hinged on his attention to the "events between stations" rather than to intelligible sounds of conversation and dialogue.[4] Fascinated with feedback and interference, he recorded and manipulated static. In the 1980s, Duncan's location in Japan allowed him access to shortwave radio broadcasts from Soviet stations. These audio elements quickly became the basic material of his compositions, including the *Move Forward* soundtrack.

Thanks to the Cold War, it was a sort of free-for-all when one side would transmit a signal and the other side would try to block it and somewhere in between you would get this sort of mixed buzz; you could hear the transmission, you could hear the block, and these crossed over and under each other. At times there was just this really sensual drone, and elsewhere you could hear voices that would sing like ghosts.[5]

He described how Plan B's limited sound equipment heightened this cacophony.

It wasn't possible to get a PA [public address] system. They just couldn't afford it, so they got me a couple of guitar amplifiers. I ran each channel into one of these guitar amplifiers. The sound was coming from a Walkman and from a cassette player. Each channel was being amplified and turned up until it was viscerally loud.

Jarring sound vibrations assailed the audience seated in darkness on the sharply gritty floor. Juxtaposed with the absence of visual stimulation and the uncomfortable physical situation, this auditory overload overwhelmed listeners with an uneven and painful sound quality.

After ten minutes of listening to this composition in darkness, the artist "stumbled over everybody, got to the projector, and turned it on." Shot on Super 8 film and projected at a very slow speed, the film flashed for about eight minutes. Long, blank stretches of plain black screen were punctuated with quick cuts that revealed black-and-white still images assembled from mass media publications, variously sexual, violent, unsettling, or simply ominous. Graphic sexual scenes figured prominently, from soft-core porn to sadomasochism (SM) and child pornography. A leather-clad woman pressed her black high heels into a man's back; men and women performed oral sex; naked boys engaged in sex acts; penises appeared repeatedly, in many guises. Other images depicted the militarism of recent history: medical photographs documenting Hiroshima victims' radiation injuries, bomb blast diagrams, and men holding large guns. Duncan described his film.

> The film was animated stills taken from magazines. *Scientific American* had an article about nuclear strategies and why Star Wars was such a ridiculous idea. I animated the drawings that were describing this kind of strategy and projected them and put that together with pornography, with ad images that would reinforce this idea of SM and games of power. The idea was to link all these things happening as a sort of nightmarish human activity.

As *Move Forward* neared its conclusion, the film reached a visual crescendo. The film's lengthy stretches of black screen increasingly gave way to clusters of more images, flashed more quickly. The final frames of the film alternated between black frames and the light-saturated image of a woman with a cigarette hanging from her lips. Her blank stare expressed a trance-like, drugged, or simply indifferent state of dissociation.[6] The visual stutter between the black screen and the woman formed a kind of black-and-white strobe, which, Duncan said, "worked as a sort of a hypnotic effect to try to emphasis the idea that we are being hypnotized by all of these things." Finally, a photographic self-portrait of Duncan appeared, remaining on the screen for a few heartbeats. In this grainy, Super 8 shot of an altered Polaroid photograph, with the words "watching and learning" scrawled on the bottom of the frame, most of the artist's face had been scratched and destroyed. An echo of the woman in the preceding image, the self-portrait retained only an eye, nose, cheek, and a few fingers holding a cigarette to his mouth. At the same time that the visual strobe quickened, the accompanying soundtrack aggressively intensified. Overlapping and interfering with the droning static, voices—screaming voices—became audible. These voices spliced into the soundtrack were recordings of shortwave radio broadcasts from Jim Jones's Jonestown, the site of killings and mass suicides in Guyana in 1978. Duncan detailed these excerpts.

[The *Move Forward* soundtrack] ends with a woman shouting into her microphone, "We will lay our lives on the line if it comes to that. Do you copy?" Then the last part, Jim Jones himself saying, "Don't ever say hate is your enemy!" He starts off with a very soft voice, [quoting] different lines from Martin Luther King, John Kennedy: "Love is the only weapon with which I have to fight. Bullshit, shit, bullshit. Love is the only weapon with which I have to fight. Bullshit. I got a hell of a lot of weapons to fight. I got knives. I got cutlasses. I got swords. I will fight, I will fight, I will fight, I will fight!" Everybody starts chant[ing] behind him, and at a certain moment, he stops speaking and holds the microphone out to them. You hear all these people screaming in rage. The piece ends, "Let the night roar with it! They're out there!" Cut to silence.

At this moment, as the screen fell dark and the soundtrack abruptly ended, Duncan lit the paper screen on fire. Flames quickly consumed the newsprint, and the room filled with smoke. Standing behind the screen facing the audience, Duncan activated a fire extinguisher which smothered the flames, but the force of the extinguisher's spray blew burning bits of the paper screen into the audience. Duncan noted that the fire was unexpectedly virulent.

I set the screen on fire at both sides, just took a little lighter and started at the bottom. I thought the screen would just burn across. But fire doesn't work like that, it burned up and then over at the ceiling. And then a big chunk of this screen fell onto the floor and was, of course, still burning. So I took the other fire extinguisher and sprayed it to put it out. This thing was under enough pressure to take the screen and lift it up and send it flying. It was impossible to breathe in there. It just absorbed all the oxygen.

Move Forward ended as frightened audience members fled the flaming, air-less room, crunching extinguisher grit beneath their feet.

Duncan's final, fiery action implicated him and his audience in the violent, exploitative activities depicted visually and aurally in *Move Forward*. While his denunciation participated in the 1980s punk aesthetic of rejection and nihilism, it depended on the foundational Calvinist belief in the inevitability and ubiquity of human evil. *Move Forward*'s hellish vision represented men and women as innately depraved and potentially violent. A key tenet of Calvinism since John Calvin posited reformed theology in the sixteenth century, the doctrine of total depravity expresses a deeply cynical understanding of human nature, assuming that people inevitably sin in the most disgusting of ways.[7] Calvin wrote, "The mind of man has been so completely estranged from God's righteousness that it conceives, desires, and undertakes, only that which is impious, perverted, foul, impure, and infamous."[8] American Presbyterian preacher Jonathan Edwards, whose sermons and voluminous writings continue to influence contemporary American Calvinist theologians and ministers, expressed the frequency and consistency of human evil with rhetorical flair: "The depravity of nature appears by a propensity in all to sin immediately, as soon as they are capable of it, and to sin continually and progressively."[9] Total depravity was a subject of particular concern for theologians in the twentieth century, and it shaped Duncan's childhood experience of Calvinist Presbyterianism from the 1950s to 1972.[10] In response to World War I, theologians such as Karl Barth, Paul Tillich, and Reinhold Niebuhr had developed neo-orthodoxy, a theology that emphasized the problem of human evil and total depravity.[11] By midcentury a generation of American pastors educated by neo-orthodox theologians had disseminated these views to mainstream American churches. Neo-orthodox theology was so influential that the Presbyterian Church in the U.S.A. (PCUSA) revised its children's educational materials to highlight concepts of total depravity. Released in 1948, the Christian Faith and Life curriculum explicitly offered neo-orthodox interpretations of human nature.[12] By the mid-1950s, the curriculum had been distributed to churches nationwide to encourage children—including Duncan—to absorb from an early age neo-orthodox preoccupations with human evil.[13] In addition, Rev. William F. Keesecker, the minister at Grace Presbyterian during Duncan's childhood and adolescence, was a prominent national Presbyterian leader and a vocal advocate of neo-orthodox ideology. In his popular books, he explained Calvinist approaches to evil, sin, and depravity to a broad audience.[14] Duncan grew up in a home and community dominated by Calvinist assumptions of human evil, and this attention to the innate depravity of human nature has undergirded his practice since his earliest artworks. He has consistently oriented his work toward the exposure of human evil: "Part of my work is to show that we are cruel. Not to be cruel myself but to hold up a mirror to that. Show it and say, 'This is who we are,' and to accept that." Echoing a metaphor frequently used in Calvinist discourse, Duncan compared human nature to a tree.

> You love the beauty and the shade that a tree offers you at a certain time of the year: the leaves, the form of the tree. If you love this and accept only this, that's the same as cutting the tree off from the roots, which are down in shit, down in all this decay. They're sucking it up as nutriment. This same object of beauty that you see going up toward light and to the sky is very, very entrenched in the ground. The mire that it's pulling its sustenance from is an essential part of what it is. You cut that off, you cut off the nutrient, then you kill the whole entity. We are the same. If you deny the cruelty, if you deny the horror, which is an intrinsic essential part of who we are, then you miss a key element of our existence.[15]

In this striking image, Duncan outlined his conviction in the tainted origins of all human activity.

Duncan described the aggressive sensory chaos of *Move Forward* as "a reflection of our social situation."[16] His references to the horrors of the postwar experience and to Cold War anxieties implied direct relationships among militarism, sexual exploitation, mass media, political and financial corruption, disease, religious fanaticism, indifference, and despair. His work registered fundamental anxieties around the alienation of mass consumer society, shifts in sexual relations, and Cold War Soviet-American politics, specifically the acceleration of nuclear armament under the leadership of Ronald Reagan. The Tokyo location of the performance—the site of World War II atrocities, radical shifts in cultural experience and sexual politics, and sharply escalating financial excesses in the 1980s—heightened these associations. By situating individual actions within broader social contexts, *Move Forward* recalled Calvinist elaborations of the impact of total depravity on communities. According to Calvinist doctrine, humans, as innately evil creatures, inevitably express this depravity publicly. The doctrine of total depravity thus denounces not only individual sin but also social, political, and economic forms of evil. Keesecker, in an essay titled "What Is Sin?" explicitly addressed this connection.

Sin's presence in any society has social consequences. A few of the ills it evokes are strife, murder, dishonesty, terror, despair and guilt; nationalism, racism, imperialism (communist and capitalist), inequities and inequality, poverty, and perhaps most awesome of all in our day, the specter of nuclear annihilation.[17]

In *Move Forward*, Duncan collected images and sounds of these wide-ranging public consequences of total depravity, and his depiction of what he called "nightmarish human activity" constituted a searing indictment of the present.

Move Forward marked seeing—the appetite for images—as a depraved activity in the contemporary world. By setting the screen on fire at the end of the piece, Duncan perpetrated violence against vision itself. He presented the destruction of visual media as both a condemnation of and a kind of escape from the power of images. This concern with the power of images echoed Calvinist iconoclasm; Calvin himself was suspicious of images because he recognized their power.[18] At the same time, Duncan handled these images with a fascination that reinforced their seductiveness, as in the final image of the film, in which his mutilated self-portrait proclaimed that he was watching and learning. The year after *Move Forward*, a Japanese investor approached Duncan and invited him to direct adult films. Inspired by the example of Cosey Fanny Tutti, who created sexually explicit images as pornography and incorporated these images into her art, he agreed in order to produce his own content for print and film collages.

> The idea was to go as a consumer to my local video rental shop, to the section of adult films that had this company's products. I would rent the film, take it home, and transfer it to VHS [format] to try and make a sort of subverted copy of it, a cut-up version of it. The inspiration for this was Cosey Fanny Tutti.

Just as Duncan consistently featured shortwave radio "found recordings" in his musical compositions, images from mass media publications had appeared in his earlier work from the 1970s and continued to play a significant role in his art production throughout the 1980s. In addition to the collected images in *Move Forward*'s film, he created collages for the covers of his audio releases, and he mounted the *Toilet Exhibition* (1985), in which he placed poster-sized photocopies of collages, thematically similar to the *Move Forward* images, in men's bathrooms all over Tokyo. Duncan has noted, "Juxtaposing images . . . seemed to give a more complete mirroring of human activity, of who we are, than the separate images did alone in or out of context. At the same time I didn't want to draw or paint on them, preferring instead to let their nuances come through without imposing distractions."[19] To support these and other collages, Duncan produced a series of pornographic films in the 1980s, including *Doll, Fallen Angel, Inka, Aidayuki Passion,* and *Power Love.* He assumed the name John See for these projects, defining himself by the activity of looking and emphasizing the voyeurism of his role as a director and consumer of pornographic images. Echoing his actual first name, John referred to the obfuscation and anonymity of a typical male pseudonym (John Doe) and marked him as a participant in sexual commerce by identifying him as a john, a prostitute's client. In this way, Duncan emphasized his own imbrication in producing and consuming pornographic images, contributing to and complicating his use of sexually explicit material in *Move Forward* and other performances.

PREACHING HELLFIRE

In *Move Forward* and throughout his endurance art, Duncan has mobilized a uniquely Calvinist rhetorical device in response to his perception of moral crisis: the jeremiad, a form of public address focused on spiritual and social condemnation and reform. Often associated with the Puritans, who adapted it to the American context, the jeremiad offers a bitter critique of the present moment resolving in a prophetic vision of a purified future.[20] The jeremiad has shaped American public discourse, from the sermons of Presbyterian and Calvinist ministers such as Edwards, Lyman Beecher, and Keesecker to the rhetoric of religious figures outside the tradition such as Billy Graham and Jerry Falwell, abolitionists, and civil rights activists including Martin Luther King, Jr. The jeremiad form has appeared in the speeches of political figures from Abraham Lincoln to George W. Bush and Hillary Rodham Clinton and in the texts of Nathaniel Hawthorne, Edith Wharton, Marilynne Robinson, and the rapper Mr. Lif.[21] Art historian Michael Fried appropriated the conventions of the jeremiad for an academic audience in his essay "Art and Objecthood."[22]

The form of the jeremiad operates by inducing and sustaining anxiety.[23] Duncan's *Move Forward* and Edwards's exemplary Calvinist sermon "Sinners in the Hands of an Angry God" implemented similarly confrontational rhetorical strategies to create this sense of crisis.[24] Through vivid, visceral appeals to the senses, both "Sinners" and *Move Forward* built and sustained an atmosphere of palpable fear and horror situated in the body.

In "Sinners," Edwards drew on embodied experience, especially tactility, to unsettle assumptions of safety and salvation. He argued that, at this moment, God is holding you in his hand above the fiery pit of hell. You deserve to be destroyed and could drop into hell at any time: "That world of misery, that lake of burning brimstone is extended abroad under you. . . . Your wickedness makes you . . . heavy as lead, and to tend downwards with great weight and pressure towards hell."[25] In *Move Forward*, Duncan mimicked and extended Edwards's threatening sensory appeal. The piece assailed the audience with a cacophony of jarring, chaotic, and painful sensory inputs: uncomfortable seating; droning, viscerally loud audio; and the confined space of a pitch-black room punctuated with disturbing visual information and the acrid scent and taste of burning paper and smoke. By deliberately overwhelming each sensory channel, directing his fire extinguisher at the audience, and covering it with burning bits of paper, Duncan created a mounting tension, an increased perception of danger that neither dissipated nor resolved but rather exploded, pushing outside the boundaries of the room. The pacing of both sermon and artwork created maximum rhetorical momentum. In the text of "Sinners," this momentum occurred through tense shifts (from past to present to present progressive) and the liberal use of temporal words like *suddenly* and *immediately*.[26] Edwards increasingly personalized his text with the use of the second person and by addressing specific groups of audience members in turn: the healthy, the elderly, young men, young women, and finally children.[27] The visual and aural crescendo near the end of *Move Forward* fostered a similarly compelling sense of urgency. The speed and emotional intensity of the film and the audio composition quickened, and the final visual strobe heightened the artwork's oscillation of sensory overload and understimulation.

The jeremiad offers the potential for gripping content and spectacular responses, yet the solemnity of the Calvinist preaching tradition can encourage audience disengagement. Edwards preached "Sinners in the Hands of an Angry God" twice; as a visiting preacher in Enfield, Connecticut, the congregation reacted with screams and fits, but in his own church several weeks earlier the sermon had produced no comment.[28] While these differing receptions depended on immediate historical and community contexts, audiences' communal expectations, and other local phenomena, they mark a frequent pairing in the presentation and reception of the jeremiad: spectacle and indifference. According to his biographer, George Marsden, Edwards himself moderated the passion of his words by delivering them in a monotone, "as though he were staring at the bell-rope in the back of the meetinghouse."[29] Duncan remembered the sermons of his youth as abysmally tedious: "I used to fall asleep during the sermons. Most of the time I thought the sermons were useless. I remember them as being very tedious, very hypnotic. I thought that was like somebody put a hand over my nose and mouth. All of the sudden it was very claustrophobic, just a horrible trap." *Move Forward* re-created both of these extremes, urgency and boredom. With the juxtaposition of too much and too little sensory data, the choking smoke, and the monotonous droning of the audio soundtrack, Duncan literalized his feelings of constriction, airlessness, and suffocation.

Both Duncan's performance and Edwards's sermon offer compelling visions of hell. Following John Milton's correlation of hell with the elements of earth and fire, Edwards's sermon presented only imagery of earth and particularly fire.[30] In his vision, men "kindle and flame out in hellfire," souls are transformed into "fiery oven[s]," hell's "flames gather and flash," and God's wrath "burns like fire."[31] Duncan made hell present in *Move Forward* using the same elements of earth and fire: the underground basement, the grit on the floor, the actual smoke and fire. Edwards was explicit about the goal of his vivid imagery: "The use may be of awakening to unconverted persons in this congregation."[32] Duncan echoed this motive: "All these things were an attempt to get people to wake up, because in Japan—even more than the United States—people follow each other. There is this tendency to go along with things. I was trying to suggest that there would be another way. Wake up!" Like Edwards, Duncan was concerned with ethical revival, but he focused his rage on patriarchy. Since the 1970s, aggressive male sexuality has been the ongoing object of Duncan's jeremiad. From his early endurance actions to his recent sound-based artworks, Duncan has displayed and critiqued American assumptions of masculinity. In artworks that converge on his own body, relationships, human interactions, and encounters, Duncan has stood as prophetic witness to the dehumanizing, destructive impact of patriarchy on men, women, and children. Two related experiences influenced the artist's profound sensitivity to male aggression and shaped his critique: his personal experience of sexual trauma and his encounter with feminism and feminist art practices. As a result, both the visual marks of trauma and the visual rhetoric of feminism have suffused his work.

MUTILATING THE SELF

Duncan introduced his desolate view of American masculinity in an early work, *Bed* (1973). In this ten-minute video, an unmoving camera focused on

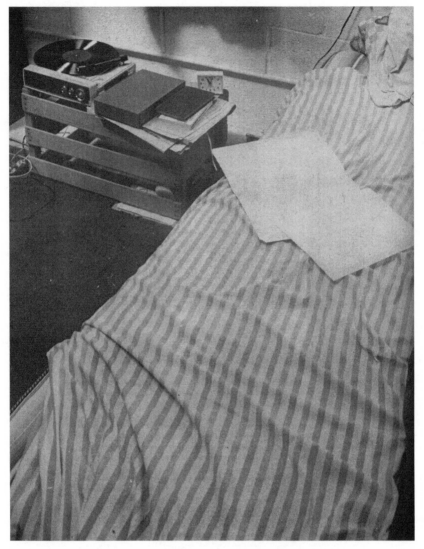

Fig. 12. John Duncan, *Untitled* (1976). (Copyright © John Duncan)

the artist's bed. He described the details that emerged through long contemplation of the still bed: "I see that two people have recently gotten out of it in different directions and that they haven't really slept together but have just occupied the same space."[33] He continued, "There was a real sadness I was having at that time. . . . Staring at the bed . . . thinking about the decay of actions that had taken place there. . . . A graveyard of feelings."[34]

A later work, *Untitled* (1976), published in Paul McCarthy's newsprint *Criss Cross Double Cross*, re-created this image and clarified Duncan's gendered reading of the scene.[35] In this black-and-white photograph, a single mattress rests directly on the floor. The bed looms, occupying all but the upper left corner of the photo frame, where a few objects are visible: a makeshift crate crowded with an alarm clock and record player and a small square of floor littered with wires, crumbs, papers, and dirt. Of this scene, and the absent human figure—which might remain just outside the frame, behind the camera—the artist observed, "It's rough and lonely, and the combination of nonchalance and loneliness seemed very male to me."

The issues of masculinity introduced in *Bed* and *Untitled* preoccupied Duncan throughout the 1970s and into the present. In these early works, he visualized male sexuality as absence, removing human figures and linking sex with isolation and death. His artworks articulated the destructive consequences of male gender socialization, the cultural process by which boys internalize masculine attributes and behaviors and by which these standards are policed in adult men. Duncan has described his critique of this inflexible masculine ideology in terms of conflicts between internal states and cultural expectations.

> The idea was to be focused on work, to repress sensual pleasure and, more than sensual pleasure experiences, emotions. Displays of emotions were considered a personal threat. . . . The dangerous thing about that entire form of training was the repressed impulses. They become concentrated and boil up and explode and are sometimes impossible to control.

The artist identified the totalizing narrative of male gender socialization—repressing emotions, avoiding the appearance of vulnerability, and internalizing cultural expectations—with the eruption of uncontrollable urges, particularly coercive sexuality. Duncan has explored the personal and social consequences of male gender socialization throughout his oeuvre, hypothesizing culturally constructed notions of masculinity as instrumental in the generation of violent aggressive sexual behavior. Since the early 1970s, his art has condemned gender socialization and insisted on the reality and rights of male victimhood. These insights were confirmed by research psychologists in the late 1980s and early 1990s. Psychologist David Lisak, who pioneered research with male survivors of sexual abuse, has argued that "male gender socialization . . . is implicated in the genesis of interpersonal violence."[36] In particular, Lisak has suggested a direct connection among male gender socialization, sexual victimization of boys, and sexual aggression.[37] Given Lisak's charge that clinical "research on male sexual victimization lags more than a decade behind that of female victimization," Duncan's early work could be considered an avant-garde form of research about male survivors.[38]

Duncan recognized the correspondence between masculine socialization and violent sexuality from personal experience. Early sexual abuse motivated his critique of aggressive male sexuality. Throughout his childhood and adolescence, he was sexually victimized by several men in his life. He described his violent home life: "I experienced my father's attentions of punishment. He would spank us when we did something that he didn't like. There was [a] very odd sort of sexual tension in the sessions. With me they happened quite a bit more than I thought they should." Similar to Linda Montano's spare discussion of her sexual trauma, Duncan has been circumspect about the extent of his abuse. Reflecting the distance afforded by dissociation and affect constriction common to many survivors of sexual trauma, his reticence also coincides with gendered modes of communication that restrain male disclosures of vulnerability.[39] Neither this reserve nor the seemingly "normal" context of 1960s parental discipline and punishment should mask the abusive nature of Duncan's childhood and its impact on his life and work.[40] With his volatile and repeated attentions, Duncan's father betrayed his role as a caretaking adult, assailed his son's sense of physical and psychic wholeness and personhood, and maintained an atmosphere of unpredictability and fear. In addition to this domestic violence, Duncan's early life was marked by an elementary school teacher's abuse.

> In sixth grade, the last year of elementary school, I had my first male teacher and I was delighted. He was an attractive man, witty, intelligent, sarcastic, all of which I really admired and liked. I thought the world of this guy. Over the course of the year, he chose five boys for particular attention. One of the boys became a delinquent. One of the boys had a nervous breakdown and was committed to a hospital for several weeks. Another should have been committed to a hospital but wasn't; I don't know what's happened to him since. One boy and his family moved, suddenly.[41]

Duncan was the fifth boy targeted by the teacher; he indicated that several of these boys were sexually molested, while others—including Duncan— were victims of "psychological torture," which continued for months. The teacher was eventually fired, but Duncan endured the extended psychological aftermath of this abusive situation: "For years, I thought that if I met this teacher again, I would probably kill him. After a while, I realized that it just didn't make any difference. It taught me that it's just not in me to commit murder." The virulence of Duncan's anger underscored the deep contradictions and long-term impact of male victimhood.

At the core of male survivors' traumatic struggles is the conflict between the experience of victimization and cultural assumptions about masculinity. Male victims' feelings of overwhelming fear and helplessness starkly contrast with traditional notions of masculine agency and invulnerability. Despite the multiplicities and complexities of masculine identities in late-twentieth-century America, Duncan and other survivors have described the process of gender socialization as extremely rigid. For these men, masculinity appeared monolithic. For male children and adolescents, victimization intensifies the already painful process of assimilating gender norms and constricting "nonmasculine" traits. In addition to excising those behaviors deemed unacceptably "feminine" by their peers and families, these boys also must reject the fear and grief associated with their traumatic vulnerability.[42] In Duncan's early photograph *Unititled*, the absent male figure marked this self-erasure. Following the repression of traumatic affect, many adult survivors, including Duncan, are left with rage, the only response to victimhood sanctioned by cultural notions of masculine behavior.[43] Rage is a characteristic, powerful, and multivalent force in the trauma discourses of male and female survivors, who may struggle with modulating their anger and aggression. For male survivors, anger functions broadly, standing in for other emotions that these men, as a result of gender socialization, deem unacceptable.[44] Rage is a striking element of Duncan's artwork, and it appears in especially virulent form in his early work. The performance and installation *If Only We Could Tell You* (1980), also known as *The Black Room*, gave voice to his anger, self-hatred, and self-destructive impulses engendered by trauma.[45] The installation suggested the presence of a male child, a substitute for his childhood self, locked in a closet.

> The entire room was painted black. The closet was padlocked shut and made a constant, painfully loud rattling noise caused by something unseen (an electric sander mounted to the door inside). A framed, typewritten page hung on the opposite wall.[46]

This text, written as if spoken to a child, documented a hateful, stream-of-consciousness dialogue. The title of the piece introduced the text: "If only we could tell you . . ." The silence at the end of this sentence, the ellipsis, was deliberate. Duncan observed:

> The line was never finished because at the time it did not need to be finished. "If only we could tell you how we feel. . . . If only we could tell you . . . what is in our heart." And that is the answer. "We hate you, we hate you, we hate you, we hate you, we hate you, we hate you, we hate you, we hate you," over and over and over and over.

The text continued: "We hate you, little boy. . . . Ugly little body with the sex exposed. . . . Why don't you do everyone a favor and kill yourself. . . . DIE DIE DIE DIE DIE."[47] In the performance that took place in the installation, Duncan read this text aloud, rehearsing the abusive scripts of his youth. Addressing these words to the imagined figure in the closet, railing against the hidden, captive child, Duncan assumed the role of the abusive father, the perpetrator of this child abuse. With *If Only We Could Tell You*, Duncan attempted to destroy the victimized part of himself. This murderous self-hatred has been described by another male survivor: "It's not so much I want to kill myself, but I want to kill that little boy that caused all the pain. It wasn't me. It's like that little boy is just a different person than me. I'm just a shell, but that little boy is living it, is what it is. And I wanted to kill him immediately."[48] *If Only We Could Tell You* externalized the victim inside himself, projecting this figure out of sight, into the closet. Further, through the uneven, noisy grating of the sander, Duncan located himself and aligned viewers' sympathies *against* the imagined child behind the door. Rather than an object of pity—a boy alone and scared in the dark— the rattling door suggested the presence of a threatening, unnatural, and possibly inhuman entity reiterated by the text "We always knew you'd be a half-human baggage." Though invisible, the figure behind the door asserted its mysterious presence noisily; though hidden, it constantly and frighteningly intruded, inchoate, in the aural register. By subjecting his childhood self to his own unremitting rage, Duncan's endurance action witnessed to his firsthand view of total depravity within family life, to male victimhood, and to the dehumanizing effects of patriarchy.

FEMINISM, DIALOGUE, CONFRONTATION

The expression of anger and witness to personal abuse in Duncan's art was shaped by his encounter with strident feminists in the Los Angeles arts

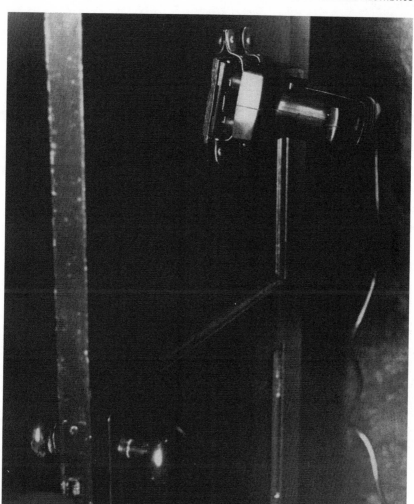

Fig. 13. John Duncan, *If Only We Could Tell You* (1980). (Copyright ©
John Duncan)

community, where women artists were experimenting with performance
as a medium that, as feminist artist Judy Chicago observed, "can be fueled
by rage in a way that painting and sculpture can't."[49] In 1972, after receiving conscientious objector status, Duncan moved to Los Angeles to attend
the California Institute of Arts (CalArts), where he studied with Allan
Kaprow and Yvonne Rainer. There he scrutinized the work of Rudolf
Schwarzkogler, Jerzy Grotowsky, Wolfgang Stoerchle, Pauline Oliveros,

and Wolf Vostell, becoming well versed in the postwar avant-garde of Europe and the United States. As a CalArts student, Duncan met Suzanne Lacy, who introduced him to Woman's Building feminist circles. He attended events at the Chouinard Art Institute location of the Woman's Building, and he helped renovate the organization's subsequent space on Spring Street. At the same time, Duncan studied feminist writings: "I was reading Jill Johnston's books, and the 'Scum Manifesto.'" He developed intimate friendships with artists such as Lacy, Laurel Klick, and Cheri Gaulke of the Feminist Art Workers, and later Barbara T. Smith, and many of these relationships yielded fruitful artistic collaborations. He attended performances by important feminists in the Southern California art scene, from Nancy Angelo and Leslie Labowitz to Linda Montano and Pauline Oliveros.[50] Duncan's fundamental concern with personal experience in his endurance art investigations derived from this feminist education. In dialogue with Los Angeles feminist artists and their artworks throughout the 1970s, and in the broader context of the Southern Californian avant-garde and its social politics, he developed the tools to deconstruct gender socialization. Working within this intellectual milieu, Duncan evaluated masculinity as a social practice, situated his personal traumatic experiences within wider political and social systems, and experimented with consciousness-raising and confrontation as artistic practices. Rather than simply appropriating feminist tools, Duncan actively participated in the rich experimentation that took place among Southern Californian feminist artists at this time, and his work continually sparked debate among and served as juxtapositions for his female collaborators. In this way, Duncan and other male artists working in this community—Paul McCarthy, Chris Burden, James Welling, and others—contributed to the work of defining and building the tools and forms of feminist performance art.[51]

In the 1970s, Duncan took seriously the feminist charge to represent the personal as political. During this period, he said, "I concentrated on a sense of myself as a member of society, one in a social order, trying to understand myself as a member of this larger society."[52] In his art actions, he began to incorporate his personal experiences of an abusive childhood and to explore the ongoing trauma of male socialization. As art historian Kristine Stiles has shown, these feminist modes of visual communication were themselves motivated and shaped by traumatic experience and thus particularly suited to the kind of personal exploration and moral consciousness-raising that Duncan sought.[53] Influenced by his friends at the Woman's Building, Duncan organized and attended male consciousness-raising meetings as early as 1975; Smith named Duncan as one of the first men she knew to participate in such a group.[54] Based on these experiences, and following Lacy, Labowitz, Smith, and others, Duncan adopted consciousness-raising as an artistic strategy. *Sanctuary* (1976) directly appropriated this format as a means of exploring male anger. He gathered a group of men and women and seated them in a circle. Then he described his experiences with rage: "Whenever I tried to figure out how my sex affected my character, which was often, the train of my thought always stopped at anger. Anger at women, at men, at advertising, at my parents, at myself, at something I could never fully understand." He invited each man in the audience to explore this issue, one by one, by discussing "how his sexuality affected his character." Duncan further destabilized gender relations by asking women to "watch men's interactions and to comment on them later."[55] In notes written after the piece, Duncan expressed disappointment at the lack of authentic interaction—possibly due to his choice to cast female audience members as judges of male commentary—and deemed the straightforward, group therapy format a failure: "I wasn't convinced that anyone had been honest with me."[56] However, Duncan continued to experiment with dialogue and group discussion. Subsequent performances (including *Blind Date*) retained an element of *Sanctuary*'s structure: following the completion and documentation of an art action, Duncan often arranged a consciousness-raising-style discussion with a public audience. His late works have relied heavily on one-on-one interactions similar to those modeled by Smith in *Feed Me* (1973), in which she invited individual audience members into a private space to dialogue verbally and physically. These autobiographical endurance actions examined specific gendered encounters in Duncan's personal life as a means of generating potentially transformative dialogue about the structures and consequences of male gender socialization. In this way, his performances have mimicked therapeutic group work; he noted that *Sanctuary* "sounds like a group therapy session because in some ways it was." Lisak's research on therapeutic approaches to male survivors has emphasized the importance of analyzing and critiquing gender socialization: "The treatment of male survivors of childhood abuse must actively and consciously confront the gender conflict that comprises part of the core of the survivor's post-abuse adaptation."[57] In this regard, artworks like *Sanctuary*, which sought to foster critical thinking about masculinity, anticipated treatment models.

At the Woman's Building, Duncan observed feminist artists practicing confrontation as an aggressive form of consciousness-raising. These artists regularly staged antagonistic performances, seeking to expose the harsh realities of sexual assault against women and the violent consequences of patriarchy. Lacy observed in 1980, "[T]he threat of violence is a current condition of every woman's life."[58] Her large-scale series of events titled *Three Weeks in May* (1977) tracked local sexual assaults against women and courted extensive media coverage with performances, including Labowitz's *All Men Are Potential Rapists*. In the collaborative performance *Ablutions* (1972), Judy Chicago, Suzanne Lacy, Sandra Orgel, and Aviva Rahmani performed a set of actions recalling the materials and tasks of Viennese Action art; blood, organs, eggs, clay, and gauze were applied to women's bodies while audio recordings detailed instances of sexual violence against women.[59] These actions joined those of global feminist artists engaged in endurance art as prophetic witness to female victimhood, including Yoko Ono's *Cut Piece* (1964), in which she invited audience members to cut her clothing from her body; Marina Abramović's *Rhythm 0* (1974), which provided viewers with a variety of objects, including weapons, to use in interacting with her; and Ana Mendieta's *Rape Scene* (1973), in which Mendieta arranged for friends to find her beaten, bloody body at her home. Motivated by intense rage, these and other artists implicated audience members in the perpetration of patriarchal violence. Duncan's explorations of masculinity similarly experimented with rage-fueled confrontation as a powerful form of education: "It was necessary to create confrontations, especially with myself and social conventions I'd always taken for granted, in order to learn from the conflicts and grow as a human being."[60] For Duncan conflict could provoke self-reflection, productive dialogue, and important cognitive shifts for both artist and audience. Parallel to feminists' deconstructions of female stereotypes, Duncan sought to reveal the destructive effects of traditional assumptions about masculinity. Like his feminist colleagues, Duncan exposed structural patriarchal oppression, condemned men's capacity for sexual violence, experimented with unsettling gender stereotypes, and advocated expanded conceptions of gender identity. His performances enacted multiple modes of maleness, exposed male victimhood as a cultural reality, and argued that traditional masculinities were inadequate to encompassing the complexity of men's experiences.

Duncan's early confrontations targeted men as a means of challenging both his own and other men's assumptions about masculinity. In *Scare* (1976), the artist knocked at the front door of a male friend's home. When the door opened, Duncan, wearing a mask that obscured his face, brandished a gun, fired blanks in his friend's face, and ran. He developed the performance in response to a mugging. When Duncan and artist James Welling were attacked on Venice Boulevard, one of their assailants cracked a broomstick over his head.

I thought I had been shot in the neck. . . . For a split second, I felt cold terror. Then I pulled my hand away and saw that there was no blood, and I felt hot anger, all in a split second. What was amazing to me was that it was possible to go from one extreme to an entirely opposite extreme within a split second. I decided I wanted to give that experience as art to other people.

Duncan wanted to bring this moment of insight to other men. He decided to wear "a mask to hide [his] identity and load a starting pistol with blanks." He continued:

I went to people that I knew well. There were two people who . . . would actually be able to see it as an art experience: Paul [McCarthy] and Tom Recchion. I performed it and didn't say anything. I called them a couple of days later to tell them what had happened. It had worked the way that I had intended.

Placing these men in vulnerable circumstances, Duncan subverted their masculine assumptions of safety and control. He later observed, "I found out much later from a lawyer that what I'd done in *Scare* was felony assault, but I looked at it more as a gift."[61] Masked and threatening, he demonstrated how the overwhelming negative affect of victimization necessarily undermines gender norms that demand the outward expression of confidence and invulnerability. Contrary to masculine stereotypes, *Scare* insisted on the reality of male victimhood. In highlighting men's dual roles in violence—as both perpetrators and victims—*Scare* generated consternation and criticism among his colleagues. In 1979 Duncan's colleague and collaborator Linda Frye Burnham, editor of *High Performance* magazine, summarized debates about the "remarkably violent nature" of his artworks.

Duncan has been called on the carpet by his feminist colleagues for "irresponsibility" in pieces like *Scare*. The charge is that the meaning of the piece is not clear to the observer and that it is in fact dangerous and threatening, even though the gun was loaded with blanks. They question Duncan's right to assault an unprepared audience with unexplained violence.[62]

Duncan responded to these legitimate concerns emphatically: "This question of who is the aggressor and who is the victim has come up often. . . . I AM THE VICTIM. That is how I see it."[63]

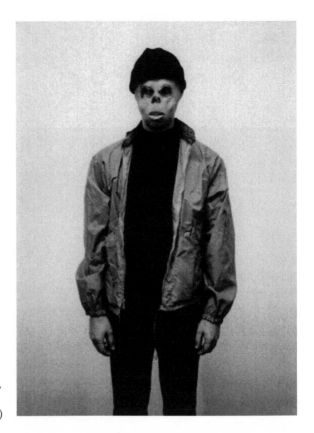

Fig. 14. John Duncan,
Scare (1976). (Copy-
right © John Duncan)

Scare asserted the fact of male victimhood, but it also allowed Duncan to perpetrate an offense—the violent mugging—that had reverted him to a state of objecthood, the unwilling recipient of violent attention. In *Scare* he attempted to countermand this experience of helplessness and masquerade as a perpetrator, obscuring his face and marking his own absence. With this deliberate move from assailed to assailant, Duncan drew attention to what Lisak and other psychologists refer to as cyclical victimization, the perpetration of interpersonal violence by victims and their repeated exposure to the risk of further victimization.[64] As adults survivors of abuse may attempt to master childhood traumas by repeating them from a position of control. However, in re-creating or participating in situations that mimic or evoke their abusive pasts, they may expose themselves to danger or exploitation, as in the illusory agency of prostitution.[65] Many of Duncan's artworks, particularly those of the 1970s, were predicated on this kind of risk and revictimization. For example, in *Every Woman*

(1978), Duncan hitchhiked on the stretch of Sunset Boulevard known for prostitution: "I wanted to feel, even for one night, the daily vulnerability to sexual attack experienced by most women. I exposed myself to sexual aggression by men—as a man one night, a woman the next, on a Hollywood street."[66] Duncan presented this work in the context of Connecting Myths, a feminist performance art festival that he organized with artist Cheri Gaulke. Dressed as a woman, he planned to observe male sexual aggression and learn about female victimhood. The reality, however, undermined this conceptual framework. His dangerous actions did render him vulnerable to sexual violence, but he observed, "[T]he irony of it is that I got more threats as a man than I got as a woman." He elaborated on the risks of performing his own gender identity.

> I got in people's cars, sure. The first time, I dressed as I would normally dress—jeans and a Lacoste shirt. That night, I hitchhiked looking like that, and I got a couple of rides. One guy who picked me up tried to rape me. I jumped out of the van while it was moving. Other than that, people just took me where I was going and that was it. Nobody picked me up when I was dressed as a woman.

Duncan presented himself simultaneously as male and sexual prey, demonstrating how male sexual aggression threatens men as well as women. In addition, by deliberately exposing himself to attack, Duncan created the conditions for re-experiencing his abusive past. This reenactment repeated previous abuses and reinforced his participation in cyclical victimization. His prophetic witness to the consequences of aggressive male sexuality revealed his feminist commitment to using himself—his body, psyche, experiences, actions, and relationships—as a means of exploring cycles of abuse.

Similarly, *For Women Only* (1979) explicitly established the conditions for revictimization. If, as many feminists argued, pornography could motivate men to commit acts of violence against women, Duncan wondered, could these patriarchal representations of sexuality also incite women to perpetrate violence against men? Seeking to index the impact of pornography on his own body, he assembled an audience of women and declared that, after projecting a pornographic film titled *Hurts So Good*, he would "make himself available" for sexual exploitation in a back room.[67] Based on his own preferences, Duncan designed the hour-long *Hurts So Good*—a series of excerpts from a variety of pornographic sources—to oscillate between arousing and repelling visual information: "The idea was to sexually arouse the audience and turn arousal into repulsion, leaving everyone polarized with themselves when they returned home."[68] Duncan was curious about the effect of this pornographic stimulation on women.

> I wanted to see what women would do, if they would become the same as the men that they were criticizing. One woman came back, and she talked about how the SM had particularly turned her on. . . . She said that she had come back to do those kinds of things to me. She wanted to see if she would actually do it. . . . When she got into the room she changed her mind.

For Women Only mimicked feminist artworks (like Ono's *Cut Piece*) that implicated audiences in acts of violence against women. However, by interrogating women's capacities for sexual violence, Duncan laid bare the essentialism of feminist narratives that associated pornography with male perpetration alone. Further, in an early draft of a text about *For Women Only*, he linked his endurance action to the exploitation and sexual victimization of boys.

> In the middle of a conversation one day I suddenly had a revelation: the memory of my circumcision came back in full color, doctor's face and all. RAPED in INFANCY! A social crime that no one recognizes, that's even encouraged. That some doctors consider medically unnecessary. That started me thinking about other social crimes committed against men, the training we get: training from infancy to become insensitive to our emotions and to treat sexually-desirable people as a commodity.[69]

In this way, Duncan equated male genital mutilation and the gender socialization process with rape, revealing the insidious consequences of sexual objectification for everyone in patriarchal societies.

Duncan's risk-taking actions coincided with his posttraumatic subjectivity, and they also resonated with an atmosphere of escalating risk among 1970s Los Angeles performance artists, who pushed the limits of physical, social, legal, sexual, and personal boundaries. Feminist artists were at the forefront of these explorations, as when a naked Barbara T. Smith invited individual audience members to interact with her in a private space, accompanied by a soundtrack with the repeated injunction "feed me."[70] Gender and sexuality figured prominently in many of these performances. Paul McCarthy, for example, in his performance and video *Contemporary Cure-All* (1979), staged a sex-change operation with dildos, ketchup, and Barbie dolls, and Johanna Went's chaotic punk club performances, beginning in 1977, simulated explicit sex.[71] Recalling the foment of this period, Duncan has insisted on the contributions of CalArts professor Wolfgang Stoerchle. In his action *Untitled* (1975), performed at John Baldessari's studio, Stoerchle exposed and interrogated the painful consequences of his own masculine assumptions and conditioning. Duncan witnessed the performance.

> The performance that really inspired me and left me weeping at the end was one where [Stoerchle] invited an audience to his studio. He told us that he wanted to suck somebody's cock. He said it was the last thing that he'd ever want to do, that he'd ever imagine that he'd want to do. He proceeded to tell an hour-long story of his life, about how he was brought up very macho and this idea was not only alien to his upbringing and his moral code, but a threat to that. That was why he wanted to do it. He gave us this entire background into his life and why this was such a repulsive action. Then he asked somebody in the audience, a male of course, to come and take their pants off and allow him to suck their cock in front of everybody. Somebody did . . . [H]e came up and Stoerchle tried to get him erect and he couldn't. They tried for a few minutes . . . and then the performance was over. For me, this was such a revelation of taking risks with what you believe in, what you've been brought up with. To take all of that, put it off to one side because it gets in the way of what you need to know. The courage to do that—I'll never forget. It really informed my worldview.[72]

For Duncan, Stoerchle served as a courageous example of the power of personal disclosure. *Untitled* modeled the way discussing and transgressing one's own sexual boundaries might have risked misunderstanding and public outcry within the insular Los Angeles arts community but could also function as moral consciousness-raising. With Stoerchle's precedent, and fueled by neo-orthodox concepts of total depravity and feminist ideologies, analyses, and strategies, Duncan's 1970s denunciation of aggressive male sexuality culminated in a pair of linked performances; his jeremiad consisted of *Blind Date* (1980) and *If Only We Could Tell You* (1980). Duncan presented both endurance actions as part of the Public Spirit performance art festival that he co-organized as part of the Highland Art Agents collective, which included Duncan, Linda Frye Burnham, Chip Chapman, Paul McCarthy, and Barbara T. Smith.[73] As in *Scare, Every Woman, For Women Only*, and others, and parallel to Stoerchle's *Untitled*, these autobiographical performances offered the artist's own example in order to educate others about the dangers and consequences of masculinity. In both performances, Duncan executed a complex series of intensely degrading, extremely self-destructive actions. While prior works had involved high levels of risk and participated in cycles of victimization, the physical and psychological perils of *Blind Date* and *If Only We Could Tell You* far exceeded those of his earlier actions—and those of previous artists, including the Viennese Action artists. Incendiary and devastating to himself and his audiences, the artist's actions clarified his stark views on the violent sources and consequences of male sexual aggression. In these performances, Duncan enacted a range of transgressive masculine identities: angry violator and lifeless corpse, abusive father and victimized child. These painful testimonies to trauma challenge even the most experienced of performance art audiences, raising troubling questions of culpability, accountability, and complicity, and often engendering aggressive rejection. However, in response to Duncan's traumatic representations, I suggest that viewers and readers witness his actions through a series of oscillations, looking and looking away in turn. Although contradictions may remain unsolved and distress unrelieved, the actions of looking and looking away can make space for affect—for disgust and pity, anger and shame—for the endurance of uncomfortable subject-to-subject encounters, and for sustained, reflective engagement with the challenges of Duncan's performance actions.

SURVIVING *BLIND DATE*

Sex with a corpse was at the center of *Blind Date*. Duncan subjected himself to this dire experience out of self-hatred and despair over the failure of his four-year relationship with girlfriend Terryl Hunter.

> I thought that I had failed at something that makes us essentially human, and that is to love somebody. *Blind Date*, for me, was about punishing myself for that failure. Making it art was bringing that sense of failure into a public arena to make it a public issue: this is a way that men deal with emotional trauma, with anger against ourselves or especially against ourselves.

He intended *Blind Date* to illustrate the violent consequences of male conditioning, "to show them as conditioning, and to use myself as an example of the conditioning gone wrong."[74] As in earlier works, he offered his own negative example in hopes of educating others about the dangers and consequences of traditional male gender socialization. Duncan described the first phase of the performance.

> I went around to different Hollywood porn shops, told the clerk I wanted to buy time with a cadaver for sex and was looking for information. Three of these guys threw me out; the fourth said he had a Tijuana phone number for sale. In Tijuana someone met me and we drove to a morgue in his car. He said, "No pictures," opened the door to a medium-sized room, then closed it again behind me. The body was on a wooden table. I put microphones at both ends, turned on the cassette recorder. I came by imagining everyone I'd wanted to have sex with and never had. When it was over I packed up the recorder and walked out of the room, and was driven back to the meeting point.[75]

Radical exposure and extreme risk characterized this phase of the performance. First, as he searched for a corpse, Duncan opened himself to humiliation, condemnation, and accusations of perversion, necrophilia, and masochism. At the morgue, beyond the legal risk of engaging in this deeply illicit activity, Duncan imperiled his physical health and debased his sexuality, exposing himself to disease, putrescence, and bodily corruption. Finally, by enduring this utterly transgressive and apocalyptic action, he risked acute psychological damage with lifelong consequences. Duncan violated a corpse, joined himself with a dead body, and contaminated his living being.

The core endurance action in this stage of the performance, Duncan's abject sex act, remained invisible. He intended to videotape the action, but when he arrived at the morgue, he said, "I wasn't allowed to take pictures at the mortuary. I would have taken a film if I could have, but I was told very strictly not to do that." The mortician's ban on photography suspended visual representation as a precaution against legal prosecution, but it also forced Duncan to document the event aurally rather than visually.[76] This substitution abstracted and objectified Duncan's desperate action. Burnham described the audio recording: "It just sounded like a bunch of furniture being moved around."[77] The sounds of Duncan's unseen act reiterated the objectification and dehumanization—the blindness—engendered by patriarchy, identifying Duncan's body with the inert matter of things, of furniture, and of the dead woman's corpse. While Duncan has argued that he "wasn't looking for a specific race, age, or gender," the availability of a female corpse must be acknowledged and testifies to the profound objectification of women's bodies.[78] For the artist, death was the body's crucial attribute. Smith supported this intention when, just after the performance, she dismissed questions of misogyny in *Blind Date*, observing that "if he fucked a man it would have been the same thing."[79] Yet Duncan's observations highlighted the exploitation of Mexican women's labor: "The first thing[s] you notice . . . are that the body is female and that it is intact. Her face shows that she worked hard for a long time."[80] This woman's body indexed the particular, physical impact of patriarchy; Duncan's action perpetrated further exploitation, implicating him in cycles of aggressive male sexuality and illustrating his neo-orthodox view of the ubiquity and inevitability of human evil. He has said, "Remaining true to my Calvinist upbringing, I intended to punish myself . . . in the most repulsive way I could come up with."[81] In *Blind Date*, Duncan represented total depravity as both human condition and punishment, transforming neo-orthodox theology into a retributive strategy.[82]

The second phase of *Blind Date* took place a few days after his return from Tijuana. At the Los Angeles Center for Birth Control, Duncan underwent a vasectomy "to make sure that the last potent seed I had was spent in a cadaver."[83] In a photograph taken by McCarthy—the only visual documentation of *Blind Date*—Duncan's body rests on a surgical table. A hospital gown covers his chest and legs. His eyes are closed, his mouth open, and his hands lay on his chest, interlaced fingers extending slightly, perhaps in response to distress or pain. A doctor, white-coated and gloved, bends over Duncan's genitals and buries his scalpel in the tissue below a barely distinguishable penis. McCarthy's photograph figures Duncan's manhood as painfully vulnerable. Manipulated by the doctor and surveyed by the cool gaze of the camera, this depiction of the penis recalls Rudolf Schwarzkogler's *Action with a Male Body* (1965), which simulated the castration of a male figure wrapped in bandages.[84] Duncan has been captured in the precise moment of incision, in the ongoing and castrating experience of male victimhood.

In the third action of the piece, Duncan organized an opportunity for public discussion. As in *Sanctuary* and other works modeled on consciousness-raising groups, he sought to generate a detailed discussion about the implications of the artwork.

An audience was invited to a small warehouse space in downtown L.A., an old triangular brick building with a tiny balcony at one end, no windows, no chairs, one exit. A microphone, cassette player, amp and speakers were set up on the balcony. When the exit door was closed and the lights were switched off, I described the process of finding the cadaver, receiving a vasectomy shortly afterward, and why I was making the action public, then played the audiotape recording of the session with the cadaver. When the tape ended, the door was opened and people could see to leave.[85]

Duncan anticipated that this format would yield a rich conversation. He earnestly hoped that his jeremiad, his own cautionary tale of "where such an upbringing can lead," would awaken audience members to their own blindness about aggressive male sexuality and victimhood.[86] However, he was taken aback, he said, when "no one said a word. No one did anything; everyone just left."[87] Overwhelmed by the shocking nature of Duncan's act, audiences then and now have overlooked his explicit aim to illustrate the violent consequences of traditional masculinities, responding instead with revulsion. His critique of patriarchy has been subsumed by the powerful affect engendered by his taboo performance, which remains one of the most infamous and reviled actions in contemporary art history.

In the dark of the theater, Duncan's friends in the Los Angeles arts community struggled to respond to his performance. Smith described the immediate, personal, emotional impact of *Blind Date* on her own life: "Each person just sat there coping with John's piece the best they could. I couldn't deal with the story myself because it was so destructive to my life. I just sat there and turned it into pure sound."[88] Smith had lived with Duncan for almost two years in the mid-1970s; the audience also included Duncan's friends, colleagues, artist-collaborators, co-organizers, and many former lovers, like Smith, who were personally, not simply ideologically, threatened by Duncan's action. By fucking a corpse, Duncan commented on his relationships with every individual in the audience, intimately associating them with death, suffering, and failure. Paul McCarthy anticipated the force of this community's negative response. Despite his own role in photographing Duncan's vasectomy, he listened from outside the room but did not enter: "I felt obliged to appear, but I felt the piece was socially self-destructive. It made John a pariah in the community."[89] Duncan has observed that, in the extremity of his pain, he did not consider the realistic consequences of his performance or its impact on his friends. He remembered that Smith tried to convince him not to go through with *Blind Date*.

I disagreed with her. I said, "I don't think I have a choice." I couldn't imagine suffering any more than I was. I thought if the art that I'm making serves any purpose, then it makes it possible for other people not to have to do something like this. That's why I made it public, so that it wouldn't be necessary for anybody else.[90]

However, *Blind Date* outraged Duncan's feminist colleagues. Suzanne Lacy, Barbara T. Smith, and others described the action as a rape and initiated legal proceedings against Duncan. When lack of evidence stalled the group's efforts, he said, "They decided on a 'media boycott,' threatening anyone who was willing to put even the mention of my work or my name in print, let alone show my work."[91] This suppression, whether deliberately orchestrated or simply responding to the shocking nature of Duncan's actions, was successful—very little has been written about *Blind Date* or his other works—and Duncan soon left the United States to live in exile, as he does today. As result, he has suggested that *Blind Date* may still be in progress: "Has it ended? I thought it would end with the vasectomy and the presentation of the whole thing. But there is still so much reaction to it, and those reactions have a very direct influence on my daily life. The life [of *Blind Date*] seems to be rather vital; it keeps touching nerves and causing responses." At the same time, *Blind Date* marked the end of an era of widespread, risky experimentation in Los Angeles performance art. Looking back on the controversy, Duncan observed:

If there is anything I regret about *Blind Date* it's that it seems [to have] stopped a lot of other people from going into that manner of research. It seemed to scare them. That's a real frustration for me, because that is what I'm interested in. That is what I want to know, that is why I'm making art, and I can't do it by myself. . . . People [have] pulled back from that kind of searching. . . . It's too bad, because there was something going on at that time that is worth looking into. We have no more answers now than we did then, and there's no absence at all of material.

Blind Date also coincided with a moment of culture change. Ronald Reagan would shortly assume the presidency, punk was in the process of commercialization, and feminist artists would soon adopt more conceptual artistic strategies. At this juncture, *Blind Date* marked and likely hastened performance artists' move away from dangerous behaviors in the early 1980s, but it profoundly influenced a younger generation of artists, including Mike Kelley and Tony Ourlser, and prefigured the morbid concerns of such recent artists as Damien Hirst and Teresa Margolles.[92]

The full trajectory of *Blind Date*—from the porn shops to the silent warehouse—took place at the limit of Duncan's physical and psychological endurance. The abject set of actions that comprised the performance embodied the overwhelming self-hatred and agony of his past and present, and it marked a suicidal inability to imagine the future. The performance threatened his own psychic annihilation: *Blind Date* curtailed Duncan's future by jeopardizing his emotional life and destroying his ability to have children. Just after the performance, he observed, "What have I risked? I've risked the ability to accept myself. I've risked the ability to have sex . . . and the ability to love."[93] In an interview with McCarthy, he added, "I won't have any kids, that's a guarantee. That's a price to pay, a small part of the price. Now I live in total fear of intimacy with anyone or of trusting anyone; that's another small part."[94] *Blind Date* also marked the artist's suicidal isolation: "I think [*Blind Date*] was a step towards my own death. Towards committing suicide."[95] Duncan verbalized his wish for death: "I didn't feel anything but self-hatred. I did it for the torture, I wanted to be thrown out of the porn shops. I wanted to be killed."[96] This investment in death continued in *If Only We Could Tell You* (also known as *The Black Room*), Duncan's first project after *Blind Date* and his second contribution to the Public Spirit festival. He conceived of the two performances together and carefully organized their timing.

> The connecting element between [*Blind Date* and *If Only We Could Tell You*] is that both of them come from me and my experiences. The timing was important in the sense that I had the seasons very much in mind. I wanted to have *Blind Date* in the spring. I wanted *The Black Room* to happen in the autumn, talking about the treatment of a young life, a little boy.[97]

Considered together, *Blind Date* and *If Only We Could Tell You* reveal Duncan's struggle with what psychiatrist Robert J. Lifton has called the death imprint. Lifton theorized that trauma survivors are plagued by vivid imaginings of grotesque, spectacular death, reenactments that re-create the unresolvable conditions of traumatic subjectivity.[98] With these paired works, Duncan manifested and performed his grotesque death imprint, systematically attacking his experience of being. Together the two performances effected the deaths of his past, present, and future. *If Only We Could Tell You* targeted his childhood self, locking that helpless little boy in a closet and asphyxiating him with commands to "DIE." In *Blind Date*, Duncan encountered the traumatized—dead—part of himself in the figure of the dead woman whom he violated. By identifying himself, particularly his penis, with death in this way, he metaphorically executed his adult masculinity, the male self that continued to experience the pain of childhood victimization. And, finally, in vasectomy surgery to "make sure that the last potent seed I had was spent in a cadaver," Duncan assaulted his future.[99] He symbolically obliterated the possibility of transformative, generative change and attempted to literally halt the cycle of violence. As the culmination of his critique, Duncan's deeply self-hating actions in *Blind Date* painfully marked men's performances of masculinity as literally deadening. In his public presentation of the performance, Duncan told his audience, "There is a point to all this. . . . Death is at the center of myths about men."[100]

Duncan's actions also served as a vivid illustration of the Calvinist doctrine of total depravity as self-destruction and death. *Blind Date* and *If Only We Could Tell You* evinced a dark, neo-orthodox conviction in the depths of human capacity for transgression, violence, and depravity, and it visualized Duncan's belief in the futility of human striving: "To paraphrase Presbyterian Calvinistic thought as I know it, we're fucked from the beginning, there's nothing we can do about it."[101] By both violating the dead woman and identifying the deepest parts of himself with her, *Blind Date* literalized this violent experience of being fucked. In the face of this despairing view, Duncan took on a prophetic stance. He intended the performance to function as a jeremiad, denouncing the violence latent in male gender socialization and awakening people to the deadly consequences of patriarchy.

> [*Blind Date* was] a form of sacrifice to humanity as a whole, to everybody waking up. If people see what you do as such a heinous act that they are repelled . . . that they are just stunned, really shocked at themselves, at something that's within themselves as well. That helps them to wake up to something within themselves that they wouldn't otherwise see, and that helps everybody.

Duncan clearly and repeatedly stated his prophetic motive in interviews and writings just after the performance. Just a few of these comments include the following.

> I wanted to show what can happen to men that are trained to ignore their emotions. I called it an art piece to objectify myself becoming self-destructive and numb.[102]

I wanted to show by example how divorced men are from their own feelings.[103]

I did it to show people's conditioning to themselves, specifically men. I did it for people to ask why and maybe look at themselves for some sort of answer.[104]

Blind Date initiated real changes in Duncan's art practice. In the aftermath of its troubled reception, he realized the depth of social resistance to ideas of male victimhood. Just after the performance, he told McCarthy, "I don't want to try to make statements about the conditioning of men in this culture or any other. What difference does it make?"[105] He moved away from the overt political approaches of his early experiments, as did many feminist artists in the 1980s, and he no longer oriented his work toward immediate social change. Although Duncan has continued to work with the theme of male victimhood, his commentary has been subtle. For example, *The Flocking* (2000), which he noted "was about child abuse, about seeing child abuse," included a four-channel audio installation with the sounds of whispering children, a human tooth, and the text from *Happy Homes*, an early performance, hanging on the wall. Duncan's relationship with his audiences also shifted following *Blind Date*. He observed, "The problem was that the onus of it fell entirely on my shoulders. . . . One of many things that I took away from the experience was that I was very, very tired of putting myself up in front of an audience and taking all the risks. I wanted to share those risks with the audience. I wanted the audience to meet me halfway." Since the 1990s, his endurance actions have sought increasingly relational and intimate partnerships with viewers as participants. However, these actions have continued to enact the cyclical dynamics of victimization and coercion. In *Voice Contact* (1998), Duncan invited participants to take off their clothes and interact with him in a pitch-black room. In the course of the performance, he was fondled and repeatedly propositioned: "One man groped me. When it was clear that it was not about sex, he left. . . . I did this in Tokyo and half of the participants were women, and at least half of them wanted sex. They left pretty soon after they realized it wasn't going to happen." Viewers who entered the small, enclosed space of *Stress Chamber* (1993) were bombarded with earthquakelike movements and explosive sound waves.[106] In *Maze* (1995), Duncan locked himself and a group of unsuspecting volunteers into the exhibition space, shut the lights off, and used an infrared camera to film their distress. During the exhibition of his installation *The Gauntlet* (2008), he programmed high-volume sirens to trigger in response to human movement. While these artworks have posited alternate modes of relational humanity and new conceptions of personal politics, Duncan's experiments remain caught in patterns of cyclical victimization.

Traditionally, a jeremiad dwells on depravity, evil and social disorder with a purpose: to contrast with the redemptive prophetic vision, the potential alternative reality, offered at the end of the sermon.[107] In *Blind Date, Move Forward*, and other jeremiads throughout his endurance art, Duncan has envisioned the possibility of interrupting cycles of male victimhood and sexual aggression. From his earliest endurance actions, his work has embodied the tensions of testifying to an abusive past while acknowledging his own complicity in perpetuating further violence. Caught within these contradictions, and complicated by his neo-orthodox conviction in the continuation of total depravity, Duncan has nevertheless stood as prophetic witness to his vision of halting cycles of violence: "I have a choice to retaliate or absorb. What I mean by absorption is not just holding on to it, but also seeing to it that it goes no further."[108] Duncan illustrated both the courage and the precarity of this position in *The Dream Room* (1982), an installation that consisted of detailed drawings on newsprint, now lost.

> The walls were entirely covered with drawings from dreams. One of them was a woman staked down, pinned down, chained, being raped by a man who was, in turn, being raped by another man bigger, who was in turn being raped by a bigger man, and in turn, and in turn, and in turn until these men turned into monsters.

Following his feminist roots, Duncan visualized the enmeshment of individuals in larger social webs of victimhood and perpetration. Extending the depiction of rape as presented in *Blind Date*, the repetition of male figures and their transformation into monsters emphasized the particular dangers of masculine sexuality. *The Dream Room* registered the messy complexity of cyclical abuse, a dynamic that Duncan attempted to escape at the conclusion of the work.

> When the exhibition was over, I took all these drawings down, wadded them up, and tossed them. It felt good to destroy all this stuff. If you had gone to see this, maybe you would remember it: that's what was left.

In this action, Duncan pictured himself, the victimized man, as an object of refuse, as remains, as absence.

Duncan's performances have regularly erased him, supplying instead a variety of objects: an empty bed, a mask, a corpse, an electric sander, and crumpled paper. His subject matter demanded these erasures and substitutions; his actions continually created victimized men—a category so contrary to traditional gender expectations as to make visualization impossible. As a result, his art actions have consistently evaded visual representation, often taking refuge in the abstraction of sound. Even allowing for the challenges of documenting ephemeral actions, Duncan's visual documentation has projected a remarkable stillness that contrasts with his intense and focused endurance actions. The photograph of *Scare* pictured the masked artist standing immobile, facing the camera. The proof sheets documenting *Every Woman* depicted anonymous, empty street scenes. *Blind Date* is remembered in an image of the artist lying on a surgical table. A shadowed photograph of an electric sander mounted on a door commemorates *If Only We Could Tell You*. Left to the imagination are Duncan's gunshot, his leap from a van to escape a rapist, his sexual encounter with a corpse, his screamed threats to an invisible child. In place of these impossible pictures, Duncan's public exposure of his own absence, his own numbing deadness, stands as prophetic witness and visual substitute for the violence, aggression, and internal death imposed on boys and men through patriarchy.

Epilogue

Endurance at the Corner of State and Bank

At the Soldiers and Sailors Monument in New London, Connecticut, an elderly man stands vigil. With his cane, Veterans for Peace t-shirt, and "War Is Not the Answer" sign, my friend Cal Robertson is a familiar sight to locals, rain or shine. Within view of the nuclear submarine manufacturer Electric Boat and just downriver from a US Navy submarine base, Cal's stooped figure has occupied the public square daily since 1986. Well known to our homeless neighbors, who seek him out for a kind word or some change, Cal waves at passing cars, offers photocopies of a Buddhist poem, and shakes the hands of passersby.[1] Sometimes, he holds a handmade sign with grubby edges full of gruesome photographs of wounded veterans and annotated with cramped, impassioned text. He frames each person he encounters as part of his project. I met Cal at Saint Francis House, an intentional community in New London with roots in the Catholic Worker movement, Gandhian peace activism, and Christian anarchist politics. I participate in the life of the house as a member of the extended community, but Cal lives there. When I visit the house for meetings, I see him continuing his vigil on the front porch, his sign over the rail, or seated in a corner with bowed head, listening carefully to the energetic din around him, participating only when directly questioned. Aphasia slows his speech and marks his survival of service in Vietnam and its posttraumatic aftermath—alcoholism and a long-ago assault. His movement is hampered by complications of diabetes and an accident; in 1996 he was hit by a truck while standing vigil outside the gates of Electric Boat. Each time I settle in to wait for him to complete his careful greeting I am learning the power of *being*. Cal's daily public witness, on the street corner and at home, is a profound act of being, an endurance of weather fair and foul, of friendship and insults, of long-held trauma, of war-induced disability, of injustice both visible and invisible.

Cal is famous in peace activist communities nationwide. When asked about his vigil, he insists, in his slow but emphatic way, on the difference

Fig. 15. Cal Robertson and Mike Hatt at the Soldiers and Sailors Monument, New London, Connecticut, 2015. (Photograph by Karen Gonzalez Rice)

between protesting and witnessing. Fellow Vietnam veteran Mike Hatt, who has been accompanying Cal during his vigils recently, described their first encounter: "When I first approached Cal back then, I asked him how long he had been protesting. He quickly and firmly corrected me. 'Not protesting, Brother; witnessing for peace.'"[2] By carefully reframing his actions beyond 1960s paradigms of protest, Cal intentionally roots his actions in centuries-long traditions of justice-directed prophetic witnessing. With a universal invitation to join his vigil and his constant injunction to "keep your eye on the prize," he calls on me to do good work and consider my daily complicity in war, oppression, and death. He makes me aware of my own desire to shut my eyes to his gruesome sign and difficult work, and he draws my attention to the courage it takes for each of us to open our eyes, look away, and open them again. He offers me the opportunity to participate in a prophetic project by witnessing, observing, and testifying.

In *Long Suffering*, I have framed endurance art as prophetic witness in order to locate it within an American tradition that also includes Cal's decades-long peace vigil and other activists' performative endurance actions. Parallel to Cal's daily commitment, Montano, Athey, and Duncan have *endured*, displaying their own bodies as material artifacts of loss and as agents of survival. Montano's passionate pursuit of sainthood, Athey's spectacles of suffering, and Duncan's fiery denunciation of gender socialization have all witnessed to injustice in the prophetic forms of their religious backgrounds. The medium of endurance art has allied them with the prophetic witness of activists like Cal. By using their bodies to bend the arc of the moral universe toward justice, endurance artists in the United States participate in deep traditions of American radicalism, creating possibilities for performing dissent as survival, generating productive and sometimes unbearable tensions, and challenging us, as witnesses, to add our own weight to the balance.

Notes

CHAPTER 1

1. Kristine Stiles, "Performance," in *Critical Terms for Art History*, ed. Robert Nelson and Richard Shiff (Chicago: University of Chicago Press, 2003), 95. See also Kristine Stiles, "Uncorrupted Joy: International Art Actions," in *Out of Actions: Between Performance and the Object, 1949–1979*, ed. Paul Schimmel (Los Angeles: Los Angeles Museum of Contemporary Art, 1998), 226–328.

2. For an overview of approaches to endurance art, see Jennie Klein, "Endurance Performance," in *Reading Contemporary Performance: Theatricality across Genres*, ed. Gabrielle Cody and Meiling Cheng (New York: Routledge, 2016), 22–23.

3. This action was publicized in the West through Malcolm Browne's Pulitzer Prize–winning photograph for the Associated Press.

4. Jacques Derrida and Gil Anidjar, eds., *Acts of Religion* (New York: Routledge, 2001), 38.

5. Stiles has addressed this point in Kristine Stiles, "Burden of Light," in *Chris Burden*, ed. Paul Schimmel (Newcastle: Merrel and Locus Plus, 2007); and "Wangechi Mutu's Family Tree," in *Wangechi Mutu: A Fantastic Journey*, ed. Trevor Schoonmaker (Durham: Nasher Museum of Art, Duke University, 2013).

6. In a word, politics.

7. For a transcript of this exchange, see Mark H. C. Bessire, ed., *William Pope.L: The Friendliest Black Artist in America* (Cambridge: MIT Press, 2002), 174–75.

8. Derrida and Anidjar, *Acts of Religion*, 387.

9. Derrida observed, "Nothing is more illegible than the wound." Jacques Derrida and Thomas Dutoit, eds., *On the Name*, trans. David Wood, John P. Leavey Jr., and Ian MacLeod (Stanford: Stanford University Press, 1995), 60.

10. Stephen Heyman, "Pulp Friction," *T: The New York Times Style Magazine*, August 19, 2012, M2108.

11. "Religion shapes and is shaped by cognitive (*beliefs*), moral (*values*), and affective (*emotions*) processes. . . . [T]he devout offer assertions about the nature of things and prescribe moral codes to guide conduct." Thomas A. Tweed, *Crossing and Dwelling: A Theory of Religion* (Cambridge: Harvard University Press, 2006), 67–68. This aligns with Derrida's view: "The fundamental concepts that often permit us to isolate or to *pretend* to isolate the political . . . remain religious or in any case theologico-political. . . . The unprecedented forms

of today's wars of religion . . . constitute a response to everything that our idea of democracy, for example, with all its associated juridical, ethical and political concepts, including those of the sovereign state, of the citizen-subject, of public and private space, etc. still entails that is religious, inherited in truth from a determinate religious stratum." Derrida and Anidjar, *Acts of Religion*, 63–64.

12. Many scholars have elaborated on the prophetic tradition in radical American politics, including Robert H. Abzug, Robert N. Bellah, David L. Chappell, Robert H. Craig, Dan MacKanan, Greil Marcus, Charles Marsh, Doug Rossinow, George M. Shulman, Cornel West, and Gayraud S. Wilmore.

13. George M. Shulman, *American Prophecy: Race and Redemption in American Political Culture* (Minneapolis: University of Minnesota Press, 2008), 5.

14. For a survey of these topics, see Robert H. Abzug, *Cosmos Crumbling: American Reform and the Religious Imagination* (New York: Oxford University Press, 1994); Gastón Espinosa, Virgilio P. Elizondo, and Jesse Miranda, *Latino Religions and Civic Activism in the United States* (New York: Oxford University Press, 2005); Dan McKanan, *Prophetic Encounters: Religion and the American Radical Tradition* (Boston: Beacon Press, 2011); Greil Marcus, *The Shape of Things to Come: Prophecy of the American Voice* (New York: Farrar, Straus and Giroux, 2006); Cornel West and Christa Buschendorf, eds., *Black Prophetic Fire* (Boston: Beacon Press, 2014); and Gayraud S. Wilmore, *Black Religion and Black Radicalism: An Interpretation of the Religious History of African Americans* (Maryknoll, NY: Orbis Books, 1998).

15. According to historian Robert H. Abzug, antebellum reformers "did not abandon the realm of the sacred in championing 'social' causes. Rather, they made religious sense of society, economy, race, politics, gender, and physiology. . . . [T]hey made it their business to clarify the ways in which the most personal and the most cosmic issues interconnected" (*Cosmos Crumbling*, 4).

16. For more on the role of trauma in nineteenth-century American prophetic religious discourse, see Abzug, *Cosmos Crumbling*.

17. Martin Luther King, Jr., "Address at the Thirty-Sixth Annual Dinner of the War Resisters League," in *The Papers of Martin Luther King, Jr.: Threshold of a New Decade, January 1959–December 1960*, ed. Clayborne Carson, Ralph Luker, and Penny A. Russell (Berkeley: University of California Press, 1992), 124.

18. King's statement is currently on display in President Barack Obama's Oval Office, woven into a rug with other favorite quotes. Melissa Block, "Theodore Parker and the 'Moral Universe,'" *All Things Considered*, National Public Radio, September 2, 2010.

19. Theodore Parker, "Justice and the Conscience," in *Ten Sermons on Religion* (Boston: Crosby, Nichols, 1853), 84–85.

20. I am grateful to peace activist Frida Berrigan for describing her experience of holding space: "The prophetic part is the belief that there will be more of you in the future. I am guarding the space, and others will fill it. The timing, strategy, message, optics are up to someone else. But I am holding this space for a week, for a year, for a generation, for a lifetime. This space needs to be filled with this. I can do it and other people can't, so I stand here and hold this space." Personal communication, November 12, 2014. Berrigan's editorial column "Lit-

tle Insurrections" can be found at *Waging Nonviolence*, http://wagingnonvio lence.org/column/little-insurrections/ (accessed November 12, 2014).

21. For Cornel West's reading of this "sanitization" of King's legacy and his view of King as a prophetic witness, see West and Buschendorf, *Black Prophetic Fire*, 65–87.

22. Mierle Laderman Ukeles, "Touch Sanitation," in *Issue: Social Strategies by Women Artists, an Exhibition*, ed. Lucy Lippard (London: Institute of Contemporary Arts, 1980), n.p.

23. For more on this performance, see Maurice Berger, "The Critique of Pure Racism: An Interview with Adrian Piper," *Afterimage* 18, no. 3 (1990): 5–9.

24. Montano's work has been addressed in the important scholarship of Jennifer Fisher, Jennie Klein, Moira Roth, and Jenni Sorkin and has been shown in recent feminist art exhibitions, including *WACK! Art and the Feminist Revolution*, The Geffen Contemporary at the Museum of Contemporary Art [MOCA], 2007.

25. These publications include Jennifer Doyle, *Hold It against Me: Difficulty and Emotion in Contemporary Art* (Durham: Duke University Press, 2013); Dominic Johnson, ed., *Pleading in the Blood: The Art and Performances of Ron Athey* (London and Bristol: Live Art Development Agency and Intellect Ltd., 2013); Amelia Jones, "Holy Body: Erotic Ethics in Ron Athey and Juliana Snapper's 'Judas Cradle,'" *TDR/The Drama Review* 50, no. 1 (2006): 159–69; and Amelia Jones, "Performing the Wounded Body: Pain, Affect, and the Radical Relationality of Meaning," *Parallax* 15, no. 4 (2009): 45–67.

26. See, for example, Eleanor Heartney, *Postmodern Heretics: The Catholic Imagination in Contemporary Art* (New York: Midmarch Arts Press, 2004); Johnson, *Pleading in the Blood*; and Lewis MacAdams, *Blind Date* (Los Angeles: Am Here Books and Immediate Editions, 1981).

27. These include Talal Asad, *Formations of the Secular: Christianity, Islam, Modernity* (Stanford: Stanford University Press, 2003), 120–21; and Linda Frye Burnham, "'High Performance,' Performance Art, and Me," *TDR/The Drama Review* 30, no. 1 (Spring 1986): 39.

28. The formation of the journal *Material Religion* in 2005 and recent conferences, including Art + Religion (Concordia University, Montreal, 2010) and Why Have There Been No Great Modern Religious Artists? (Association of Scholars of Christianity in the History of Art, New York, 2011), suggest rising interest in these topics among art historians.

29. For histories of the secularization thesis, see José Casanova, *Public Religions in the Modern World* (Chicago: University of Chicago Press, 1994); and Mark C. Taylor, *After God* (Chicago: University of Chicago Press, 2009).

30. For critiques of these perspectives, see Jonathan Z. Smith, "Religion, Religions, Religious," in *Critical Terms for Religious Studies*, ed. Mark C. Taylor (Chicago: University of Chicago Press, 1998); and Ann Taves, *Fits, Trances, and Visions: Experiencing Religion and Explaining Experience from Wesley to James* (Princeton: Princeton University Press, 1999).

31. Consequently, modern art historians have studied artists' intellectual engagements with such spiritual philosophies as theosophy or anthroposophy; this intellectual approach to artists' religious investments is well explored in

Maurice Tuchman, ed. *The Spiritual in Art: Abstract Painting, 1890–1985* (New York: Abbeville Press, 1986).

32. Taylor has noted that the western Judeo-Christian tradition produced the notion of secularity itself (*After God*, xvi).

33. For an early example of this attitude, see Hume's discussion of "enthusiasticke" religious expression in David Hume, *The Natural History of Religion* (Stanford: Stanford University Press, 1957). President Barack Obama also expressed this view when he claimed that working-class voters "cling to guns or religion or [racism] . . . to explain their frustrations." Ed Pilkington, "Obama Angers Midwest Voters with Guns and Religion Remark," *The Guardian*, April 14, 2008).

34. Sigmund Freud, "The Future of an Illusion," in *The Freud Reader*, ed. Peter Gay (New York: Norton, 1989), 685–722; Karl Marx, "Contribution to the Critique of Hegel's Philosophy of Right: Introduction," in *The Marx-Engels Reader*, ed. Robert C. Tucker (New York: W. W. Norton, 1978), 54.

35. See, for example, Jane Blocker, *Seeing Witness: Visuality and the Ethics of Testimony* (Minneapolis: University of Minnesota Press, 2009), xxii.

36. David Morgan and James Elkins, eds., *Re-Enchantment* (New York: Routledge, 2009), 17. Amelia Jones, in her important theory of difference, *Seeing Differently*, observed, "[T]here were few art historians or art critics visible in the US or UK to address [the issue of religion and faith-based identifications] as it relates to contemporary art." Amelia Jones, *Seeing Differently: A History and Theory of Identification and the Visual Arts* (New York: Routledge, 2012), 149. In this way, her book noted but did not explore the role of religious difference in her visual theory.

37. Religious studies scholar Thomas A. Tweed has theorized religions as spatial practices and religious studies as a space for exploring movement and relation (Tweed, *Crossing and Dwelling*). Other approaches to lived religion include David D. Hall, ed., *Lived Religion in America: Toward a History of Practice* (Princeton: Princeton University Press, 1997); Thomas A. Tweed, *Our Lady of the Exile: Diasporic Religion at a Cuban Catholic Shrine in Miami* (New York: Oxford University Press, 1997); Robert A. Orsi, *The Madonna of 115th Street: Faith and Community in Italian Harlem, 1880–1950* (New Haven: Yale University Press, 1985); Robert A. Orsi, *Thank You, St. Jude: Women's Devotion to the Patron Saint of Hopeless Causes* (New Haven: Yale University Press, 1996); Stephen Prothero, *American Jesus: How the Son of God Became a National Icon* (New York: Farrar, Straus and Giroux, 2003); R. Marie Griffith, *Born Again Bodies: Flesh and Spirit in American Christianity* (Los Angeles: University of California Press, 2004); and R. Marie Griffith, *God's Daughters: Evangelical Women and the Power of Submission* (Berkeley: University of California Press, 1997). My methodological approach to religions reflects a Jamesian, pragmatic concern with subjective religious experience yet rejects both abstract ideas of "religion in general" as posited by phenomenologists of religion such as Mircea Eliade and the Weberian notion that scholars have access to these subjective states. See William James, *The Varieties of Religious Experience: A Study in Human Nature* (New York: Longmans Green, 1902); Mircea Eliade, *The Sacred and the Profane: The Nature of Religion*, trans. Willard R. Trask (San Diego: Harcourt Brace Jovanovich, 1959); and Max

Weber, *The Sociology of Religion*, trans. Ephraim Fischoff (Boston: Beacon Press, [1922] 1963).

38. In this way, *Long Suffering* contributes to dialogues about American art that limn issues of religion and/or trauma, including, for example, Debra Bricker Balken, *Dove/O'Keeffe: Circles of Influence* (Williamstown, MA: Sterling and Francine Clark Art Institute, 2009); Charles Colbert, *Haunted Visions: Spiritualism and American Art* (Philadelphia: University of Pennsylvania Press, 2011); and Gwendolyn DuBois Shaw, *Seeing the Unspeakable: The Art of Kara Walker* (Durham: Duke University Press, 2004).

39. For more on religious improvisation in the United States, see R. Laurence Moore, *Religious Outsiders and the Making of Americans* (New York: Oxford University Press, 1986); and Nathan O. Hatch, *The Democratization of American Christianity* (New Haven: Yale University Press, 1989). For the foundational analysis of denominational decline in midcentury America, see Robert Wuthnow, *The Restructuring of American Religion: Society and Faith since World War II* (Princeton: Princeton University Press, 1988), 71–99.

40. Kathy O'Dell, *Contract with the Skin: Masochism, Performance Art, and the 1970s* (Minneapolis: University of Minnesota Press, 1998).

41. Sigmund Freud, "Autobiographical Study," in *The Freud Reader*, ed. Peter Gay (New York: W. W. Norton, 1989), 21. In 1897 Freud abandoned the "seduction theory," his original understanding of hysteria as induced by adults' sexual assault of children, and later developed his theory of the oedipal complex. For a controversial reading of Freud's rejection of the seduction theory, see Jeffrey Moussaieff Masson, *The Assault on Truth: Freud's Suppression of the Seduction Theory* (New York: Farrar, Straus and Giroux, 1984).

42. Kristine Stiles has mobilized clinical psychology in her studies of performance art, as in her "Barbara Turner Smith's Haunting," in *The 21st Century Odyssey, Part II: The Performances of Barbara T. Smith*, ed. Rebecca McGrew and Jennie Klein (Claremont, CA: Pomona College Museum of Art, 2005). The theoretical frame of psychoanalysis may resonate with the personal experiences of particular artists, such as Jackson Pollock, who were directly influenced by psychoanalytic theory. In contrast, the artists in this book have been engaged with psychology and psychiatry. Montano, for example, sent her artwork to psychiatrist and anorexia nervosa specialist Hilde Bruch, Duncan participated in sensory deprivation experiments during the 1970s, and Athey has been involved with therapy and recovery communities since the 1980s.

43. Robert J. Lifton, "From Hiroshima to the Nazi Doctors: The Evolution of Psychoformative Approaches to Understanding Traumatic Stress Syndromes," in *International Handbook of Traumatic Stress Syndromes*, ed. John P. Wilson and Beverly Raphael (New York: Plenum, 1993), 12.

44. For an overview of traumatic memory research and debates, see James A. Chu, *Rebuilding Shattered Lives: Treating Complex PTSD and Dissociative Disorders*, 2nd ed. (New York: John Wiley & Sons, 2011), 78–106.

45. Nanette C. Auerhahn and Dori Laub, "Intergenerational Memory of the Holocaust," in *International Handbook of Multigenerational Legacies of Trauma*, ed. Yael Danieli (New York: Plenum Press, 1998), 23.

46. For important discussions of posttraumatic responses, see Chu, *Rebuild-*

ing Shattered Lives; Judith Lewis Herman, *Trauma and Recovery: The Aftermath of Violence from Domestic Abuse to Political Terror* (New York: Basic Books, 1992); and Bessel A. van der Kolk, ed., *Post-traumatic Stress Disorder: Psychological and Biological Sequelae* (Washington, DC: American Psychiatric Press, 1984).

47. For an early elaboration on this idea, see Kristine Stiles, "Shaved Heads and Marked Bodies: Representations from Cultures of Trauma," *Strategie II: Peuples Mediterraneens*, nos. 64–65 (July–December 1993): 95–117.

48. Kristine Stiles, "I/Eye/Oculus: Performance, Installation, Video," in *Themes in Contemporary Art*, ed. Gill Perry and Paul Woods (New Haven: Yale University Press, 2004), 186.

49. Stiles, "Performance," 90.

50. Ron Athey, interview with Karen Gonzalez Rice, August 15, 2007.

51. Ann Scott, "Trauma, Skin: Memory, Speech," in *Memory in Dispute*, ed. Valerie Sinason (London: Karnac Books, 1998), 43.

52. Van der Kolk, *Post-traumatic Stress Disorder*, 22.

53. Auerhahn and Laub, "Intergenerational Memory of the Holocaust," 22.

54. Martin Luther King, Jr., "Letter from a Birmingham City Jail," in *A Testament of Hope: The Essential Writings and Speeches of Martin Luther King, Jr.*, ed. James Melvin Washington (New York: HarperCollins, 1986), 295.

CHAPTER 2

1. Linda Montano, *Art in Everyday Life* (Los Angeles: Astro Artz, 1981), 25.

2. Ibid., 99.

3. Hilary Robinson, "God! I Love Time: An Interview with Linda Montano," *n.paradoxa* 5 (January 2000): 64. Montano here referred to the martyrdom of Saint Agatha.

4. Linda M. Montano, "Roman Catholic Performance Artist Manifesto: An Email Sent to Pope Benedict," *Linda Mary Montano* (blog), accessed January 2009, http://lindamarymontano.blogspot.com/2009/12/roman-catholic-performance-artist_08.html.

5. For an introduction to the extensive and varied scholarship on this topic, see Robert H. Craig, *Religion and Radical Politics: An Alternative Christian Tradition in the United States* (Philadelphia Temple University Press, 1992); Gastón Espinosa, Virgilio P. Elizondo, and Jesse Miranda, *Latino Religions and Civic Activism in the United States* (New York: Oxford University Press, 2005); Dan McKanan, *Prophetic Encounters: Religion and the American Radical Tradition* (Boston: Beacon Press, 2011); and Mel Piehl and Peter Maurin, *Breaking Bread: The Catholic Worker and the Origin of Catholic Radicalism in America* (Philadelphia Temple University Press, 1982).

6. For details of Day's activities, see Dan McKanan, *The Catholic Worker after Dorothy: Practicing the Works of Mercy in a New Generation* (Collegeville, MN: Liturgical Press, 2008); and Piehl and Maurin, *Breaking Bread*.

7. For descriptions of New Monasticism, see Piehl and Maurin, *Breaking Bread*; Jonathan Wilson-Hartgrove, *School(s) for Conversion: 12 Marks of a New Monasticism* (Eugene, OR: Cascade, 2005); and Jonathan Wilson-Hartgrove,

New Monasticism: What It Has to Say to Today's Church (Grand Rapids, MI: Brazos, 2008).

8. For more on American Catholicism and racial justice, see Amy L. Koehlinger, *The New Nuns: Racial Justice and Religious Reform in the 1960s* (Cambridge: Harvard University Press, 2007).

9. For the 1980s activism of the Plowshares Movement, see Sharon Erickson Nepstad, *Religion and War Resistance in the Plowshares Movement* (Cambridge: Cambridge University Press, 2008).

10. Montano and I have discussed our differing points of view on this term extensively in conversations that continue to the present.

11. For a brief discussion of Montano's concern with these subjects, see Kristine Stiles, "Performance Art and the Experiential Present: Irregular Ways of Being," in *The Third Mind: American Artists Contemplate Asia*, ed. Alexandra Munroe (New York: Guggenheim Museum, 2009), 337.

12. Montano regularly returned to the Zen Mountain Monastery to live part time or full time between 1984 and 1991.

13. Robinson, "God! I Love Time," 70.

14. Linda M. Montano and Jennie Klein, eds., *Letters from Linda M. Montano* (New York: Routledge, 2005), 60.

15. Eleanor Heartney's important study of Catholicism in contemporary art includes a brief examination of the Catholic nature of Montano's work. See her *Postmodern Heretics: The Catholic Imagination in Contemporary Art* (New York: Midmarch Arts Press, 2004), 54–57. Jennie Klein's compilation of Montano's writings, *Letters from Linda M. Montano*, has facilitated the study of Catholicism in Montano's work.

16. The authors of *Practicing Catholic* described Catholicism as "a religion whose core theology, individual believer's inner spiritual experiences, and a great variety of parochial and other social entities such as social, communal identities come alive preeminently though participation in and a sense of ownership of rite." Bruce T. Morrill, Joanna E. Ziegler, and Susan Rodgers, eds., *Practicing Catholic: Ritual, Body, and Contestation in Catholic Faith* (New York: Palgrave Macmillan, 2006), 3. I follow these authors, and other religious studies scholars, such as R. Marie Griffith, David Morgan, Robert Orsi, Stephen Prothero, and Thomas Tweed, in exploring lived religion.

17. Bonnie Marranca et al., "Art as Spiritual Practice," *PAJ: A Journal of Performance and Art* 24, no. 3 (September 2002): 27.

18. Montano and Klein, *Letters from Linda M. Montano*, 123. In addition to *Letters from Linda M. Montano*, this brief biographical sketch is drawn from Linda Montano, "Spirituality and Art," *Women Artists' News* 10, no. 3 (Spring 1985): 8; Lyn Blumenthal, "On Art and Artists: Linda Montano," *Profile* 4, no. 6 (December 1984): 2; Linda Montano, interview with Karen Gonzalez Rice, June 25–29, 2007; Linda Montano, "Linda Montano," *Bob's Art* (website), accessed June 2007, http://www.bobsart.org/montano/more/vita.html. My conversation with Montano took place at her home in Saugerties, New York, and at her studio, the Art/Life Institute, in Kingston, New York, where we worked to organize her personal archive. I recorded our discussions in extensive notes. In addition, Montano and I maintain an active correspondence through letters and e-mail.

19. Blumenthal, "On Art and Artists," 2.

20. Montano and Klein, *Letters from Linda M. Montano*, 18.

21. Ibid., 123. These words are excerpted from a lecture on endurance art; the artist's use of quotation marks highlighted the connection between her artistic and religious activities. There is a discrepancy of dates here: if Montano entered the convent in 1960, she would have been eighteen years of age, not twenty.

22. This population reached its peak in 1965; between 1950 and 1966, the number of women religious increased by 25 percent, from 147,000 to 181,421. Helen Rose Fuchs Ebaugh, *Women in the Vanishing Cloister: Organizational Decline in Catholic Religious Orders in the United States* (New Brunswick, NJ: Rutgers University Press, 1993), 1.

23. In 1950, 381 novices did not take their final vows; in 1965, the number was 1,562 (ibid., 50). Like other religious organizations in the United States, the American Catholic Church grew dramatically in the 1950s and early 1960s, only to decline quickly in the late 1960s and 1970s.

24. Patricia Curran, *Grace before Meals: Food Ritual and Body Discipline in Convent Culture* (Urbana: University of Illinois Press, 1989), 136.

25. Lora Ann Quinonez and Mary Daniel Turner, *The Transformation of American Catholic Sisters* (Philadelphia: Temple University Press, 1992), 3–4.

26. Montano, "Spirituality and Art," 8.

27. Barbara Hendricks, "The Legacy of Mary Josephine Rogers," *International Bulletin of Missionary Research* 21, no. 2 (1997): 77.

28. Ibid., 76.

29. Ibid.

30. Angelyn Dries, "American Catholic 'Woman's Work for Woman' in the Twentieth Century," in *Gospel Bearers, Gender Barriers: Missionary Women in the Twentieth Century*, ed. Dana L. Robert (Maryknoll, NY: Orbis Books, 2002), 140. Maryknoll nuns' participation in the direct apostolate took place due to the urging of Bishop Francis Ford in China's Kaying province. The nuns adopted common practices of lay evangelization in China at the time (139).

31. According to the Catholic Mission Association, Maryknoll supported 555 separate institutes in countries across Asia, Latin America, and Africa, while the organization with the second-most missionary sisters supported only 168 institutes (ibid., 130). Due to its flexible, embedded, intersubjective missionary practices already in place, the Maryknoll order was less troubled than others by Vatican II. Many present-day Maryknoll sisters embrace social and political activism; for example, they have been highly involved in Latin American civil society and social movements. See Bernice Kita, "Maryknoll Sisters in Latin America, 1943–1993," *Missiology* 26, no. 4 (October 1998): 419–30.

32. Some features of this distinction between religious and lay communities are suggested in Ebaugh, *Women in the Vanishing Cloister*, 89.

33. Ibid., 90.

34. Ibid., 24.

35. Montano, *Art in Everyday Life*, 7.

36. After leaving the convent, Montano attended the College of New Rochelle in New York, studied sculpture in Italy in 1965, and earned her MFA in sculpture from the University of Wisconsin–Madison in 1969.

37. Montano, *Art in Everyday Life,* 87.

38. Blumenthal, "On Art and Artists," 8.

39. For documentation and discussion of these and other artworks, see Tehching Hsieh and Adrian Heathfield, *Out of Now: The Lifeworks of Tehching Hsieh* (Cambridge: MIT Press, 2009).

40. Alex Grey and Allyson Grey, "Linda Montano and Tehching Hsieh's One Year Performance: Alex and Allyson Grey Ask Questions about the Year of the Rope," *High Performance* 7, no. 3 (1984): 25.

41. Max Weber, *The Protestant Ethic and the "Spirit" of Capitalism: and Other Writings* (New York: Penguin Classics, 2002), 109.

42. Robinson, "God! I Love Time," 67.

43. Maya Houng, email exchange with Karen Gonzalez Rice, July 10, 2009. Hsieh communicated with me through his assistant, Maya Houng.

44. Tehching Hsieh, *Tehching Hsieh: One Year Performance Art Documents 1978–1999,* DVD. New York, 2000; distributed by Tehching Hsieh.

45. Linda Montano, "Art/Life Counseling," *High Performance* 4, no. 2 (Summer 1981): 53.

46. Montano, *Art in Everyday Life,* 55. I am grateful to David Morgan for indicating that this attitude echoed the sacrilization of everyday life observed by nuns such as the nineteenth-century Carmelite Thérèse of Lisieux, who wrote that dialogue with Christ infused daily life with divine presence. See St. Thérèse of Lisieux, *Story of a Soul: The Autobiography of St. Thérèse of Lisieux, a New Translation from the Original Manuscripts,* trans. John Clarke (Washington, DC: ICS Publications, 1996).

47. Montano and Hsieh, "Statement," in Tehching Hsieh, *Tehching Hsieh: One Year Performance Art Documents 1978–1999,* DVD. New York, 2000; distributed by Tehching Hsieh.

48. Maya Houng, email exchange with Karen Gonzalez Rice, July 10, 2009.

49. Grey and Grey, "Linda Montano and Tehching Hsieh's One Year Performance," 27.

50. Ibid., 29.

51. Ibid., 26.

52. Jill Johnston, "Hardship Art," *Art in America* 72, no. 8 (September 1984): 179.

53. Blumenthal, "On Art and Artists," 30.

54. Johnston, "Hardship Art," 179.

55. Maya Houng, email exchange with Karen Gonzalez Rice, July 10, 2009. Photographic documentation is available in Hsieh and Heathfield, *Out of Now;* and Hsieh, *Tehching Hsieh.*

56. Grey and Grey, "Linda Montano and Tehching Hsieh's One Year Performance," 25.

57. Montano and Klein, *Letters from Linda M. Montano,* 245. Despite their equal conception of and participation in the work, Montano recently has referred to the piece as Hsieh's (58, 66, 164).

58. Ibid., 27.

59. Linda Montano, interview with Karen Gonzalez Rice, June 25–29, 2007.

60. Robinson, "God! I Love Time," 67.

61. Montano and Klein, *Letters from Linda M. Montano*, 9.

62. Ibid., xii.

63. Robinson, "God! I Love Time," 68.

64. See Linda Montano, Annie Sprinkle, and Veronica Vera, "Summer Saint Camp 1987: With Annie Sprinkle and Veronica Vera," *TDR/The Drama Review* 33, no. 1 (1989): 94–103.

65. Montano and Klein, *Letters from Linda M. Montano*, 26.

66. See St. Marguerite Marie Alacoque, *The Autobiography of St. Marguerite Marie Alacoque*, trans. Sisters of the Visitation (Rockford, IL: Tan Books and Publishers, 1986). Thanks to David Morgan for this reference.

67. Montano, *Art in Everyday Life*, 63.

68. Ibid. Montano placed the acupuncture needles in her lower abdomen.

69. Linda M. Montano, "Love Sex: The Ecstatic Writings of Linda M. Montano," (1995), n.p. Montano shared this unpublished manuscript with me during our interview in Saugerties, New York.

70. "1+1=1," *The Act* 1, no. 3 (Winter–Spring 1988–99): 44–48; Linda Montano, interview with Karen Gonzalez Rice, June 25–29, 2007.

71. Judith Lewis Herman, *Father-Daughter Incest* (Cambridge: Harvard University Press, 2000), 70; Anna C. Salter, *Transforming Trauma: A Guide to Understanding and Treating Adult Survivors of Child Sexual Abuse* (Thousand Oaks, CA: Sage Publications, 1995), 182.

72. Herman, *Father-Daughter Incest*, 33.

73. Montano, *Art in Everyday Life*, 63.

74. From an overview of the history of and current research on dissociation, see James A. Chu, *Rebuilding Shattered Lives: Treating Complex PTSD and Dissociative Disorders,* 2nd ed. (New York: John Wiley & Sons, 2011), 41–64.

75. Nanette C. Auerhahn and Dori Laub, "Intergenerational Memory of the Holocaust," in *International Handbook of Multigenerational Legacies of Trauma*, ed. Yael Danieli (New York: Plenum Press, 1998), 22.

76. Susan Roth and Leslie Lebowitz. "The Experience of Sexual Trauma," *Journal of Traumatic Stress* 1, no. 1 (1988): 97.

77. Ibid.

78. Ann Kearney-Cooke, "Group Treatment of Sexual Abuse among Women with Eating Disorders," *Women and Therapy* 7, no. 1 (1998): 11. The survivor who created this sculpture had been molested by a priest.

79. Blumenthal, "On Art and Artists," 3.

80. Linda Montano, interview with Karen Gonzalez Rice, June 25–29, 2007.

81. Montano has challenged Catholic resistance to female leadership, its enervating narratives of female participation, and its rejection of nonnormative sexualities. Her criticism of the policies of the Catholic Church has appeared in interviews, writings, and performances throughout her career. She anthologized her critique in Montano, "Roman Catholic Performance Artist Manifesto."

82. It is not uncommon for survivors of sexual trauma to initiate drastic changes in their life circumstances (moving, changing jobs, etc.) within a few years of the traumatic experience. Ann Wolbert Burgess and Lynda Lytle

Holmstrom, "Adaptive Strategies and Recovery from Rape," *American Journal of Psychiatry* 136, no. 10 (1979): 1280.

83. Montano, "Love Sex," n.p.

84. Ibid.

85. Sister Maria del Rey, *Bernie Becomes a Nun* (New York: Farrar, Straus & Cudahy, 1956), n.p.

86. Linda Montano, interview with Karen Gonzalez Rice, June 25–29, 2007.

87. Michael W. Wiederman, " Women, Sex, and Food: A Review of Research on Eating Disorders and Sexuality," *Journal of Sex Research* 33, no. 4 (1996): 306; Burgess and Holmstrom, "Adaptive Strategies and Recovery from Rape," 1282. See also John N. Briere and Diana M. Elliott, "Immediate and Long-Term Impacts of Child Sexual Abuse," *The Future of Children* 4, no. 2 (Summer–Autumn 1994): 54–69; and Susan Roth and Elana Newman, "The Process of Coping with Sexual Trauma," *Journal of Traumatic Stress* 4, no. 2 (1991): 279–97.

88. Montano and Klein, *Letters from Linda M. Montano*, 18.

89. Blumenthal, "On Art and Artists," 3.

90. Ibid.

91. Ibid.

92. Ibid.

93. Kearney-Cooke, "Group Treatment of Sexual Abuse," 7. For a reading of dissociation in the work of performance artist Lynn Hershman Leeson, see "1.1.78–2.2.78: Lynn Hershman's *Roberta Breitmore*," in Kristine Stiles, *Concerning Consequences: Studies in Art, Destruction, and Trauma* (Chicago: University of Chicago Press, 2016), 109–20.

94. Curran, *Grace before Meals*, 120.

95. Blumenthal, "On Art and Artists," 3.

96. Quoted by Montano in Marranca et al., "Art as Spiritual Practice," 25.

97. See Caroline Walker Bynum, *Holy Feast and Holy Fast: The Religious Significance of Food to Medieval Women* (Berkeley: University of California Press, 1987). Bynum has suggested that medieval notions of the embodied self have resurfaced in the contemporary era due to a condition of threat to the body. See her "Death and Resurrection in the Middle Ages: Some Modern Implications," *Proceedings of the American Philosophical Society* 142, no. 4 (1998): 595.

98. Marranca et al., "Art as Spiritual Practice," 72.

99. Curran, *Grace before Meals*, 141.

100. Ibid., 131.

101. Ibid.

102. Ibid., 120.

103. Linda Montano, *Anorexia Nervosa*, artist's film, 1981. Distributed by Video Data Bank, Chicago.

104. Linda Montano to Karen Gonzalez Rice, February 17, 2009 (Montano's emphasis).

105. Ibid.

106. Ibid. (Montano's quotations).

107. The full paragraph reads, "During the year you have seen Sister several times, and I think you know either from having seen her, or by letter, that Sister

has lost a great deal of weight. We have observed this with great concern, especially after learning that it was due to deliberate undereating. Since Sister was working out-of-doors for one period each day, which would normally help to create a hearty appetite, we have been waiting for this to happen and to see her regain the round cheeks that were hers last Fall. This has not happened. Yesterday Sister could not promise to eat normally, not because of physical reasons, but because she could not make up her mind to do it. It is difficult for me to write this to you, because I feel that it will be a disappointment to you, but it is the general consensus of opinion here that Sister Rose Augustine is out of place in religious life. Sister herself is among those who are of this opinion, and has never felt, even as a postulant 'this is it.' We also feel that this non-eating program is an expression of the resistance—even perhaps sub-conscious—'a square peg in a round hole.' At any rate she and we are aware that it could be unwise for her to continue any longer in the novitiate." Sister Paul Miriam to Henry and Mildred Montano, July 6, 1962.

108. Blumenthal, "On Art and Artists," 4.

109. Ibid., 2.

110. Montano, *Anorexia Nervosa*.

111. Linda Montano, interview with Karen Gonzalez Rice, June 25–29, 2007.

112. Roth and Lebowitz, "The Experience of Sexual Trauma," 100.

113. Kearney-Cooke, "Group Treatment of Sexual Abuse," 7. See also Joanne T. Everill and Glenn Waller, "Reported Sexual Abuse and Eating Psychopathology: A Review of the Evidence for a Causal Link," *International Journal of Eating Disorders* 18, no. 1 (1995): 1–11. Practitioners continue to debate the relationship between eating disorders and sexual trauma. Psychologists Rachel Calam and Peter Slade have noted the difficulty of identifying an incontrovertible link between sexual trauma and eating disorders because "eating difficulties and unwanted sexual experiences . . . both occur with such high rates in the female population as a whole and so there is a high probability that many women have experienced both." Rachel Calam and Peter Slade, "Eating Patterns and Unwanted Sexual Experiences," in *Why Women? Gender Issues and Eating Disorders*, ed. Bridget Dolan and Inez Gizinger (Atlantic Highlands, NJ: Athlone Press, 1994), 102. Current research suggests that, while not all anorexics have experienced sexual trauma, many sexually traumatized women are anorexic and that a history of sexual trauma is "likely to be relevant to the development and maintenance of an eating disorder." Everill and Waller, "Reported Sexual Abuse and Eating Psychopathology," 7.

114. Montano, *Anorexia Nervosa*.

115. See Hilde Bruch, *The Golden Cage: The Enigma of Anorexia Nervosa* (Cambridge: Harvard University Press, 1978); and Bruch, "Anorexia Nervosa: Therapy and Theory," *American Journal of Psychiatry* 139, no. 12 (December 1982): 1531–38.

116. R. A. Gordon, "Concepts of Eating Disorders: A Historical Reflection," in *Neurobiology in the Treatment of Eating Disorders*, ed. Hans Wijbrand Hoek, Janet L. Treasure, and Melanie A. Katzman (New York: John Wiley & Sons, 1998), 9.

117. Paula Saukko, *The Anorexic Self: A Personal, Political Analysis of a Diagnostic Discourse* (Albany: State University of New York Press, 2008), 39.

118. Drawing on Bruch's concern with identity, some scholars argue for the recognition of the role of religious self-understandings in the development and treatment of anorexia. See Caroline Giles Banks, "The Imaginative Use of Religious Symbols in Subjective Experiences of Anorexia Nervosa," *Psychoanalytic Review* 84, no. 2 (April 1997): 227–36; Caroline Giles Banks, "'There is No Fat in Heaven': Religious Asceticism and the Meaning of Anorexia Nervosa," *Ethos* 24, no. 1 (March 1996): 107–35; David Rampling, "Ascetic Ideals and Anorexia Nervosa," *Journal of Psychiatric Research* 19, nos. 2–3 (1985): 89–94; S. Huline-Dickens, "Anorexia Nervosa: Some Connections with the Religious Attitude," *British Journal of Medical Psychology* 73, no. 1 (March 2000): 67–76; P. Marsden, E. Karagianni, and J. F. Morgan, "Spirituality and Clinical Care in Eating Disorders: A Qualitative Study," *International Journal of Eating Disorders* 40, no. 1 (January 2007): 7–12; and J. F. Morgan, P. Marsden, and J. H. Lacey, "'Spiritual Starvation?': A Case Series Concerning Christianity and Eating Disorders," *International Journal of Eating Disorders* 28, no. 4 (December 2000): 476–80.

119. While Bruch did not respond to the artist, Montano's letter, video, and book have been archived in the University of Houston's collection of Bruch's papers. Papers of Hilde Bruch, Manuscript Collection no. 7, John P. McGovern Historical Collections and Research Center, University of Houston.

120. Bruch, "Anorexia Nervosa: Therapy and Theory," 1536–37.

121. Montano and Klein, *Letters from Linda M. Montano*, 18. The use of the third person was common among the anorexics studied by Bruch, who called this style of communicating a "confusion of pronouns." Bruch, *The Golden Cage*, 35.

122. Montano and Klein, *Letters from Linda M. Montano*, 123.

123. St. Augustine, *Concerning the City of God, against the Pagans* (New York: Penguin Putnam, 2003), 139. For more on Catholic notions of pain before the twentieth century, see Caroline Walker Bynum, *Fragmentation and Redemption: Essays on Gender and the Human Body in Medieval Religion* (New York: Zone Books, 1992); and Manuele Gragnolati, "From Decay to Splendor: Body and Pain in Bonvesin de la Riva's *Book of the Three Scriptures*," in *Last Things: Death and the Apocalypse in the Middle Ages*, ed. Caroline Walker Bynum (Philadelphia: University of Pennsylvania Press, 2000).

124. Robert A. Orsi, *Between Heaven and Earth: The Religious Worlds People Make and the Scholars Who Study Them* (Princeton: Princeton University Press, 2005), 21.

125. Ibid., 43.

126. Ibid., 23.

127. Ibid., 34.

128. Linda Montano, interview with Karen Gonzalez Rice, June 25–29, 2007.

129. Marranca et al., "Art as Spiritual Practice," 25.

130. Montano, *Art in Everyday Life*, 96.

131. Orsi, *Between Heaven and Earth*, 42.

132. Paula M. Kane, "'She Offered Herself Up': The Victim Soul and Victim Spirituality in Catholicism," *Church History* 71, no. 1 (2002): 118.

133. Ibid., 117.

134. A recording of Montano's 1977 broadcast for *Close Radio* can be found at the J. Paul Getty Museum http://www.getty.edu/art/exhibitions/evidence_movement/close_radio.html (accessed July 16, 2009).

135. Blumenthal, "On Art and Artists," 11.

136. John Duncan, discussed later in this book, was present at this performance; it moved him to tears. John Duncan, interview with Karen Gonzalez Rice, August 2–7, 2009.

137. Bynum, *Fragmentation and Redemption*, 181–238. These medieval women's visions often reveal a fluidity of gender mimicked in Montano's transgendered self-portrait as Christ.

138. Robinson, "God! I Love Time," 69.

139. Ibid., 64. Here Montano was referring to the martyr St. Agatha, who was tortured in this fashion.

140. Orsi, *Between Heaven and Earth*, 27.

141. Montano and Klein, *Letters from Linda M. Montano*, 124.

142. Robinson, "God! I Love Time," 67.

143. Robert J. Lifton, "From Hiroshima to the Nazi Doctors: The Evolution of Psychoformative Approaches to Understanding Traumatic Stress Syndromes," in *International Handbook of Traumatic Stress Syndromes*, ed. John P. Wilson and Beverly Raphael (New York: Plenum, 1993), 17.

144. Montano, "Spirituality and Art," 8. For a brief discussion of the traumatic implications of the gauze-wrapped body in performance art, see Kristine Stiles, *amaLIA perjovschi* (Bucharest: Soros Center of Contemporary Art, 1996), 49, 56; and "Notes on Rudolf Schwartzkogler's Images of Healing," *Whitewalls* 25 (Spring 1990): 10–26. For more on the white nun's habit, see Elizabeth Kuhns, *The Habit: A History of the Clothing of Catholic Nuns* (New York: Doubleday, 2003).

145. Montano and Klein, *Letters from Linda M. Montano*, 59.

146. Montano, *Art in Everyday Life*, 102. This language recalls her description of *Erasing the Past.*

147. Similar to Montano's chicken woman performances, Barbara T. Smith, in *Piercing the Corporate Veil* (1980), lay in a coffin for twenty hours wearing a pink dress. Kristine Stiles analyzed Smith's piece in terms of traumatic dissociation in "Barbara Turner Smith's Haunting," in *The 21st Century Odyssey, Part II: The Performances of Barbara T. Smith*, ed. Rebecca McGrew and Jennie Klein (Claremont, CA: Pomona College Museum of Art, 2005), 437–40.

148. Moira Roth, "Matters of Life and Death: Linda Montano Interviewed by Moira Roth," *High Performance* 1, no. 4 (1978): 7; Montano and Klein, *Letters from Linda M. Montano*, 238.

149. Suzanne Foley, *Space/Time/Sound-1970s: A Decade in the Bay Area* (Seattle: University of Seattle Press, 1979), 87.

150. Montano and Klein, *Letters from Linda M. Montano*, 124.

151. Dori Laub, "An Event without a Witness: Truth, Testimony, and Sur-

vival," in *Testimony: Crises of Witnessing in Literature, Psychoanalysis, and History*, ed. Shoshana Felman and Dori Laub (New York: Routledge, 1992), 78 (Laub's emphasis).

152. Ibid. (Laub's emphasis).

153. Ibid., 70.

154. Montano, *Art in Everyday Life*, 41.

155. Ibid.

156. "Mission Woods Death Becomes Murder Case," *Kansas City Star*, September 20, 1977, 1.

157. Montano and Klein, *Letters from Linda M. Montano*, 6.

158. Marranca et al., "Art as Spiritual Practice," 25.

159. Robinson, "God! I Love Time," 68.

160. Montano and Klein, *Letters from Linda M. Montano*, 166.

161. Montano, "Spirituality and Art," 8. Montano's phrasing echoes the Sermon on the Mount: "Blessed are the pure in heart, for they shall see God" (Matt. 5:8).

162. Linda Montano, "Letter Number One," in *Franko B: Blinded by Love*, ed. Dominic Johnson (Bologna: Damiani, 2006), 177 (Montano's emphasis).

163. Linda Montano, "Letter Number Two," in *Franko B: Blinded by Love*, ed. Dominic Johnson (Bologna: Damiani, 2006), 177.

164. Blumenthal, "On Art and Artists," 30.

165. Montano and Klein, *Letters from Linda M. Montano*, 25.

166. Ibid., 97, 104.

167. Linda Montano, interview with Karen Gonzalez Rice, June 25–29, 2007.

168. Montano's description of this event can be found at *Linda Mary Montano* (blog), http://lindamarymontano.blogspot.com/2013/01/linda-mary-montano-as-mother-teresa-of.html. See also Karen Gonzalez Rice, "Linda Montano, Student of Real Presence," *In Media Res: A Media Commons Project* (April 10, 2010), http://mediacommons.futureofthebook.org/imr/2010/04/15/linda-montano-student-real-presence.

169. Although her art/life observance of Catholic ritual is strict, Montano's actions have retained the marks of her encounters with other religious traditions. At a public reading of "Roman Catholic Performance Artist Manifesto: An Email Sent to Pope Benedict" (2008), Montano appeared with her head wrapped in an orange scarf. This abstracted habit recalled both her convent experience and her spiritual travels in India, where her guru advised her to wear orange as a mark of her spiritual achievement. Linda Montano, interview with Karen Gonzalez Rice, June 25–29, 2007.

CHAPTER 3

1. See, for example, Richard A. Kaye, "Losing His Religion: Saint Sebastian as Contemporary Gay Martyr," in *Outlooks: Lesbian and Gay Sexualities and Visual Cultures*, ed. Peter Horne and Reina Lewis (New York: Routledge, 1996), 86–105; Talal Asad, *Formations of the Secular: Christianity, Islam, Modernity* (Stan-

ford: Stanford University Press, 2003), 119–21; and Fintan Walsh, *Male Trouble: Masculinity and the Performance of Crisis* (Basingstoke: Palgrave Macmillan, 2010), 109–30.

2. Ron Athey, "Deliverance: Introduction, Foreword, Description, and Selected Text," in *Acting on AIDS: Sex, Drugs, and Politics,* ed. Joshua Oppenheimer and Helena Reckitt (London: Serpent's Tail, 1997), 434.

3. Billy Graham, "We Need Revival," in *Encyclopedia of Religious Revival in America,* ed. Michael McClymond (Westport, CT: Greenwood Press, 2007), 290. Graham's articulation of these political ends was unusual among Christian evangelists generally and within his own Southern Baptist tradition specifically.

4. For Pentecostal evangelist A. A. Allen's integration policies, see Don Stewart, *Only Believe: An Eyewitness Account of the Great Healing Revivals of the 20th Century* (Shippensburg, PA: Revival Press, 1999), 89–91.

5. This account of Athey's autobiography draws on the following interviews and written texts: Ron Athey, "Gifts of the Spirit," in *Unnatural Disasters: Recent Writings from the Golden State,* ed. Nicole Panter (San Diego: Incommunicado Press, 1996), 70–80; Ron Athey, "Raised in the Lord: Revelations at the Knee of Miss Velma," *L.A. Weekly,* June 30–July 6, 1995, 20–25; Ron Athey, "Artist's Notes," in *Out of Character: Rants, Raves, and Monologues from Today's Top Performance Artists,* ed. Mark Russell (New York: Bantam Books, 1997), 32–37; Athey, "Deliverance: Introduction"; "Ron Athey Biography," www.ronathey. com (accessed October 15, 2004); *Hallelujah! Ron Athey: A Story of Deliverance,* directed by Catherine Gund (New York: Aubin Pictures, 1999, videocassette); and Ron Athey, interview with Karen Gonzalez Rice, August 15, 2007. My discussion with Athey took place in the artist's Los Angeles home and was audiorecorded. Further conversation continued via e-mail. Significantly revised versions of Athey's early texts can be found in Dominic Johnson, ed., *Pleading in the Blood: The Art and Performances of Ron Athey* (London and Bristol: Live Art Development Agency and Intellect Ltd., 2013).

6. Athey, "Raised in the Lord," *L.A. Weekly,* 25.

7. My analysis of the *Torture Trilogy* draws on video documentation of the following performances: *Martyrs and Saints* at Los Angeles Contemporary Exhibitions (Los Angeles 1992); *4 Scenes* at the Los Angeles Theater Center (Los Angeles, 1993), the Walker Arts Center (Minneapolis, 1994), and Ex-Teresa (Mexico City, 1995); and *Deliverance* at the Institute of Contemporary Art (London, 1995) and Cankarjev Dom (Zagreb, Slovenia, 1997). Athey performed and reperformed the *Torture Trilogy* throughout the 1990s.

8. Ron Athey, interview with Karen Gonzalez Rice, August 15, 2007. In the 1990s, Athey deliberately crafted this autobiographical approach despite his awareness of critical resistance to autobiography in performance. He observed, "I saw people stopping their story, stopping their own interpretation of how their work should be seen, and I rebelled. I decided [to] sincerely tell . . . my biography to make sense of why I was making the work. I decided to continue doing that even though I saw people not wanting to be known as an HIV-positive artist, not wanting to be known as an 'I'm telling my story' artist, which in that period was being rejected" (ibid).

9. In the early twentieth century, this kind of baptism in the spirit experience was almost exclusively associated with Pentecostalism. However, in the Charismatic Revival of the 1960s–80s, mainline faiths, including Catholicism and diverse Protestant denominations, began to incorporate Pentecostal practices. Derived from the Pentecostal baptism in the spirit, these activities have disseminated Pentecostal actions broadly across diverse religious populations. For more, see Stanley M. Burgess, "Charismatic Revival and Renewal," in *Encyclopedia of Religious Revivals in America*, ed. Michael McClymond (Westport, CT: Greenwood Press, 2007); and P. D. Hocken, "Charismatic Movement," in *The New International Dictionary of Pentecostal and Charismatic Movements*, ed. Stanley M. Burgess and Eduard M. van der Maas (Grand Rapids, MI: Zondervan, 2003).

10. Margaret M. Poloma, *Main Street Mystics: The Toronto Blessing and Reviving Pentecostalism* (New York: Altamira Press, 2003), 26 (Poloma's emphasis). Following Poloma, religious studies scholars, medievalists, and Renaissance art historians, I do not take a stand on theological questions of the natural or supernatural origins of believers' experiences, which lie outside the scope of this project. Instead, this chapter is concerned with lived religion, in particular how these self-reported beliefs and practices, situated in their specific historical contexts, have shaped Athey's performance art.

11. Harvey Cox, *Fire from Heaven: The Rise of Pentecostal Spirituality and the Reshaping of Religion in the Twenty-First Century* (New York: Addison-Wesley, 1995), 95.

12. C. M. Robeck Jr., "Prophecy, Gift Of," in *The New International Dictionary of Pentecostal and Charismatic Movements*, ed. Stanley M. Burgess and Eduard M. van der Maas (Grand Rapids, MI: Zondervan, 2003), 1002.

13. Laying on of hands facilitates this connection, but believers may also connect with a point of contact in the form of an object, for example, by holding an anointed handkerchief or touching a radio or television. See J. R. Williams, "Laying on of Hands," in *The New International Dictionary of Pentecostal and Charismatic Movements*, ed. Stanley M. Burgess and Eduard M. van der Maas (Grand Rapids, MI: Zondervan, 2003), 834; and David Edwin Harrell, Jr., *All Things Are Possible: The Healing and Charismatic Revivals in Modern America* (Bloomington: Indiana University Press, 1975), 92. Harrell's text contains the most comprehensive scholarly treatment of the healing revival and its aftermath to date.

14. Oral Roberts, "Oral Roberts's Life Story," in *Encyclopedia of Religious Revival in America*, ed. Michael McClymond (Westport, CT: Greenwood Press, 2007), 300.

15. Bodily manifestations of the baptism in the spirit vary with historical circumstances and geography. Being slain in the spirit, for example, was a frequent experience in Southern California in the mid-twentieth century, but is much less common in the twenty-first. The Toronto Blessing revival in 1994 introduced many new gifts of the spirit, including animal sounds and being drunk in the spirit. See Benjamin Wagner, "Bodily Manifestations in Revivals," in *Encyclopedia of Religious Revivals in America*, ed. Michael McClymond (Westport, CT: Greenwood Press, 2007), 57; Ruth Burgess, "Enculturation," in *Ency-*

clopedia of Pentecostal and Charismatic Christianity, ed. Stanley M. Burgess (New York: Routledge, 2006), 163–64; and Poloma, *Main Street Mystics*, 70–74.

16. Athey, "Gifts of the Spirit," in *Unnatural Disasters*, 70.

17. Daniel E. Albrecht, "Worshiping and the Spirit: Transmuting Liturgy Pentecostally," in *The Spirit in Worship, Worship in the Spirit*, ed. Teresa Berger and Bryan D. Spinks (Collegeville, MN: Liturgical Press, 2009), 239.

18. Cox, *Fire from Heaven*, 100.

19. Ibid., 17.

20. J. R. Williams, "Baptism in the Holy Spirit," in *The New International Dictionary of Pentecostal and Charismatic Movements*, ed. Stanley M. Burgess and Eduard M. van der Maas (Grand Rapids, MI: Zondervan, 2003), 356.

21. Ibid. Wacker noted that electricity and fire are also common metaphors. See Grant A. Wacker, *Heaven Below: Early Pentecostals and American Culture* (Cambridge: Harvard University Press, 2001), 39.

22. Jenny Moore in *Apostolic Faith* (May 1907), quoted in Wacker, *Heaven Below*, 38.

23. Roberts, "Oral Roberts's Life Story," 299. Roberts began his career as a Pentecostal minister but later joined the United Methodist Church.

24. Georges Bataille, *Visions of Excess: Selected Writings, 1927–1939*, trans. Allan Stoekl (Minneapolis: University of Minnesota Press, 1993), 31. Athey's solo performance *Solar Anus* (1998) visualized Bataille's text "L'anus solaire" (1931). See Dominic Johnson, "Ron Athey's Visions of Excess: Performance after Georges Bataille," *Papers of Surrealism*, no. 8 (Spring 2010): 1–12, http://www.surrealismcentre.ac.uk/papersofsurrealism/journal8/index.htm (accessed August 13, 2014).

25. Aimee Semple McPherson, "This Is That," in *Encyclopedia of Religious Revival in America*, ed. Michael McClymond (Westport, CT: Greenwood Press, 2007), 268.

26. Athey, "Deliverance: Introduction," 437.

27. Amelia Jones, "Holy Body: Erotic Ethics in Ron Athey and Juliana Snapper's Judas Cradle," *TDR/The Drama Review* 50, no. 1 (Spring 2006): 163.

28. Albrecht, "Worshiping and the Spirit," 239.

29. These layered associations of the baptism in the spirit with self-injury, drugs, and sex radically extend the physicality of the Pentecostal gifts of the spirit. However, the baptism in the spirit has been linked with self-injury, drugs, and sex since the beginnings of Pentecostalism in 1906, when disagreements about the propriety of the gifts of the spirit precipitated Pentecostals' split from their parent organization, the Holiness Wesleyans. As radical evangelicals, Holiness Wesleyans, like the incipient Pentecostals in their midst, emphasized individual religious experience. However, they were dismayed when some believers began to manifest extremely physical experiences of the Holy Spirit such as speaking in tongues and being slain in the spirit. See Grant A. Wacker, "Travail of a Broken Family: Radical Evangelical Responses to the Emergence of Pentecostalism in America, 1906–16," in *Pentecostal Currents in American Protestantism*, ed. Edith L. Blumhofer, Russell P. Spittler, and Grant A. Wacker (Chicago: University of Illinois Press, 1999), 25–26. Suspicious of these embodied practices, Holiness Wesleyans claimed that these new forms of the

baptism in the spirit led to "shocking impropriety," including the mixing of classes, races, and genders; sexual promiscuity (specifically homosexuality); and physical harm: "[R]adical evangelicals charged . . . [that] Pentecostal religion endangered one's physical body" (ibid., 31–33). In the midst of the Toronto Blessing revival in the 1990s, believers were moved to make animal noises during the baptism in the spirit, causing consternation among many Pentecostals, who expressed the fear that this new manifestation was the result of demonic possession (Poloma, *Main Street Mystics*, 70). Like incipient Pentecostals and these more recent revivalists, Athey took embodiment beyond the boundaries of social normativity. At the same time, his actions took seriously the central Pentecostal belief in the embodiment of religious experience: all aspects of the body, from despised effluvia and marginalized behaviors to demonized urges, might become vehicles of the Holy Spirit.

30. Athey, "Raised in the Lord," *L.A. Weekly*, 21.

31. For more on fasting in the context of Pentecostal healing, see Benjamin Wagner, "Fasting and Revivals," in *Encyclopedia of Religious Revivals in America*, ed. Michael McClymond (Westport, CT: Greenwood Press, 2007), 167; and Harrell, *All Things Are Possible*, 81. For an account of Pentecostal women's narratives of suffering, see R. Marie Griffith, "Female Suffering and Religious Devotion in American Pentecostalism," in *Women and Twentieth-Century Protestantism*, ed. Margaret Lamberts Bendroth and Virginia Lieson Brereton (Chicago: University of Illinois Press, 2002).

32. Ron Athey, interview with Karen Gonzalez Rice, August 15, 2007. Similarly, Athey has written, "To me, her tongues were indistinguishable from her epileptic mumblings" ("Gifts of the Spirit," in *Unnatural Disasters*, 73).

33. Athey "Gifts of the Spirit," in *Unnatural Disasters*, 70.

34. Ibid., 78.

35. Ibid., 79.

36. Ibid., 78–79.

37. Athey, "Deliverance: Introduction," 434.

38. The presence of medical instruments, rubber gloves, and sterilization equipment in these actions underscored the medicalized narrative surrounding abuse in Athey's home. This visualization of cleanliness and medical order also reflected late-twentieth-century legal and public-health issues in the context of AIDS, and it echoed the visual language of medical fetish subcultures. See John Edward McGrath, "Trusting in Rubber: Performing Boundaries during the AIDS epidemic," *TDR/The Drama Review* 39, no. 2 (1995): 21–39.

39. Ron Athey, "Wounded: The Transformation of Franko B," in *Franko B: Blinded by Love*, ed. Dominic Johnson (Bologna: Damiani, 2006), 28.

40. From an early draft of the introduction to Kristine Stiles, *Concerning Consequences: Studies in Art, Destruction, and Trauma* (Chicago: University of Chicago Press, 2016), 2.

41. Athey, "Gifts of the Spirit," in *Unnatural Disasters*, 72.

42. Athey, "Artist's Notes," 37.

43. Ibid., 35.

44. Colleen M. Lang and Komal Sharma-Patel, "The Relation between Childhood Maltreatment and Self-Injury: A Review of the Literature on Conceptual-

ization and Intervention," *Trauma Violence Abuse* 12, no. 1 (2011): 28; E. David Klonsky et al., *Nonsuicidal Self-Injury* (Cambridge, MA: Hogrefe Publishing, 2011), 33; Armando Favazza, *Bodies under Siege: Self-Mutilation, Nonsuicidal Self-Injury, and Body Modification in Culture and Psychiatry*, 3rd ed. (Baltimore: Johns Hopkins University Press, 2011), 197.

45. James A. Chu, *Rebuilding Shattered Lives: Treating Complex PTSD and Dissociative Disorders* 2nd ed. (New York: John Wiley & Sons, 2011), 132.

46. Ron Athey, "Ron Athey Biography," www.ronathey.com (accessed October 15, 2004).

47. E. David Klonsky, "The Functions of Deliberate Self-Injury: A Review of the Evidence," *Clinical Psychology Review* 27 (2007): 227; Rebecca C. Groshwitz, "The Neurobiology of Non-suicidal Self-Injury (NSSI): A Review," *Suicidology Online* 3 (2012): 28, http://www.suicidology-online.com/pdf/SOL-2012-3-24-32. pdf (accessed April 24, 2012); Armando Favazza, "A Cultural Understanding of Nonsuicidal Self-Injury," in *Understanding Nonsuicidal Self-Injury*, ed. Matthew K. Nock (Washington, DC: American Psychological Association, 2009), 27.

48. Lang and Sharma-Patel, "Relation between Childhood Maltreatment and Self-Injury," 27; Klonsky, "Functions of Deliberate Self-Injury," 229; Klonsky et al., *Nonsuicidal Self-Injury*, 29; Chu, *Rebuilding Shattered Lives*, 132.

49. The particular nature of the relationship between maltreatment and NSSI has been theorized but is not well understood. See Lang and Sharma-Patel, "Relation between Childhood Maltreatment and Self-Injury."

50. Ibid., 29; Chu, *Rebuilding Shattered Lives*, 134.

51. Favazza, "A Cultural Understanding of Nonsuicidal Self-Injury," 108; Lang and Sharma-Patel, "Relation between Childhood Maltreatment and Self-Injury," 26; Chu, *Rebuilding Shattered Lives*, 132.

52. Favazza has observed that "self-injury is a morbid form of self-help" (*Bodies under Siege*, xv).

53. Klonsky, "Functions of Deliberate Self-Injury," 236. See also Chu, *Rebuilding Shattered Lives*, 113, 34; Judith Lewis Herman, *Trauma and Recovery: The Aftermath of Violence from Domestic Abuse to Political Terror* (New York: Basic Books, 1992), 109; and Bessel A. van der Kolk, ed., *Post-traumatic Stress Disorder: Psychological and Biological Sequelae* (Washington, DC: American Psychiatric Press, 1984), 20.

54. Ron Athey, interview with Karen Gonzalez Rice, August 15, 2007.

55. Performance studies scholar Jennifer Doyle, who served as Athey's attendant during *Incorruptible Flesh (Dissociative Sparkle)* (2006), has reflected extensively on the dynamics of care in Athey's work. See her *Hold It Against Me: Difficulty and Emotion in Contemporary Art* (Durham: Duke University Press, 2013), 49–68.

56. Tom Liesegang, "Perforating Saint: Interview with Ron Athey," *FAD* 30 (1993): 48–49.

57. Ron Athey, interview with Karen Gonzalez Rice, August 15, 2007.

58. Ibid.

59. Ibid. For more on Athey and sadomasochistic sexuality, see Lynda Hart, "Blood, Piss, and Tears: The Queer Real," *Textual Practice* 9, no. 1 (1995): 56–59.

Athey continued, "I think some people don't understand that I have boundaries. I think you get in this contest to outdo yourself every time. People will never stop wincing and projecting the pain on themselves, but likewise there is a pathology in it. It's tricky to explain. You're somehow looking for it to be a sickness and self-destruction." Ron Athey, interview with Karen Gonzalez Rice, August 15, 2007.

60. Favazza, "A Cultural Understanding of Nonsuicidal Self-Injury," 22.

61. Caroline Kettlewell, *Skin Game* (1999), quoted in Favazza, *Bodies under Siege*, 278.

62. Favazza, "A Cultural Understanding of Nonsuicidal Self-Injury," 28.

63. Favazza, *Bodies under Siege*, 272.

64. The figure of the Holy Woman reflected characteristics of several female deliverance ministers, including Kathryn Kuhlman, Velma Jaggers, and Aimee Semple McPherson.

65. Athey, "Raised in the Lord," *L.A. Weekly*, 22.

66. The Pentecostal healing revival set the groundwork for the Charismatic Revival of the 1960s–80s, when Catholics and mainstream Protestants began to incorporate the embodied, affective elements of Pentecostal worship into their liturgies. See Burgess, "Charismatic Revival and Renewal"; and Hocken, "Charismatic Movement." Outside these institutional relations, the Athey family's improvisational practice of Pentecostalism posited a connection to Catholicism later visualized in Athey's work. Throughout his childhood, Athey observed his Aunt Vena incorporating Catholic worship practices such as the veneration of saints, the Stations of the Cross, and especially the late medieval *imitatio Christi*, or "imitation of Christ," into her daily worship. These deeply personal, reflective exercises encouraged believers to actually relive the suffering of Christ and the saints by various physical, mental, or emotional means. For more on these practices, see Carolyn Walker Bynum, *Fragmentation and Redemption: Essays on Gender and the Human Body in Medieval Religion* (New York: Zone Books, 1992), 181–238; Peter Brown, *The Cult of the Saints: Its Rise and Function in Latin Christianity* (Chicago: University of Chicago Press, 1981); and Caroline Walker Bynum, *Holy Feast and Holy Fast: The Religious Significance of Food to Medieval Women* (Berkeley: University of California Press, 1987), 255–59. Although Vena considered herself a strict Pentecostal, she embraced the Catholic icons that were readily available in the Latino stores in her neighborhood. Athey observed, "She stood by the conviction that she could have the fire of the Holy Spirit . . . and the bloody martyr saints" (Athey, "Gifts of the Spirit," in *Unnatural Disasters*, 75). In the *Torture Trilogy*, Athey deployed NSSI in the performance of *imitatio Christi*, bringing to life the gruesome actions of Christian martyrs. St. Sebastian's traditional Catholic iconography—a nude figure tied to a tree or column and shot full of arrows—appeared in both *Martyrs and Saints* and *4 Scenes*. Elements of the Passion propelled the narrative action in *Martyrs and Saints*; flogged, mocked, crowned with thorns, and pierced in the side, Athey overtly performed Christ's sufferings. By enduring the torments of these martyrs—figures acknowledged in western culture to embody ultimate suffering—Athey invested these already highly physical, bloody, and emotionally charged biblical narratives with renewed violence.

67. Reflecting on Los Angeles history, Lou Engle, minister of the Harvest Rock Church in Pasadena, preached in 1998, "This city has been the cradle of revivals" (quoted in Poloma, *Main Street Mystics*, 173).

68. A. A. Allen and others commonly used the phrase "old-time revival service" to describe this kind of healing revival meeting (Harrell, *All Things Are Possible*, 114).

69. Athey, "Artist's Notes," 37.

70. Liesegang, "Perforating Saint," 48.

71. Athey, "Raised in the Lord," *L.A. Weekly*, 21.

72. Ibid., 22.

73. Athey, "Gifts of the Spirit," in *Unnatural Disasters*, 75.

74. A. A. Allen, *Prisons with Stained Glass Windows* (1963), quoted in Harrell, *All Things Are Possible*, 114.

75. Ron Athey, interview with Karen Gonzalez Rice, August 15, 2007.

76. For more on Kathryn Kuhlman, see Dan L. Thrapp, "Miss Kuhlman: Preacher Sways Throngs with Healing Service," *Los Angeles Times*, February 16, 1970, A1; Roberta Osteroff, "The Old Evangelism: Hard-Sell Salvation," *Los Angeles Times*, September 19, 1971, A9; and Wayne E. Warner, *Kathryn Kuhlman: The Woman behind the Miracles* (Ann Arbor, MI: Servant Publications, 1993).

77. Osteroff, "Old Evangelism," A9. Athey described the family's regular trips to the Universal World Church: "We would go see the girl with white hair and ballroom gowns, and spinning, gold-crowned angels. It was like a literal interpretation of the psychedelic numerology of the book of Revelations, done in 3D in an airplane hanger. It was like being raised on Salvador Dalí, with all rhinestones" (Ron Athey, interview with Karen Gonzalez Rice, August 15, 2007). Athey also discussed his experiences at the Universal World Church in Ron Athey, "Raised in the Lord: Revelations at the Knee of Miss Velma," in *Pleading in the Blood: The Art and Performances of Ron Athey*, ed. Dominic Johnson (London, Bristol: Live Art Development Agency, Intellect Ltd., 2013). He explored other female Pentecostal evangelists in Athey, "Artist's Notes"; and Ron Athey, "Reading Sister Aimee," in *Live Art and Performance*, ed. Adrian Heathfield (New York: Routledge, 2004).

78. Images of Kathryn Kuhlman can be found at www.kathrynkuhlman.com.

79. Albrecht, "Worshiping and the Spirit," 236.

80. Harrell, *All Things Are Possible*, 92–93.

81. Ibid., 6.

82. Ibid., 92.

83. William Hedgepeth, "Brother A. A. Allen on the Gospel Trail: He Feels, He Heals, and He Turns You on with God," *Look*, October 7, 1969, 27.

84. Gund, *Hallelujah!*

85. Harrell, *All Things Are Possible*, 69.

86. Ibid. For more on the controversies surrounding evangelists and the public sphere, see Susan Friend Harding, *The Book of Jerry Falwell: Fundamentalist Language and Politics* (Princeton: Princeton University Press, 2001).

87. Charles T. Powers, "Rev. A. A. Allen: He Shakes, Sways Hallelujah Trail," *Los Angeles Times*, March 8, 1970, A1.

88. Don Stewart, Allen's successor, discussed this problem in his *Only Be-*

lieve: An Eyewitness Account of the Great Healing Revivals of the 20th Century (Shippensburg, PA: Revival Press, 1999), 117.

89. Athey, "Artist's Notes," 35.

90. "Deliverance: Introduction," 434.

91. Ron Athey, interview with Karen Gonzalez Rice, August 15, 2007.

92. Ibid. Athey made this comment during a discussion of the *Torture Trilogy*'s aesthetics.

93. Stewart, *Only Believe*, 129.

94. Powers, "Rev. A. A. Allen," A2.

95. "Faith Healers: Getting Back Double from God," *Time*, March 7 1969, 64.

96. Ron Athey, interview with Karen Gonzalez Rice, August 15, 2007.

97. Ibid.

98. Harrell, *All Things Are Possible*, 69.

99. Ibid., 200.

100. Ibid., 69; Warner, *Kathryn Kuhlman*, 139. In the documentary *Marjoe* (1972), evangelist Marjoe Gortner described how he used an ointment to create this effect during his sermons. *Marjoe*, directed by Sarah Kernochan and Howard Smith (1972; New York: Docurama, 2006), DVD.

101. LeRoy Jenkins, quoted in Harrell, *All Things Are Possible*, 87. Athey recounted a similar memory: "The first woman in line stepped forward to the minister; she was turned around and announced to the congregation: 'I have stomach cancer.' After the laying on of oil-drenched hands by the minister . . . the sister vomited onto the carpet. The minister announced that she had thrown up the evil cancer, roots and all, and was healed. The minister's wife flung a square of shiny light green fabric over the mess" (Athey, "Gifts of the Spirit," in *Pleading in the Blood*, 45).

102. Stewart, *Only Believe*, 83.

103. Athey, "Raised in the Lord," *L.A. Weekly*, 22.

104. Ron Athey, "Deliverance: The 'Torture Trilogy' in Retrospect," in *Pleading in the Blood: The Art and Performances of Ron Athey*, ed. Dominic Johnson (London, Bristol: Live Art Development Agency, Intellect Ltd., 2013), 109.

105. Athey, "Artist's Notes," 36.

106. Stewart, *Only Believe*, 75.

107. The image can be found in Harrell, *All Things Are Possible*, 121.

108. Stewart, *Only Believe*, 130.

109. Ibid., 74, 146.

110. Warner, *Kathryn Kuhlman*, 211. Don Stewart noted, "Toward the end of her ministry, auditoriums were packed with the terminally ill" (Stewart, *Only Believe*, 165).

111. For more on the central role of AIDS in Athey's work, see Johnson, *Pleading in the Blood*; David Harradine, "Abject Identities and Fluid Performances: Theorizing the Leaking Body," *Contemporary Theatre Review* 10, no. 3 (2000): 69–85; David Román, "Solo Performance and the Body on Stage," in *Acts of Intervention: Performance, Gay Culture, and AIDS* (Bloomington: Indiana University Press, 1998). In the 1990s AIDS also figured prominently in public discourses around Athey's performances. In 1994 reports of AIDS blood at a performance of *4 Scenes*—supported by the Walker Arts Center in Minneapolis and mini-

mally funded by the National Endowment for the Arts—ignited a national controversy over public arts funding. For a detailed account of these debates, see Dominic Johnson, "'Does a Bloody Towel Represent the Ideals of the American People?' Ron Athey and the Culture Wars," in *Pleading in the Blood: The Art and Performances of Ron Athey*, ed. Dominic Johnson (London, Bristol: Live Art Development Agency, Intellect Ltd., 2013), 64–93.

112. Athey, "Raised in the Lord," *L.A. Weekly*, 25.

113. Ron Athey, interview with Karen Gonzalez Rice, August 15, 2007. For more on independent Pentecostals, see Grant A. Wacker, "The Pentecostal Tradition," in *Caring and Curing: Health and Medicine in the Western Religious Traditions*, ed. Ronald L. Numbers and Darrel W. Amundsen (Baltimore: Johns Hopkins University Press, 1986), 527–28; and Vinson Synan, *The Holiness-Pentecostal Tradition* (Grand Rapids, MI: Willliam P. Eerdmans , 1997), 212.

114. Allen stridently advocated the autonomy of healing evangelists, claiming that deliverance ministries "will continue to fill the gap between revealed truth and the butchered truth of denominational religion. Our revivals will continue to glorify God with singing, dancing, shouting, speaking in tongues, falling prostrate before the Lord" (A. A. Allen, quoted in Harrell, *All Things Are Possible*, 195). Following Allen's insistence on the spiritual possibilities of revival, Athey observed, "I feel like Pentecostalism was over when [it became] a church, like it is actually rooted in revivalism and movement. The turn-of-the-century revival meetings, the church in L.A. in 1911 with the one-eyed black minister on the street that is now Little Tokyo, a mixed congregation in 1911, which was a horrible period in race relations, under the Spirit. That radicalism was lost. . . . That was a downfall of Aimee Semple McPherson, once she landed right over here on the lake [in Los Angeles]" (Ron Athey, interview with Karen Gonzalez Rice, August 15, 2007). Religious studies scholar Russell E. Richey has observed how the powerful experience of revival "readily displaces other ways of being the church." Russell E. Richey, "Revivalism: In Search of a Definition," *Wesleyan Theological Journal* 28, nos. 1–2 (Spring–Fall 1993): 170.

115. For more on the role of prophecy in the Latter Rain Movement, see Vinson Synan, *The Century of the Holy Spirit: 100 Years of Pentecostal and Charismatic Renewal, 1901–2001* (Nashville: Thomas Nelson, 2001), 253.

116. To some secular readers, these claims may seem ludicrous. However, in a reflection on secular journalists' reactions to his ministry, Allen cautioned that derisive comments risked dehumanizing believers: "Ridicule of the congregation—usually portraying them as a very ignorant, low-type, almost sub-human rabble" (A. A. Allen, quoted in Harrell, *All Things Are Possible*, 197).

117. Athey, "Raised in the Lord," *L.A. Weekly*, 21. These prophecies eventually contributed to Athey's disillusionment with his family's Pentecostal faith: "There was never a reality check until I was fifteen and became socialized. Then it all just fell apart. And Elvis died" (Ron Athey, interview with Karen Gonzalez Rice, August 15, 2007). He observed, "In direct opposition to my Pentecostal upbringing . . . I had firm evidence to conclude that God no longer ran my life. And because I was undeniably a homosexual, neither did my family, so I left." Ron Athey, "The Missing Link," *The Advocate*, August 15, 2000, 50.

118. Athey, "Raised in the Lord," *L.A. Weekly*, 21. The documentary *Marjoe*

profiled another Pentecostal prodigy, child evangelist Marjoe Gortner, and examines the aftermath of his upbringing.

119. Athey, "Raised in the Lord," *L.A. Weekly*, 25.

120. Ron Athey, interview with Karen Gonzalez Rice, August 15, 2007. Athey described the persistence of this early training in trance states and ecstatic practices: "I see all our life issues like a carousel: they keep coming back with different masks on. . . . I was always prone to ecstasy since I was a young, young child. You could just look at me and I was enraptured and crying. I lived in another realm that didn't really fit in with the world. Later, when I got into music and art, I recognized that I did the same exact thing; I went directly into another realm. These vibrations were still in me; they would never leave me. I still responded exactly the same way to stimulation and life issues. So I seriously sought how to understand this thing and what was mine, in the aftermath of it. I finally realized that I'm an ecstatic and I'm always going to click out into another world, from a meditative state to a dancing-in-the-spirit state" (ibid). Trancelike states appeared in Athey's actions throughout the *Torture Trilogy*, for example, speaking in tongues while pierced with arrows in *Martyrs and Saints*, agitated rocking during the enactment of his overdose suicide attempt in *4 Scenes*, and repeating his confession before the "Black Buddha" character in *Deliverance*.

121. Ibid. Kathryn Kuhlman, Franklin Hall, and the Latter Rain Movement endorsed prolonged fasting. See Harrell, *All Things Are Possible*, 81; and Wacker, "Pentecostal Tradition," 525. Athey described how his grandmother's biblical interpretation of events invested the family's suffering with authority: "My grandmother very much believed that our family was being persecuted like Job, and that we should expect to face tribulations such as painful diseases, uneven legs, and, of course, psychic warfare with demons. My mother's schizophrenia, for which she was institutionalized much of her life, was a sign of our persecution. . . . But she also believed that the Lord felt we had suffered long enough, and the 'Deliverance' was at hand. . . . Deliverance, for my grandmother, went beyond release from the oppression we had suffered . . . [for] with Deliverance, we would come into our respective ministries. We would come into our power" (Athey, "Raised in the Lord," *L.A. Weekly*, 22).

122. Athey, "Raised in the Lord," *L.A. Weekly*, 25.

123. Michael Warner, "Tongues Untied: Memoirs of a Pentecostal Boyhood," in *Curiouser: On the Queerness of Children*, ed. Steven Bruhm and Natasha Hurley (Minneapolis: University of Minnesota Press, 2004), 216.

124. Ron Athey, interview with Karen Gonzalez Rice, August 15, 2007.

125. Athey, "Deliverance: Introduction," 432. In 2013 Athey revised this text to read "Why the fucking bloodbath? The shit? The vomit? All performed on a well-lit stage so that, while stylized, no details will be missed. I want a public to bear witness" (Athey, "Deliverance: The 'Torture Trilogy,'" 101).

126. R. Marie Griffith, *God's Daughters: Evangelical Women and the Power of Submission* (Berkeley: University of California Press, 1997), 90.

127. Ron Athey, interview with Karen Gonzalez Rice, August 15, 2007.

128. For a legalistic reading of witnessing in Athey's performances, see Alison Young, *Judging the Image: Art, Value, Law* (New York: Routledge, 2005), 110.

129. Program, *4 Scenes in a Harsh Life,* Patrick's Cabaret, Minneapolis, 1994, quoted in Doyle, *Hold It against Me,* 25–26.

130. *Incorruptible Flesh (Dissociative Sparkle)* was performed in Glasgow and New York.

131. Ron Athey, interview with Karen Gonzalez Rice, August 15, 2007.

132. Ibid.

133. See Piero Camporesi, *The Incorruptible Flesh: Bodily Mutation and Mortification in Religion and Folklore,* trans. Tania Croft-Murray (New York: Cambridge University Press, 1988); and André Vauchez, *Sainthood in the Later Middle Ages,* trans. Jean Birrell (New York: Cambridge University Press, 1997). While preparing for the first iteration of *Incorruptible Flesh* in 1996–97, Athey and Lawrence Steger studied the histories of saints and materiality of relics during a joint residency at the Centre for Contemporary Art in Glasgow in 1996. Athey was already familiar with some elements of Catholic worship; his Aunt Vena, as part of her personal religious practice, venerated the Catholic saints and the Virgin Mary. According to Athey, she "co-opted the glam of Catholicism" (Ron Athey, interview with Karen Gonzalez Rice, August 15, 2007).

134. Ron Athey, interview with Karen Gonzalez Rice, August 15, 2007. Adrian Heathfield observed the contradictions in Athey's figure as both death mask and living face in Adrian Heathfield, "Illicit Transit," in *Pleading in the Blood: The Art and Performances of Ron Athey,* ed. Dominic Johnson (London, Bristol: Live Art Development Agency, Intellect Ltd., 2013), 211.

CHAPTER 4

1. To date art historical attention to Duncan's work has been limited to short discussions of *Blind Date,* including Kristine Stiles's important commentary, in performance art survey texts. See Kristine Stiles, "Uncorrupted Joy: International Art Actions," in *Out of Actions: Between Performance and the Object, 1949–1979,* ed. Paul Schimmel (Los Angeles: Los Angeles Museum of Contemporary Art, 1998), 241–42; Carl E. Loeffler, ed., *Performance Anthology: Source Book of California Performance Art* (San Francisco: Last Gasp, 1989); and Tracey Warr, *The Artist's Body: Themes and Movements* (London: Phaidon, 2000), 105.

2. Unless otherwise noted, quotations from the artist are from John Duncan, interview with Karen Gonzalez Rice, August 2–7, 2009. I spoke with Duncan daily over the course of six days at his home and studio in Bologna, Italy. I digitally audio-recorded our conversations; further discussion, which has continued to the present, has taken place through e-mails.

3. Thomas Bey William Bailey, *Micro Bionic: Radical Electronic Music and Sound Art in the 21st Century* (London: Creation Books, 2009), 14–15.

4. Ibid., 15.

5. Marcelo Aguirre, "John Duncan: Ghost Patterns Rising," *e/i* 7 (Spring–Summer 2006), reprinted under "Bio and Press" at the website for John Duncan, http://johnduncan.org/comments.html#Aguirre (accessed July 10, 2009).

6. This image may be a photograph of feminist performance artist Laurel Klick.

7. Baird Tipson, "Calvinist Heritage," in *Encyclopedia of the American Reli-*

gious Experience, ed. Charles Lippy and P. W. Williams (New York: Charles Scribner's Sons, 1988), 453.

8. John Calvin, quoted in William F. Keesecker, ed., *A Calvin Treasury: Selections from Institutes of the Christian Religion* (New York: Harper & Brothers, 1961), 124–25.

9. Jonathan Edwards, *Great Doctrine of Original Sin Defended* (1758), part I, section IV, quoted in William K. B. Stoever, "The Calvinist Theological Tradition," in *Encyclopedia of the American Religious Experience,* ed. Charles Lippy and P. W. Williams (New York Charles Scribner's Sons, 1988), 1046. American Calvinist leaders in the 1950s, for example, considered Edwards representative of the Calvinist tradition. See Jacob T. Hoogstra, *American Calvinism: A Survey* (Grand Rapids: Baker Book House, 1957), 20.

10. Before 1958 Duncan's congregation, Grace Presbyterian Church, was affiliated with the Presbyterian Church in the U.S.A. (PCUSA). In 1958 this organization merged with other Presbyterian groups to form the United Presbyterian Church in the U.S.A. (UPCUSA).

11. Edward L. Queen II, "Neoorthodoxy," in *Encyclopedia of American Religious History,* ed. Stephen R. Prothero and Gardiner H. Shattuck Jr. (New York: Facts on File, 2001), 496.

12. William B. Kennedy, "Neo-orthodoxy Goes to Sunday School: The Christian Faith and Life Curriculum," *Journal of Presbyterian History* 58 (Winter 1980): 326–70.

13. Duncan's home church, Grace Presbyterian, subscribed to these materials. James Ayers, email to Karen Gonzalez Rice, January 29, 2010; Donald F. Owens, interview with Karen Gonzalez Rice, January 12, 2010.

14. Keesecker pastored Grace Presbyterian Church between 1958 and 1979. James Ayers, email to Karen Gonzalez Rice, January 29, 2010. In 1975 he was elected to the highest position in the American Presbyterian leadership, the moderator of the 187th General Assembly of the UPCUSA. His books for popular audiences include *A Calvin Treasury; The Wisdom of the Psalms: Selections and Expositions Based on Commentary by John Calvin* (New York: World Publishing, 1970); *A Layperson's Guide to the Theology of the Book of Confessions* (New York: General Assembly of the United Presbyterian Church in the United States of America, 1976); and *A Calvin Reader: Reflections on Living* (Philadelphia: Westminster Press, 1985).

15. This metaphor echoes Jonathan Edwards's description of human evil: "Depravity of heart is to be considered two ways in Adam's posterity. The first existing of a corrupt disposition in their hearts, is not to be looked upon as a sin belonging to them, distinct from their participation of Adam's first sin; it is as if it were the extended pollution of that sin, through the whole tree, by virtue of the constituted union of the branches with the root; or the inherence of the sin of that head of the species in the members." Jonathan Edwards, *Great Doctrine of Original Sin Defended* (1758), part IV, section III, quoted in Jacob T. Hoogstra, *American Calvinism: A Survey* (Grand Rapids: Baker Book House, 1957), 24.

16. Boris Wlassoff, "John Duncan," *Revue & Corrigée* 51 (March 2002), reprinted under "Bio and Press" at the website for John Duncan, http://johndun can.org/wlassoff.rc1.html (accessed July 10, 2009).

17. Keesecker, *A Layperson's Guide to the Theology of the Book of Confessions*, 39.

18. William A. Dyrness, *Reformed Theology and Visual Culture: The Protestant Imagination from Calvin to Edwards* (New York: Cambridge University Press, 2004), 301.

19. John Duncan, e-mail to Karen Gonzalez Rice, January 26, 2010.

20. Sacvan Bercovitch, "The Ends of American Puritan Rhetoric," in *The Ends of Rhetoric: History, Theory, Practice*, ed. John Bender and David E. Wellberry (Stanford: Stanford University Press, 1990), 172; Sacvan Bercovitch, *The American Jeremiad* (Madison: University of Wisconsin Press, 1978), 16; Andrew R. Murphy, *Prodigal Nation: Moral Decline and Divine Punishment from New England to 9/11* (New York: Oxford University Press, 2009), 6.

21. For more on the jeremiad in American culture, see Bercovitch, *American Jeremiad*; Andrew R. Murphy and Jennifer Miller, "The Enduring Power of the American Jeremiad," in *Religion, Politics, and Religious Identity: New Directions, New Controversies*, ed. David S. Gutterman and Andrew R. Murphy (New York: Lexington Books, 2006); Murphy, *Prodigal Nation*; Mark Stephen Jendrysik, *Modern Jeremiahs: Contemporary Visions of American Decline* (New York: Lexington Books, 2008); and Paul Williams, "Twenty-First-Century Jeremiad: Contemporary Hip-Hop and American Tradition," *European Journal of American Culture* 27, no. 2 (2008): 111–32.

22. Michael Fried, "Art and Objecthood," *Artforum* 5.10 (Summer 1967): 12–23.

23. Bercovitch, *American Jeremiad*, 23.

24. Preached in Enfield, Connecticut, in 1741, Edwards's sermon contains traditional elements of both the jeremiad and the revivalist conversion address popular during the Great Awakening. As a result, rather than the Puritan jeremiad's direct focus on political and social aims, "Sinners" implied the connection between individual conversion and social and political purification. However, "Sinners" contains those features of the jeremiad relevant to Duncan's work, has enduring resonance with mainstream Calvinist ministers and congregations such as Grace Presbyterian Church, and has been generally considered to represent the jeremiad form in anthologies of American literature, in cross-disciplinary scholarship, and in American public discourse.

25. Jonathan Edwards, "Sinners in the Hands of an Angry God," in *A Jonathan Edwards Reader*, ed. John E. Smith, Harry S. Stout, and Kenneth P. Minkema (New Haven: Yale University Press, 1995), 95–96.

26. Stephen Richard Turley, "Awakened to the Holy: "Sinners in the Hands of an Angry God" in Ritualized Context," *Christianity and Literature* 57, no. 4 (Summer 2008): 514–15.

27. Edwin H. Cady, "The Artistry of Jonathan Edwards," *New England Quarterly* 22, no. 1 (March 1949): 70; Edwards, "Sinners in the Hands of an Angry God," 103–4.

28. George M. Marsden, *Jonathan Edwards: A Life* (New Haven: Yale University Press, 2003), 224.

29. Ibid., 220.

30. Thomas J. Steele and Eugene R. Delay, "Vertigo in History: The Threaten-

ing Tactility of 'Sinners in the Hands,'" *Early American Literature* 18, no. 3 (Winter 1983–84): 246.

31. Edwards, "Sinners in the Hands of an Angry God," 92–93, 95.

32. Ibid., 95.

33. Linda Frye Burnham, "John Duncan 3-26-79 Interview with Linda Burnham," unpublished manuscript, Manuscript no. 2006.M8, Getty Research Institute archives, 1979, 3.

34. Ibid.

35. Paul McCarthy, ed., *Criss Cross Double Cross*, vol. 1 (Los Angeles: Paul McCarthy, 1976), n.p.

36. David Lisak, Jim Hopper, and Pat Song, "Factors in the Cycle of Violence: Gender Rigidity and Emotional Constriction," *Journal of Traumatic Stress* 9, no. 4 (1996): 723.

37. See David Lisak, "Sexual Aggression, Masculinity, and Fathers," *Signs* 16, no. 2 (1991): 238–62.

38. David Lisak, "Men as Victims: Challenging Cultural Myths," *Journal of Traumatic Stress* 6, no. 4 (1993): 577.

39. John N. Briere and Diana M. Elliott, "Immediate and Long-Term Impacts of Child Sexual Abuse," *The Future of Children* 4, no. 2 (Summer–Autumn 1994): 59–60.

40. David Lisak, "Integrating a Critique of Gender in the Treatment of Male Survivors of Childhood Abuse," *Psychotherapy* 32, no. 2 (Summer 1995): 260. From a clinical perspective, childhood sexual abuse may include a spectrum of contact and noncontact activities, from penetration and fondling to sexualized speech and emotionally seductive behavior. David Lisak and Laura Luster, "Educational, Occupational, and Relationship Histories of Men Who Were Sexually and/or Physically Abused as Children," *Journal of Traumatic Stress* 7, no. 4 (1994): 513; Matthew Parynik Mendel, *The Male Survivor: The Impact of Sexual Abuse* (Thousand Oaks, CA: Sage Publications, 1995), 56.

41. Boys are more likely than girls to experience the sexual predation of several adults (Mendel, *Male Survivor*, 69).

42. Lisak, "Sexual Aggression, Masculinity, and Fathers," 246; David Lisak, "Male Survivors of Trauma," in *New Handbook of Psychotherapy and Counseling with Men*, ed. Glenn E. Good and Gary R. Brooks (San Francisco: Jossey-Bass, 2005), 152.

43. David Lisak, "Male Gender Socialization and the Perpetration of Sexual Abuse," in *Childhood Socialization*, ed. Gerald Handel (New Brunswick, NJ: Aldine Transaction, 2006), 327.

44. David Lisak, "The Psychological Impact of Sexual Abuse: Content Analysis of Interviews with Male Survivors," *Journal of Traumatic Stress* 7, no. 4 (1994): 537.

45. Stiles, "Uncorrupted Joy," 241–43. See also John Duncan, "John Duncan: If Only We Could Tell You . . . ," *High Performance* 3, nos. 3–4 (Fall–Winter 1980): 34–35. Duncan confirmed the title of the work as *If Only We Could Tell You*, but in conversation he often used the alternate title *The Black Room*.

46. Wlassoff, "John Duncan."

47. Duncan, "John Duncan," 34.

48. Lisak, "Psychological Impact of Sexual Abuse," 543.

49. Moira Roth, *The Amazing Decade: Women and Performance Art in America* (Los Angeles: Astro Artz, 1983), 18.

50. Histories of Southern California feminist arts communities are well documented. See Lisa Gabrielle Mark, ed., *Wack! Art and the Feminist Revolution* (Cambridge: MIT Press, 2007); Diana Burgess Fuller and Daniela Salvioni, *Art/Women/California* (Berkeley: University of California Press, 2002); Loeffler, *Performance Anthology*; Roth, *Amazing Decade*; and others.

51. Suzanne Lacy has defined these men (notably omitting Duncan) not as participants in the feminist scene but rather as artists who "reflected and reacted to . . . feminist discourse" (Fuller and Salvioni, *Art/Women/California*, 96).

52. Carl Abrahamsson, "Interview," *Flashback,* April 2002, reprinted under "Bio and Press" at the website for John Duncan, http://johnduncan.org/abrahamsson.html (accessed July 10, 2009).

53. Kristine Stiles, "Never Enough Is Something Else: Feminist Performance Art, Probity, and the Avant-Garde," in *Contours of the Theatrical Avant-Garde: Performance and Textuality,* ed. James M. Harding (Madison: University of Wisconsin Press, 2000).

54. John Duncan, interview with Karen Gonzalez Rice, August 2–7, 2009; Lewis MacAdams, *Blind Date* (Los Angeles: Am Here Books/Immediate Editions, 1981), n.p.

55. John Duncan, "Sanctuary" (1976).

56. Ibid.

57. Lisak, "Integrating a Critique of Gender in the Treatment of Male Survivors of Childhood Abuse," 263.

58. Moira Roth, "Visions and Re-visions: A Conversation with Suzanne Lacy," *Artforum,* November 1980, 44.

59. Roth, *Amazing Decade*, 86.

60. Massimo Ricci, "John Duncan," *Paris Transatlantic,* January 2005, http://www.paristransatlantic.com/magazine/interviews/duncan.html (accessed July 10, 2009).

61. Lewis MacAdams, "The Law and the Power," *High Performance* 5, no. 4 (Fall 1982): 39.

62. Loeffler, *Performance Anthology*, 418.

63. John Duncan, "A Secret Project for the People of the United States," *Grok* 7 (July 1984): n.p.

64. Lisak, "Male Gender Socialization and the Perpetration of Sexual Abuse"; Lisak, Hopper, and Song, "Factors in the Cycle of Violence."

65. For more on reenactment, see Briere and Elliott, "Immediate and Long-Term Impacts of Child Sexual Abuse"; James A. Chu, *Rebuilding Shattered Lives: Treating Complex PTSD and Dissociative Disorders,* 2nd ed. (New York: John Wiley & Sons, 2011); Peter T. Dimock, "Adult Males Sexually Abused as Children: Characteristics and Implications for Treatment," *Journal of Interpersonal Violence* 3 (June 1988): 203–21; Judith Lewis Herman, *Trauma and Recovery: The Aftermath of Violence from Domestic Abuse to Political Terror* (New York: Basic Books, 1992); Mendel, *Male Survivor*; and Anna C. Salter, *Transforming Trauma: A Guide to*

Understanding and Treating Adult Survivors of Child Sexual Abuse (Thousand Oaks, CA: Sage Publications, 1995).

66. John Duncan and Cheri Gaulke, "Connecting Myths," *High Performance* 2, no. 1 (June 1978): 41.

67. The artist has also said, "[I] invited the audience to abuse me sexually" (Duncan, "A Secret Project for the People of the United States," n.p).

68. Ibid., n.p.

69. John Duncan, "For Women Only" (1979).

70. For more on this performance, see Rebecca McGrew and Jennie Klein, eds., *The 21st Century Odyssey, Part II: The Performances of Barbara T. Smith* (Claremont, CA: Pomona College Museum of Art, 2005).

71. McCarthy took on the role of the surgeon while Duncan performed as the subject of the operation in this work. See Loeffler, *Performance Anthology*, 422.

72. For more on Stoerchle's *Untitled* performance, see Karen Gonzalez Rice, "Cocking the Trigger: Explicit Male Performance and Its Consequences " in *Scenes of the Obscene: Representations of Obscenity in Art, Middle Ages to Today*, ed. Kassandra Nakas and Jessica Ullrich (Weimar: Verlag und Datenbank für Geisteswissenschaften, 2014), 147–62.

73. For more on Public Spirit, see Linda Frye Burnham, "What about Public Spirit?," *High Performance* 3, nos. 3–4 (Fall–Winter 1980): 1, 164–65.

74. Duncan, "A Secret Project for the People of the United States," n.p.

75. Giuliana Stefani, "Ideas on 'Blind Date': Interview with John Duncan," (1997), 1.

76. Duncan's turn to the aural in *Blind Date* also corresponded to his long-time commitment to the medium of sound; from the early 1970s to the present, he has been best known, in experimental music circles, as a musician and sound artist.

77. Lewis MacAdams, "Sex with the Dead," *Wet* 30 (March–August 1981): 60. The *Blind Date* audio recording exists in Duncan's archive and was briefly commercially distributed on the cassette *Pleasure-Escape*, but he has attempted to curtail its availability. "I have made it almost entirely impossible to hear," he said, in order to avoid people seeking it "for perverse reasons." In recent years, however, YouTube users have uploaded excerpts from *Pleasure-Escape*, including the *Blind Date* audio.

78. Stefani, "Ideas on Blind Date," 2.

79. MacAdams, "Sex with the Dead," 61.

80. Ibid., 60.

81. Aguirre, "John Duncan."

82. Calvinist theologians have addressed this problem, warning that total depravity "does not mean absolute depravity . . . that one expresses the evil of his sinful nature as much as possible at all times." Duane E. Spencer, *Tulip: The Five Points of Calvinism in the Light of Scripture* (Grand Rapids, MI: Baker Books, 1979), 32.

83. MacAdams, "Sex with the Dead," 60.

84. Kristine Stiles, "Notes on Rudolf Schwartzkogler's Images of Healing," *Whitewalls* 25 (Spring 1990): 14.

85. Wlassoff, "John Duncan." Duncan's text has been lost, although short excerpts are documented in MacAdams, "Sex with the Dead"; and MacAdams, *Blind Date*.

86. Aguirre, "John Duncan."

87. Stefani, "Ideas on Blind Date," 1.

88. MacAdams, "Sex with the Dead," 60.

89. Ibid., 61.

90. In response to an article about *Blind Date* in the Los Angeles publication *Wet*, artist Alex Grey wrote a letter to the editor describing his performance *Necrophilia* (1976), in which, photographed by his wife, he had sex with a mutilated corpse. He wrote, "Perhaps John Duncan would not have had to put himself through the mental agony, had he seen that I had done the piece several years before. . . . A day has not gone by that I haven't thought of the necrophilia piece" (Alex Grey, "More Sex with the Dead," *Wet*, July–August 1981, n.p.). Duncan was unaware of *Necrophilia* when he performed *Blind Date*, but given his emphasis on individual experience, it is unlikely that he would have been deterred. For more on Alex Grey, see Lewis MacAdams, "It Started Out with Death," *High Performance* 5, no. 3 (Spring–Summer 1982): 43–49.

91. Stefani, "Ideas on Blind Date," 1.

92. For a discussion of Kelley's and Oursler's interest in Duncan's work, see MacAdams, "Sex with the Dead."

93. Ibid., 61.

94. John Duncan, *Pleasure-Escape*, audiocassette (Tokyo: B-Sellers, 1985).

95. MacAdams, "Sex with the Dead," 61.

96. Duncan, *Pleasure-Escape*.

97. Stiles theorized the traumatic link between these two works in "Uncorrupted Joy," 241.

98. Robert J. Lifton, *The Broken Connection: On Death and the Continuity of Life* (New York: Simon & Schuster, 1979), 171.

99. MacAdams, "Sex with the Dead," 60.

100. Ibid.

101. Here Duncan was referring to total depravity and the Calvinist doctrine of predestination. Calvinist theology posits the salvation of select individuals chosen by God at the beginning of time. Only a limited, predetermined number of specific souls will receive salvation, and believers have no way of either knowing or changing this predestined outcome. For more on predestination from a popular source concurrent with *Blind Date*, see Spencer, *Tulip*.

102. MacAdams, "Sex with the Dead," 61.

103. MacAdams, *Blind Date*, n.p.

104. Duncan, *Pleasure-Escape*.

105. Ibid.

106. Duncan has described the experience of *Stress Chamber* differently: "[F]rom the outside it looks like a torture chamber because you can feel the ground vibrating. But, if you're inside, if you're at the vortex of this source, then it's like a massage. So it's just the opposite of torture; it's very sensual, it's very pleasant."

107. Bercovitch, *American Jeremiad*, 16.
108. Abrahamsson, "Interview."

EPILOGUE

1. For more on Cal Robertson's history, see Steven Slosberg, "Robertson's 20-Year Vigil for Peace," *The Day*, October 5, 2006; Kathleen Edgecomb, "A Soldier Fighting for Peace," *The Day*, November 23, 2008; Phil Butta, "Garden Named in Peace Advocate's Honor," *Mystic River Press*, September 15, 2011; and Tess Townsend, "Christmas Vigil a Show of Solidarity for Peace," *The Day*, December 25, 2014.
2. Mike Hatt, "Keeping Our Eyes on the Prize," *Troubadour*, Fall–Winter 2014, 1.

Bibliography

Abrahamsson, Carl. "Interview." *Flashback,* April 2002, n.p. Reprinted under "Bio and Press" at the website for John Duncan, http://johnduncan.org/abrahamsson.html, accessed July 10, 2009.

Abzug, Robert H. *Cosmos Crumbling: American Reform and the Religious Imagination.* New York: Oxford University Press, 1994.

Aguirre, Marcelo. "John Duncan: Ghost Patterns Rising." *e/i* 7 (Spring–Summer 2006), n.p. Reprinted under "Bio and Press" at the website for John Duncan, http://johnduncan.org/comments.html#Aguirre, accessed July 10, 2009.

Ahlstrom, Sydney. *A Religious History of the American People.* New Haven: Yale University Press, 2004.

Albrecht, Daniel E. "Worshiping and the Spirit: Transmuting Liturgy Pentecostally." In *The Spirit in Worship, Worship in the Spirit,* edited by Teresa Berger and Bryan D. Spinks, 223–44. Collegeville, MN: Liturgical Press, 2009.

American Psychiatric Association. *Diagnostic and Statistical Manual of Mental Disorders: DSM-5.* Washington, DC: American Psychiatric Association, 2013.

Anawalt, K. "Why Not L.A." *High Performance* 3, nos. 3–4 (Fall–Winter 1980): 132–35.

Anderson, Patrick. *So Much Wasted: Hunger, Performance, and the Morbidity of Resistance.* Durham: Duke University Press, 2010.

Anderson, Robert Mapes. *Vision of the Disinherited: The Making of American Pentecostalism.* New York: Oxford University Press, 1979.

Asad, Talal. *Formations of the Secular: Christianity, Islam, Modernity.* Stanford: Stanford University Press, 2003.

Athey, Ron. "Artist's Notes." In *Out of Character: Rants, Raves, and Monologues from Today's Top Performance Artists,* edited by Mark Russell, 32–37. New York: Bantam Books, 1997.

Athey, Ron. "Casebook: Four Scenes in a Harsh Life." *TheatreForum* 6 (Winter–Spring 1995): 62–63.

Athey, Ron. "Deliverance: Introduction, Foreword, Description, and Selected Text." In *Acting on Aids: Sex, Drugs, and Politics,* edited by Joshua Oppenheimer and Helena Reckitt, 431–44. London: Serpent's Tail, 1997.

Athey, Ron. "Deliverance: The 'Torture Trilogy' in Retrospect." In *Pleading in the Blood: The Art and Performances of Ron Athey,* edited by Dominic Johnson, 100–109. London, Bristol: Live Art Development Agency, Intellect Ltd., 2013.

Athey, Ron. "Gifts of the Spirit." In *Unnatural Disasters: Recent Writings from the Golden State,* edited by Nicole Panter, 70–80. San Diego: Incommunicado Press, 1996.

Athey, Ron. "Gifts of the Spirit." In *Pleading in the Blood: The Art and Performances of Ron Athey*, edited by Dominic Johnson, 42–54. London, Bristol: Live Art Development Agency, Intellect Ltd., 2013.

Athey, Ron. "The Missing Link." *The Advocate*, August 15, 2000, 50.

Athey, Ron. "Raised in the Lord: Revelations at the Knee of Miss Velma." *L.A. Weekly*, June 30–July 6, 1995, 20–25.

Athey, Ron. "Raised in the Lord: Revelations at the Knee of Miss Velma." In *Pleading in the Blood: The Art and Performances of Ron Athey*, edited by Dominic Johnson, 180–93. London, Bristol: Live Art Development Agency, Intellect Ltd., 2013.

Athey, Ron. "Reading Sister Aimee." In *Live Art and Performance*, edited by Adrian Heathfield, 86–91. New York: Routledge, 2004.

Athey, Ron. "Under My Skin." In *Strategic Sex: Why They Won't Keep It in the Bedroom*, edited by D. Travers Scott, 23–27. New York: Harrington Park Press, 1999.

Athey, Ron. "Wounded: The Transformation of Franko B." In *Franko B: Blinded by Love*, edited by Dominic Johnson, 27–29. Bologna: Damiani, 2006.

Ron Athey. "Ron Athey Biography." www.ronathey.com, accessed October 15, 2004.

Auerhahn, Nanette C., and Dori Laub. "Intergenerational Memory of the Holocaust." In *International Handbook of Multigenerational Legacies of Trauma*, edited by Yael Danieli, 21–41. New York: Plenum Press, 1998.

Bailey, Thomas Bey William. *Micro Bionic: Radical Electronic Music and Sound Art in the 21st Century*. London: Creation Books, 2009.

Balken, Debra Bricker. *Dove/O'Keeffe: Circles of Influence*. Williamstown, MA: Sterling and Francine Clark Art Institute, 2009.

Banks, Caroline Giles. "The Imaginative Use of Religious Symbols in Subjective Experiences of Anorexia Nervosa." *Psychoanalytic Review* 84, no. 2 (April 1997): 227–36.

Banks, Caroline Giles. "'There Is No Fat in Heaven': Religious Asceticism and the Meaning of Anorexia Nervosa." *Ethos* 24, no. 1 (March 1996): 107–35.

Barnstone, Aliki, Michael Tomasek Manson, and Carol J. Singley, eds. *The Calvinist Roots of the Modern Era*. Hanover, NH: University Press of New England, 1997.

Bataille, Georges. *Visions of Excess: Selected Writings, 1927–1939*. Translated by Allan Stoekl. Minneapolis: University of Minnesota Press, 1993.

Bellah, Robert N. *Prophetic Religion in a Democratic Society: Essays on Deepening the American Dream*. Kalamazoo, MI: Fetzer Institute, 2006.

Bennett, Jill. *Empathic Vision: Affect, Trauma, and Contemporary Art*. Stanford: Stanford University Press, 2005.

Bercovitch, Sacvan. *The American Jeremiad*. Madison: University of Wisconsin Press, 1978.

Bercovitch, Sacvan. "The Ends of American Puritan Rhetoric." In *The Ends of Rhetoric: History, Theory, Practice*, edited by John Bender and David E. Wellberry, 171–90. Stanford: Stanford University Press, 1990.

Berger, Maurice. "The Critique of Pure Racism: An Interview with Adrian Piper." *Afterimage* 18, no. 3 (1990): 5–9.

Bessire, Mark H. C., ed. *William Pope.L: The Friendliest Black Artist in America.* Cambridge: MIT Press, 2002.

Biernoff, Suzannah. *Sight and Embodiment in the Middle Ages.* New York: Palgrave Macmillan, 2002.

Bishop, Claire. *Artificial Hells: Participatory Art and the Politics of Spectatorship.* New York: Verso, 2012.

Block, Melissa. "Theodore Parker and the 'Moral Universe.'" *All Things Considered*, National Public Radio, September 2, 2010.

Blocker, Jane. *Seeing Witness: Visuality and the Ethics of Testimony.* Minneapolis: University of Minnesota Press, 2009.

Blocker, Jane. *What the Body Cost: Desire, History, and Performance.* Minneapolis: University of Minnesota Press, 2004.

Blumenthal, Lyn. "On Art and Artists: Linda Montano." *Profile* 4, no. 6 (December 1984): 2–25.

Blumhofer, Edith L. *Restoring the Faith: The Assemblies of God, Pentecostalism, and American Culture.* Chicago: University of Illinois Press, 1993.

Blumhofer, Edith L., and Randall Balmer, eds. *Modern Christian Revivals.* Chicago: University of Illinois Press, 1993.

Blumhofer, Edith L., R. P. Spittler, and Grant Wacker, eds. *Pentecostal Currents in American Protestantism.* Chicago: University of Illinois Press, 1999.

Brandenburg, Alisa Anne. "Inducing Knowledge by Enduring Experience: The Function of a Postmodern Pragmatic Aesthetic in Linda Montano's 'Living Art.'" M.A. Thesis, East Tennessee State University, 2004.

Brawner, Lydia. "Linda Montano, Anorexia Nervosa, and an Art of Hunger." *Women & Performance* 18, no. 2 (July 2008): 127–32.

Briere, John N., and Diana M. Elliott. "Immediate and Long-Term Impacts of Child Sexual Abuse." *The Future of Children* 4, no. 2 (Summer–Autumn 1994): 54–69.

Brown, Candy Gunther. "Healing and Revival." In *Encyclopedia of Religious Revivals in America*, edited by Michael McClymond, 201–4. Westport, CT: Greenwood Press, 2007.

Brown, Peter. *The Cult of the Saints: Its Rise and Function in Latin Christianity.* Chicago: University of Chicago Press, 1981.

Bruch, Hilde. "Anorexia Nervosa: Therapy and Theory." *American Journal of Psychiatry* 139, no. 12 (December 1982): 1531–38.

Bruch, Hilde. *The Golden Cage: The Enigma of Anorexia Nervosa.* Cambridge: Harvard University Press, 1978.

Burgess, Ann Wolbert, A. Nicholas Groth, Lynda Lytle Holmstrom, and Suzanne Sgroi. *Sexual Assault of Children and Adolescents.* Lexington, MA: Lexington Books, 1978.

Burgess, Ann Wolbert, and Lynda Lytle Holmstrom. "Adaptive Strategies and Recovery from Rape." *American Journal of Psychiatry* 136, no. 10 (October 1979): 1278–82.

Burgess, Ruth. "Enculturation." In *Encyclopedia of Pentecostal and Charismatic Christianity*, edited by Stanley M. Burgess, 162–65. New York: Routledge, 2006.

Burgess, Stanley M. "Charismatic Revival and Renewal." In *Encyclopedia of Re-*

ligious Revivals in America, edited by Michael McClymond, 99–102. Westport, CT: Greenwood Press, 2007.

Burnham, Linda Frye. "Close Radio." *High Performance* 4, no. 1 (Winter 1978): 12–15.

Burnham, Linda Frye. "Editor's Note." *High Performance* 3, nos. 3–4 (Fall–Winter 1980): 140.

Burnham, Linda Frye. "'High Performance,' Performance Art, and Me." *TDR/ The Drama Review* 30, no. 1 (Spring 1986): 15–51.

Burnham, Linda Frye. "John Duncan 3-26-79 Interview with Linda Burnham." Unpublished manuscript, Manuscript no. 2006.M8, Getty Research Institute archives, 1979.

Burnham, Linda Frye. "What about Public Spirit?" *High Performance* 3, nos. 3–4 (Fall–Winter 1980): 1, 164–65.

Butta, Phil. "Garden Named in Peace Advocate's Honor." *Mystic River Press*, September 15, 2011, A3.

Bynum, Caroline Walker. "Death and Resurrection in the Middle Ages: Some Modern Implications." *Proceedings of the American Philosophical Society* 142, no. 4 (1998): 589–96.

Bynum, Caroline Walker. *Fragmentation and Redemption: Essays on Gender and the Human Body in Medieval Religion*. New York: Zone Books, 1992.

Bynum, Caroline Walker. *Holy Feast and Holy Fast: The Religious Significance of Food to Medieval Women*. Berkeley: University of California Press, 1987.

Bynum, Caroline Walker. *The Resurrection of the Body in Western Christianity, 200–1336*. New York: Columbia University Press, 1995.

Cady, Edwin H. "The Artistry of Jonathan Edwards." *New England Quarterly* 22, no. 1 (March 1949): 61–72.

Calam, Rachel, and Peter Slade. "Eating Patterns and Unwanted Sexual Experiences." In *Why Women? Gender Issues and Eating Disorders*, edited by Bridget Dolan and Inez Gizinger, 101–9. Atlantic Highlands, NJ: Athlone Press, 1994.

Campbell, Donna M. "Forms of Puritan Rhetoric: The Jeremiad and the Conversion Narrative." *Literary Movements*, 2009. http://www.wsu.edu/~campbelld/amlit/jeremiad.htm, accessed February 2, 2010.

Camporesi, Piero. *The Incorruptible Flesh: Bodily Mutation and Mortification in Religion and Folklore*. Translated by Tania Croft-Murray. New York: Cambridge University Press, 1988.

Carr, Cynthia. *Fire in the Belly: The Life and Times of David Wojnarowicz*. New York: Bloomsbury, 2012.

Carr, Cynthia. *On Edge: Performance at the End of the Twentieth Century*. Middletown, CT: Wesleyan University Press, 1993.

Caruth, Cathy, ed. *Trauma: Explorations in Memory*. Baltimore: Johns Hopkins University Press, 1995.

Casanova, José. *Public Religions in the Modern World*. Chicago: University of Chicago Press, 1994.

Cascella, Daniela. "John Duncan: From Noise, Installations, Shortwave Radio, Field Recordings, One of the Masters of Experimentation of the Last 20 Years." *Blow Up*, November 2000. Reprinted under "Bio and Press" at the website for John Duncan, http://johnduncan.org/BlowUp.articolo.html, accessed July 10, 2009.

Cash, Stephanie. "Ron Athey at P.S. 122." *Art in America* 83, no. 2 (February 1995): 99.

Caskey, Noelle. "Interpreting Anorexia Nervosa." *Poetics Today* 6, nos. 1–2 (1985): 259–73.

Cembalest, R. "Ritualistic Physical Mortification." *Artnews* 93, no. 6 (Summer 1994): 56.

Chappell, David L. *A Stone of Hope: Prophetic Religion and the Death of Jim Crow.* Chapel Hill: University of North Carolina Press, 2004.

Chicago, Judy. *Through the Flower: My Struggle as a Woman Artist.* Garden City, NY: Doubleday, 1975.

Chris, Cynthi. "Girls on the Re-Make." *Afterimage* 28, no. 5 (March–April 2001): 11.

Chu, James A. *Rebuilding Shattered Lives: Treating Complex PTSD and Dissociative Disorders.* 2nd ed. New York: John Wiley & Sons, 2011.

Coalter, Milton J. , John M. Mulder, and Louis B. Weeks, eds. *The Confessional Mosaic: Presbyterians and 20th Century Theology.* Louisville: Westminster/John Knox Press, 1990.

Colbert, Charles. *Haunted Visions: Spiritualism and American Art.* Philadelphia: University of Pennsylvania Press, 2011.

Cox, Harvey. *Fire from Heaven: The Rise of Pentecostal Spirituality and the Reshaping of Religion in the Twenty-First Century.* New York: Addison-Wesley, 1995.

Craig, Robert H. *Religion and Radical Politics: An Alternative Christian Tradition in the United States.* Philadelphia: Temple University Press, 1992.

Cranston, Meg, and John Baldessari. *100 Artists See God.* London: Institute of Contemporary Arts, 2004.

Cronacher, Karen. "Something about Fear and Desire." *Theatre Journal* 42, no. 3 (October 1990): 367–68.

Curran, Patricia. *Grace before Meals: Food Ritual and Body Discipline in Convent Culture.* Urbana: University of Illinois Press, 1989.

Dayton, Donald W. *Theological Roots of Pentecostalism.* Grand Rapids, MI: Francis Asbury Press, 1987.

Derrida, Jacques. *Acts of Religion.* Edited by Gil Anidjar. New York: Routledge, 2001.

Derrida, Jacques. *On the Name.* Edited by Thomas Dutoit; translated by David Wood, John P. Leavey Jr., and Ian MacLeod. Stanford: Stanford University Press, 1995.

Dimock, Peter T. "Adult Males Sexually Abused as Children: Characteristics and Implications for Treatment." *Journal of Interpersonal Violence* 3 (June 1988): 203–21.

Dolan, Jay P., R. Scott Appleby, and Debra Campbell. *Transforming Parish Ministry: The Changing Roles of Catholic Clergy, Laity, and Women Religious.* New York: Crossroad, 1990.

Doyle, Jennifer. *Hold It against Me: Difficulty and Emotion in Contemporary Art.* Durham: Duke University Press, 2013.

Doyle, Jennifer. "Ron Athey's Dissociated Sparkle." In *Cruising the Archive:*

Queer Art and Culture in Los Angeles, 1945–1980, edited by Ann Cvetkovich, 140–57. Los Angeles: ONE National Gay and Lesbian Archives, 2011.

Doyle, Jennifer. *Sex Objects: Art and the Dialectics of Desire.* Minneapolis: University of Minnesota Press, 2006.

Doyle, Jennifer. "Sex with Ron." In *Pleading in the Blood: The Art and Performances of Ron Athey,* edited by Dominic Johnson, 124–29. London, Bristol: Live Art Development Agency, Intellect Ltd., 2013.

Dries, Angelyn. "American Catholic 'Woman's Work for Woman' in the Twentieth Century." In *Gospel Bearers, Gender Barriers: Missionary Women in the Twentieth Century,* edited by Dana L. Robert, 127–42. Maryknoll, NY: Orbis Books, 2002.

Drobnick, Jim, and Jennifer Fisher. *Museopathy.* Kingston, ON: Agnes Etherington Art Centre, 2001.

Duncan, John. "Events, Installations," at the website for John Duncan, www.johnduncan.org/instalmenu.html, accessed September 16, 2008.

Duncan, John. "For Women Only." Unpublished document, Duncan personal archive, 1979.

Duncan, John. "John Duncan: If Only We Could Tell You . . ." *High Performance* 3, nos. 3–4 (Fall–Winter 1980): 34–35.

Duncan, John. *John Duncan: Work, 1975–2005.* Milan: Errant Bodies Press, 2006.

Duncan, John. *Pleasure-Escape.* Tokyo: B-Sellers, 1985. Audiocassette.

Duncan, John. "Sanctuary." Unpublished document, Duncan personal archive, 1976.

Duncan, John. "A Secret Project for the People of the United States." *Grok* 7 (July 1984): n.p.

Duncan, John, and Cheri Gaulke. "Connecting Myths." *High Performance* 2, no. 1 (Summer 1978): 40–41.

Dyrness, William A. *Reformed Theology and Visual Culture: The Protestant Imagination from Calvin to Edwards.* New York: Cambridge University Press, 2004.

Ebaugh, Helen Rose Fuchs. *Women in the Vanishing Cloister: Organizational Decline in Catholic Religious Orders in the United States.* New Brunswick, NJ: Rutgers University Press, 1993.

Eckhart, Christian, Osvaldo Romberg, Harry Philbrick, and Eleanor Heartney, eds. *Faith: The Impact of Judeo-Christian Religion on Art at the Millennium.* Ridgefield, CT: Aldrich Museum of Contemporary Art, 2000.

Edgecomb, Kathleen. "A Soldier Fighting for Peace." *The Day,* November 23, 2008.

Edwards, Jonathan. "Sinners in the Hands of an Angry God." In *A Jonathan Edwards Reader,* edited by John E. Smith, Harry S. Stout, and Kenneth P. Minkema, 89–105. New Haven: Yale University Press, 1995.

Eliade, Mircea. *The Sacred and the Profane: The Nature of Religion.* Translated by Willard R. Trask. San Diego: Harcourt Brace Jovanovich, 1959.

Elkins, James. *On the Strange Place of Religion in Contemporary Art.* New York: Routledge, 2004.

Espinosa, Gastón, Virgilio P. Elizondo, and Jesse Miranda. *Latino Religions and Civic Activism in the United States.* New York: Oxford University Press, 2005.

Everill, Joanne T., and Glenn Waller. "Reported Sexual Abuse and Eating Psychopathology: A Review of the Evidence for a Causal Link." *International Journal of Eating Disorders* 18, no. 1 (1995): 1–11.

"Faith Healers: Getting Back Double from God." *Time*, March 7, 1969, 64, 67.

Favazza, Armando. *Bodies under Siege: Self-Mutilation, Nonsuicidal Self-Injury, and Body Modification in Culture and Psychiatry*. 3rd ed. Baltimore: Johns Hopkins University Press, 2011.

Favazza, Armando. "A Cultural Understanding of Nonsuicidal Self-Injury." In *Understanding Nonsuicidal Self-Injury*, edited by Matthew K. Nock, 19–35. Washington, DC: American Psychological Association, 2009.

Fisher, Jennifer. "Linda Montano: Seven Years of Living Art." *Parachute* 64 (October–December 1991): 23–28.

Foley, Suzanne. *Space/Time/Sound: Conceptual Art in the San Francisco Bay Area, the 1970s*. San Francisco: San Francisco Museum of Modern Art, 1981.

Foucault, Michel. *Abnormal: Lectures at the College de France, 1974–1975*. New York: Picador, 2003.

Foucault, Michel. *The Foucault Reader*. Edited by Paul Rabinow. New York: Pantheon Books, 1984.

Francis, Richard, ed. *Negotiating Rapture*. Chicago: Museum of Contemporary Art, 1996.

Freud, Sigmund. "Autobiographical Study." In *The Freud Reader*, edited by Peter Gay, 3–44. New York: W. W. Norton, 1989.

Freud, Sigmund. "The Future of an Illusion." In *The Freud Reader*, edited by Peter Gay, 685–722. New York: W. W. Norton, 1989.

Fried, Michael. "Art and Objecthood." *Artforum* 5, no. 10 (Summer 1967): 12–23.

Fuller, Diana Burgess, and Daniela Salvioni. *Art/Women/California*. Berkeley: University of California Press, 2002.

Gilchrist, Roberta. *Gender and Material Culture: The Archaeology of Religious Women*. New York: Routledge, 1993.

Gilchrist, Roberta. "Medieval Bodies in the Material World: Gender, Stigma, and the Body." In *Framing Medieval Bodies*, edited by Sarah Kay and Miri Rubin, 43–61. New York: Manchester University Press, 1994.

Gonzalez Rice, Karen. "Cocking the Trigger: Explicit Male Performance and Its Consequences." In *Scenes of the Obscene: Representations of Obscenity in Art, Middle Ages to Today*, edited by Kassandra Nakas and Jessica Ullrich, 147–62. Weimar: Verlag und Datenbank für Geisteswissenschaften, 2014.

Gonzalez Rice, Karen. "Linda Montano, Student of Real Presence." *In Media Res: A Media Commons Project* (April 10, 2010). http://mediacommons.future ofthebook.org/imr/2010/04/15/linda-montano-student-real-presence, accessed April 10, 2010.

Gonzalez Rice, Karen. "Linda Montano and the Tensions of Monasticism." In *Beyond Belief: Theoaesthetics or Just Old-Time Religion?*, edited by Ronald R. Bernier. 25–43. Eugene, OR: Wipf and Stock, Pickwick Publications, 2010.

Gonzalez Rice, Karen. "'No Pictures': Blind Date and Abject Masculinity." *Performance Research* 19, no. 1 (June 2014): 15–24.

Gordon, R. A. "Concepts of Eating Disorders: A Historical Reflection." In *Neu-*

robiology in the Treatment of Eating Disorders, edited by Hans Wijbrand Hoek, Janet L. Treasure, and Melanie A. Katzman, 5–25. New York: John Wiley & Sons, 1998.

Gragnolati, Manuele. "From Decay to Splendor: Body and Pain in Bonvesin de la Riva's *Book of the Three Scriptures*." In *Last Things: Death and the Apocalypse in the Middle Ages*, edited by Caroline Walker Bynum, 84–97. Philadelphia: University of Pennsylvania Press, 2000.

Graham, Billy. "We Need Revival." In *Encyclopedia of Religious Revival in America*, edited by Michael McClymond, 288–91. Westport, CT: Greenwood Press, 2007.

Grey, Alex. "More Sex with the Dead." *Wet*, July–August 1981, n.p.

Grey, Alex, and Allyson Grey. "Linda Montano and Tehching Hsieh's One Year Performance: Alex and Allyson Grey Ask Questions about the Year of the Rope." *High Performance* 7, no. 3 (Fall 1984): 24–27.

Griffith, R. Marie. *Born Again Bodies: Flesh and Spirit in American Christianity*. Los Angeles: University of California Press, 2004.

Griffith, R. Marie. "Female Suffering and Religious Devotion in American Pentecostalism." In *Women and Twentieth-Century Protestantism*, edited by Margaret Lamberts Bendroth and Virginia Lieson Brereton, 184–208. Chicago: University of Illinois Press, 2002.

Griffith, R. Marie. *God's Daughters: Evangelical Women and the Power of Submission*. Berkeley: University of California Press, 1997.

Groshwitz, Rebecca C. "The Neurobiology of Non-suicidal Self-Injury (NSSI): A Review." *Suicidology Online* 3 (2012): 24–32. http://www.suicidology-online.com/pdf/SOL-2012-3-24-32.pdf, accessed April 24, 2012.

Hacking, Ian. *Rewriting the Soul: Multiple Personality and the Sciences of Memory*. Princeton: Princeton University Press, 1995.

Hall, David D., ed. *Lived Religion in America: Toward a History of Practice*. Princeton: Princeton University Press, 1997.

Hallelujah! Ron Athey: A Story of Deliverance. Directed by Catherine Gund. 1999. New York: Aubin Pictures, 1999. Videocassette.

Harding, Susan Friend. *The Book of Jerry Falwell: Fundamentalist Language and Politics*. Princeton: Princeton University Press, 2001.

Harradine, David. "Abject Identities and Fluid Performances: Theorizing the Leaking Body." *Contemporary Theatre Review* 10, no. 3 (2000): 69–85.

Harrell, David Edwin, Jr. *All Things Are Possible: The Healing and Charismatic Revivals in Modern America*. Bloomington: Indiana University Press, 1975.

Harris, William. "Demonized and Struggling with His Demons." *New York Times*, October 23, 1994, A1.

Hart, D. G., Sean Michael Lucas, and Stephen J. Nichols, eds. *The Legacy of Jonathan Edwards*. Grand Rapids, MI: Baker Academic, 2003.

Hart, Lynda. "Blood, Piss, and Tears: The Queer Real." *Textual Practice* 9, no. 1 (1995): 55–66.

Harvey, Doug "Corpsefucker Makes Good: Up the Hill Backwards with John Duncan and Paul McCarthy." *LA Weekly*, 25 July 2007.

Hatch, Nathan O. *The Democratization of American Christianity*. New Haven: Yale University Press, 1989.

Hatt, Mike. "Keeping Our Eyes on the Prize." *Troubadour*, Fall–Winter 2014, 1–2.

Heartney, Eleanor. *Postmodern Heretics: The Catholic Imagination in Contemporary Art*. New York: Midmarch Arts Press, 2004.

Heathfield, Adrian. "Illicit Transit." In *Pleading in the Blood: The Art and Performances of Ron Athey*, edited by Dominic Johnson, 206–25. London, Bristol: Live Art Development Agency, Intellect Ltd., 2013.

Heddon, Dierdre, and Jennie Klein, eds. *Histories and Practices of Live Art*. New York: Palgrave Macmillan, 2012.

Hedgepeth, William. "Brother A. A. Allen on the Gospel Trail: He Feels, He Heals, and He Turns You on with God." *Look*, October 7, 1969, 23–32.

Hendricks, Barbara. "The Legacy of Mary Josephine Rogers." *International Bulletin of Missionary Research* 21, no. 2 (1997): 72–80.

Herbert, Lynn M., Klaus Ottman, and Peter Schjeldahl. *The Inward Eye: Transcendence in Contemporary Art*. Houston: Contemporary Arts Museum, 2001.

Herman, Judith Lewis. *Father-Daughter Incest*. Cambridge: Harvard University Press, 2000.

Herman, Judith Lewis. *Trauma and Recovery: The Aftermath of Violence from Domestic Abuse to Political Terror*. New York: Basic Books, 1992.

Heyman, Stephen. "Pulp Friction." *T: The New York Times Style Magazine*, August 19, 2012, M2108.

Hocken, P. D. "Charismatic Movement." In *The New International Dictionary of Pentecostal and Charismatic Movements*, edited by Stanley M. Burgess and Eduard M. van der Maas, 477–519. Grand Rapids, MI: Zondervan, 2003.

Hoogstra, Jacob T. *American Calvinism: A Survey*. Grand Rapids, MI: Baker Book House, 1957.

Hsieh, Tehching. *Tehching Hsieh: One Year Performance Art Documents, 1978–1999*. New York, distributed by Tehching Hsieh, 2000. DVD-ROM.

Hsieh, Tehching, and Adrian Heathfield. *Out of Now: The Lifeworks of Tehching Hsieh*. Cambridge: MIT Press, 2009.

Hsieh, Tehching, and Linda Montano. "Statement." In *Tehching Hsieh: One Year Performance Art Documents 1978–1999*. New York, distributed by Tehching Hsieh, 2000. DVD-ROM.

Huline-Dickens, S. "Anorexia Nervosa: Some Connections with the Religious Attitude." *British Journal of Medical Psychology* 73, no. 1 (March 2000): 67–76.

Hume, David. *The Natural History of Religion*. Stanford: Stanford University Press, 1957.

James, William. *The Varieties of Religious Experience: A Study in Human Nature*. New York: Longmans Green, 1902.

Jankowski, Christian. "Transcript: The Holy Artwork, 2001," 1–5. Unpublished document, ArtPace archives, 2001.

Jendrysik, Mark Stephen. *Modern Jeremiahs: Contemporary Visions of American Decline*. New York: Lexington Books, 2008.

Johnson, Dominic. "'Does a Bloody Towel Represent the Ideals of the American People?' Ron Athey and the Culture Wars." In *Pleading in the Blood: The Art and Performances of Ron Athey*, edited by Dominic Johnson, 64–93. London, Bristol: Live Art Development Agency, Intellect Ltd., 2013.

Johnson, Dominic. *Franko B: Blinded by Love*. Bologna: Damiani, 2006.

Johnson, Dominic. "Intimacy and Risk in Live Art." In *Histories and Practices of Live Art in the UK*, edited by Jennie Klein and Dierdre Heddon, 122–48. Basingstoke: Palgrave Macmillan, 2012.

Johnson, Dominic. "Perverse Martyrologies: An Interview with Ron Athey." *Contemporary Theatre Review* 18, no. 4 (2008): 503–13.

Johnson, Dominic, ed. *Pleading in the Blood: The Art and Performances of Ron Athey*. London, Bristol: Live Art Development Agency, Intellect Ltd., 2013.

Johnson, Dominic. "Ron Athey's Visions of Excess: Performance after Georges Bataille." *Papers of Surrealism*, no. 8 (Spring 2010): 1–12, http://www.surreal ismcentre.ac.uk/papersofsurrealism/journal8/index.htm, accessed August 13, 2014.

Johnston, Jill. "Hardship Art." *Art in America* 72, no. 8 (September 1984): 176–79.

Jones, Amelia. *Body Art: Performing the Subject*. Minneapolis: University of Minnesota Press, 1998.

Jones, Amelia. "Holy Body: Erotic Ethics in Ron Athey and Juliana Snapper's 'Judas Cradle.'" *TDR/The Drama Review* 50, no. 1 (Spring 2006): 159–69.

Jones, Amelia. "How Ron Athey Makes Me Feel: The Political Potential of Upsetting Art." In *Pleading in the Blood: The Art and Performances of Ron Athey*, edited by Dominic Johnson, 152–79. London, Bristol: Live Art Development Agency, Intellect Ltd., 2013.

Jones, Amelia. "Performing the Wounded Body: Pain, Affect, and the Radical Relationality of Meaning." *Parallax* 15, no. 4 (2009): 45–67.

Jones, Amelia. *Seeing Differently: A History and Theory of Identification and the Visual Arts*. New York: Routledge, 2012.

Jones, Amelia, and Adrian Heathfield, eds. *Perform, Repeat, Record: Live Art in History*. Bristol: Intellect Ltd., 2012.

Kane, Paula M. "'She Offered Herself Up': The Victim Soul and Victim Spirituality in Catholicism." *Church History* 71, no. 1 (March 2002): 80–119.

Kaye, Richard A. "Losing His Religion: Saint Sebastian as Contemporary Gay Martyr." In *Outlooks: Lesbian and Gay Sexualities and Visual Cultures*, edited by Peter Horne and Reina Lewis, 86–105. New York: Routledge, 1996.

Kearney-Cooke, Ann. "Group Treatment of Sexual Abuse among Women with Eating Disorders." *Women and Therapy* 7, no. 1 (1998): 5–21.

Keesecker, William F., ed. *A Calvin Reader: Reflections on Living*. Philadelphia: Westminster Press, 1985.

Keesecker, William F., ed. *A Calvin Treasury: Selections from Institutes of the Christian Religion*. New York: Harper & Brothers, 1961.

Keesecker, William F. *A Layperson's Guide to the Theology of the Book of Confessions*. New York: General Assembly of the United Presbyterian Church in the United States of America, 1976.

Keesecker, William F. *The Wisdom of the Psalms: Selections and Expositions Based on Commentary by John Calvin*. New York: World Publishing, 1970.

Kennedy, William B. "Neo-orthodoxy Goes to Sunday School: The Christian Faith and Life Curriculum." *Journal of Presbyterian History* 58 (Winter 1980): 326–70.

King, Martin Luther, Jr. "Address at the Thirty-Sixth Annual Dinner of the War Resisters League." In *The Papers of Martin Luther King, Jr.: Threshold of a New*

Decade, January 1959–December 1960, edited by Clayborne Carson, Ralph Luker, and Penny A. Russell, 120–25. Berkeley: University of California Press, 1992.

King, Martin Luther, Jr. "Letter from a Birmingham City Jail." In *A Testament of Hope: The Essential Writings and Speeches of Martin Luther King, Jr.*, edited by James Melvin Washington, 289–302. New York: HarperCollins, 1986.

Kita, Bernice. "Maryknoll Sisters in Latin America, 1943–1993." *Missiology* 26, no. 4 (October 1998): 419–30.

Klein, Jennie. "Endurance Performance." In *Reading Contemporary Performance: Theatricality across Genres*, edited by Gabrielle Cody and Meiling Cheng, 22–23. New York: Routledge, 2016.

Klein, Jennie. "The Ritual Body as Pedagogical Tool: The Performance Art of the Woman's Building." In *From Site to Vision: The Woman's Building in Contemporary Culture*, edited by Sondra Hale and Terry Wolverton, 172–209. Los Angeles: Otis College of Art and Design, 2011.

Klonsky, E. David. "The Functions of Deliberate Self-Injury: A Review of the Evidence." *Clinical Psychology Review* 27 (2007): 226–39.

Klonsky, E. David, Jennifer J. Muehlenkamp, Stephen P. Lewis, and Barent Walsh. *Nonsuicidal Self-Injury.* Cambridge, MA: Hogrefe Publishing, 2011.

Koehlinger, Amy L. *The New Nuns: Racial Justice and Religious Reform in the 1960s.* Cambridge: Harvard University Press, 2007.

Krause, Elizabeth D., Ruth R. DeRosa, and Susan Roth. "Gender, Trauma Themes, and PTSD." In *Gender and PTSD*, edited by Rachel Kimerling, Paige Ouimette, and Jessica Wolfe, 349–81. New York: Guilford Press, 2002.

Kuhns, Elizabeth. *The Habit: A History of the Clothing of Catholic Nuns.* New York: Doubleday, 2003.

La Capra, Dominick. *Writing History, Writing Trauma.* Baltimore: Johns Hopkins University Press, 2001.

Lang, Colleen M., and Komal Sharma-Patel. "The Relation between Childhood Maltreatment and Self-Injury: A Review of the Literature on Conceptualization and Intervention." *Trauma Violence Abuse* 12, no. 1 (2011): 23–37.

Laub, Dori. "An Event without a Witness: Truth, Testimony, and Survival." In *Testimony: Crises of Witnessing in Literature, Psychoanalysis, and History*, edited by Shoshana Felman and Dori Laub, 75–92. New York: Routledge, 1992.

Lebowitz, Leslie, and Susan Roth. "'I Felt Like a Slut': The Cultural Context and Women's Response to Being Raped." *Journal of Traumatic Stress* 7, no. 3 (1994): 363–90.

Lernoux, Penny, Arthur Jones, and Robert Ellsberg. *Hearts on Fire: The Story of the Maryknoll Sisters.* Maryknoll, NY: Orbis Books, 1993.

Leys, Ruth. *Trauma: A Genealogy.* Chicago: University of Chicago Press, 2000.

Liesegang, Tom. "Perforating Saint: Interview with Ron Athey." *FAD* 30 (1993): 48–49.

Lifton, Robert J. *The Broken Connection: On Death and the Continuity of Life.* New York: Simon & Schuster, 1979.

Lifton, Robert J. "From Hiroshima to the Nazi Doctors: The Evolution of Psychoformative Approaches to Understanding Traumatic Stress Syndromes."

In *International Handbook of Traumatic Stress Syndromes*, edited by John P. Wilson and Beverly Raphael, 11–23. New York: Plenum, 1993.

Lippard, Lucy R. "The Pains and Pleasures of Rebirth: Women's Body Art." In *The Artist's Body*, edited by Tracey Warr, 252–56. New York: Phaidon, 2000.

Lisak, David. "Integrating a Critique of Gender in the Treatment of Male Survivors of Childhood Abuse." *Psychotherapy* 32, no. 2 (Summer 1995): 258–69.

Lisak, David. "Male Gender Socialization and the Perpetration of Sexual Abuse." In *Childhood Socialization*, edited by Gerald Handel, 311–30. New Brunswick. NJ: Aldine Transaction, 2006.

Lisak, David. "Male Survivors of Trauma." In *New Handbook of Psychotherapy and Counseling with Men*, edited by Glenn E. Good and Gary R. Brooks, 147–58. San Francisco: Jossey-Bass, 2005.

Lisak, David. "Men as Victims: Challenging Cultural Myths." *Journal of Traumatic Stress* 6, no. 4 (1993): 577–80.

Lisak, David. "The Psychological Impact of Sexual Abuse: Content Analysis of Interviews with Male Survivors." *Journal of Traumatic Stress* 7, no. 4 (1994): 525–48.

Lisak, David. "Sexual Aggression, Masculinity, and Fathers." *Signs* 16, no. 2 (1991): 238–62.

Lisak, David, Jim Hopper, and Pat Song. "Factors in the Cycle of Violence: Gender Rigidity and Emotional Constriction." *Journal of Traumatic Stress* 9, no. 4 (1996): 721–43.

Lisak, David, and Laura Luster. "Educational, Occupational, and Relationship Histories of Men Who Were Sexually and/or Physically Abused as Children." *Journal of Traumatic Stress* 7, no. 4 (1994): 507–23.

"Loathsome Performances." *New Criterion* 13, no. 1 (September 1994): 1–2.

Loeffler, Carl E., ed. *Performance Anthology: Source Book of California Performance Art*. San Francisco: Last Gasp, 1989.

MacAdams, Lewis. *Blind Date*. Los Angeles: Am Here Books/Immediate Editions, 1981.

MacAdams, Lewis. "It Started Out with Death." *High Performance* 5, no. 3 (Spring–Summer 1982): 43–49.

MacAdams, Lewis. "The Law and the Power." *High Performance* 5, no. 4 (Fall 1982): 35–39.

MacAdams, Lewis. "Sex with the Dead." *Wet* 30 (March–August 1981): 60–61.

Maggi, Armando. "Performing/Annihilating the Word: Body as Erasure in the Visions of a Florentine Mystic." *TDR/The Drama Review* 41, no. 4 (Winter 1997): 110–26.

Malony, H. Newton, and A. Adams Lovekin. *Glossolalia: Behavioral Science Perspectives on Speaking in Tongues*. New York: Oxford University Press, 1985.

Marcus, Greil. *The Shape of Things to Come: Prophecy and the American Voice*. New York: Farrar, Strauss and Giroux, 2006.

Maria del Rey, Sister. *Bernie Becomes a Nun*. New York: Farrar, Straus & Cudahy, 1956.

Marjoe. Directed by Sarah Kernochan and Howard Smith. Emerging Pictures, 1972. New York: Docurama, 2006. DVD.

Mark, Lisa Gabrielle, ed. *Wack! Art and the Feminist Revolution*. Cambridge: MIT Press, 2007.

Marranca, Bonnie, Erik Ehn, Eleanor Heartney, Alison Knowles, Meredith Monk, and Linda Montano. "Art as Spiritual Practice." *PAJ: A Journal of Performance and Art* 24, no. 3 (September 2002): 18–34.

Marsden, George M. *Fundamentalism and American Culture*. 2nd ed. New York: Oxford University Press, 2006.

Marsden, George M. *Jonathan Edwards: A Life*. New Haven: Yale University Press, 2003.

Marsden, P., E. Karagianni, and J. F. Morgan. "Spirituality and Clinical Care in Eating Disorders: A Qualitative Study." *International Journal of Eating Disorders* 40, no. 1 (January 2007): 7–12.

Marsh, Charles. *The Beloved Community: How Faith Shapes Social Justice from the Civil Rights Movement to Today*. New York: Basic Books, 2005.

Martin, David. *Pentecostalism: The World Their Parish*. Malden, MA: Blackwell Publishers, 2002.

Marx, Karl. "Contribution to the Critique of Hegel's Philosophy of Right: Introduction." In *The Marx-Engels Reader*, edited by Robert C. Tucker, 53–65. New York: W. W. Norton, 1978.

Marx, Karl, and Friedrich Engels. *On Religion*. Moscow: Progress Publishers, 1975.

Masson, Jeffrey Moussiaeff. *The Assault on Truth: Freud's Suppression of the Seduction Theory*. New York: Farrar, Straus and Giroux, 1984.

McCarthy, Paul, ed. *Criss Cross Double Cross*. Vol. 1. Los Angeles: Paul McCarthy, 1976.

McClymond, Michael J., ed. *Embodying the Spirit: New Perspectives on North American Revivalism*. Baltimore: Johns Hopkins University Press, 2004.

McEvilley, Thomas. "Art in the Dark." *Artforum* 21, no. 10 (June 1983): 62–71

McGrath, John Edward. "Trusting in Rubber: Performing Boundaries during the AIDS Epidemic." *TDR/The Drama Review* 39, no. 2 (1995): 21–39.

McGrew, Rebecca, and Jennie Klein, eds. *The 21st Century Odyssey, Part II: The Performances of Barbara T. Smith*. Claremont, CA: Pomona College Museum of Art, 2005.

McKanan, Dan. *The Catholic Worker after Dorothy: Practicing the Works of Mercy in a New Generation*. Collegeville, MN: Liturgical Press, 2008.

McKanan, Dan. *Prophetic Encounters: Religion and the American Radical Tradition*. Boston: Beacon Press, 2011.

McPherson, Aimee Semple. "This Is That." In *Encyclopedia of Religious Revival in America*, edited by Michael McClymond, 267–72. Westport, CT: Greenwood Press, 2007.

Mendel, Matthew Parynik. *The Male Survivor: The Impact of Sexual Abuse*. Thousand Oaks, CA: Sage Publications, 1995.

"Mission Woods Death Becomes Murder Case." *Kansas City Star*, September 20, 1977, 1.

Mock, Roberta. "Visions of Xs: Experiencing La Fura dels Baus's 'XXX' and Ron Athey's 'Solar Anus.'" In *Eroticism and Death in Theatre and Performance*, edited by Karoline Gritzner, 178–201. Hatfield, Hertfordshire: University of Hertfordshire Press, 2010.

Montano, Linda. *Anorexia Nervosa*. Artist's film, 1981. Distributed by Video Data Bank, Chicago.

Montano, Linda. *Art in Everyday Life*. Los Angeles: Astro Artz, 1981.

Montano, Linda. "Art/Life Counseling." *High Performance* 4, no. 2 (Summer 1981): 53.

Montano, Linda. "Death in the Art of Life." In *Voices Made Flesh: Performing Women's Autobiography*, edited by Lynn C. Miller, Jacqueline Taylor, and M. Heather Carver, 265–81. Madison: University of Wisconsin Press, 2003.

Montano, Linda. "Letter Number One." In *Franko B: Blinded by Love*, edited by Dominic Johnson, 177. Bologna: Damiani, 2006.

Montano, Linda. "Letter Number Two." In *Franko B: Blinded by Love*, edited by Dominic Johnson. 177. Bologna: Damiani, 2006.

Montano, Linda. "Linda Montano." Bob's Art. http://www.bobsart.org/montano/more/vita.html, accessed June 2007.

Montano, Linda. "Spirituality and Art." *Women Artists' News* 10, no. 3 (Spring 1985): 8.

Montano, Linda, Annie Sprinkle, and Veronica Vera. "Summer Saint Camp 1987: With Annie Sprinkle and Veronica Vera." *TDR/The Drama Review* 33, no. 1 (Spring 1989): 94–103.

Montano, Linda M. "Love Sex: The Ecstatic Writings of Linda M. Montano." Unpublished manuscript, Montano personal archive, 1995.

Montano, Linda M. "1+1=1." *The Act* 1, no. 3 (Winter–Spring 1988–89): 44–48.

Montano, Linda M., ed. *Performance Artists Talking in the Eighties*. Berkeley: University of California Press, 2000.

Montano, Linda M. "Roman Catholic Performance Artist Manifesto: An Email Sent to Pope Benedict," posted December 8, 2009, *Linda Mary Montano* (blog). http://lindamarymontano.blogspot.com/2009/12/roman-catholic-performance-artist_08.html

Montano, Linda M., and Jennie Klein, eds. *Letters from Linda M. Montano*. New York: Routledge, 2005.

Moore, R. Laurence. *Religious Outsiders and the Making of Americans*. New York: Oxford University Press, 1986.

Moorhead, James H. "Presbyterianism." In *Encyclopedia of Politics and Religion*, edited by Robert Wuthnow, 724–28. Washington, DC: CQ Press, 2007.

Moorhead, James H. "Redefining Confessionalism: American Presbyterians in the Twentieth Century." In *The Confessional Mosaic: Presbyterians and Twentieth-Century Theology*, edited by Milton J. Coalter, John M. Mulder, and Louis B. Weeks, 59–83. Louisville: Westminster/John Knox Press, 1990.

Morgan, David. *Protestants and Pictures: Religion, Visual Culture, and the Age of American Mass Production*. New York: Oxford University Press, 1999.

Morgan, David. *The Sacred Gaze: Religious Visual Culture in Theory and Practice*. Berkeley: University of California Press, 2005.

Morgan, David. "Spirit and Medium: The Video Art of Bill Viola." *Image* 26 (Spring 2000): 29–39.

Morgan, David. *Visual Piety: A History and Theory of Popular Religious Images.* Berkeley: University of California Press, 1998.

Morgan, David, and James Elkins, eds. *Re-Enchantment.* New York: Routledge, 2009.

Morgan, David, and Sally Promey. *Exhibiting the Visual Culture of American Religions.* Valparaiso, IN: Valparaiso University Press, 2000.

Morgan, J. F., P. Marsden, and J. H. Lacey. "'Spiritual Starvation?' A Case Series Concerning Christianity and Eating Disorders." *International Journal of Eating Disorders* 28, no. 4 (December 2000): 476–80.

Morrill, Bruce T., Joanna E. Ziegler, and Susan Rodgers, eds. *Practicing Catholic: Ritual, Body, and Contestation in Catholic Faith.* New York: Palgrave Macmillan, 2006.

Munroe, Alexandra. *The Third Mind: American Artists Contemplate Asia, 1860 to 1989.* New York: Guggenheim, 2009.

Murphy, Andrew R. *Prodigal Nation: Moral Decline and Divine Punishment from New England to 9/11.* New York: Oxford University Press, 2009.

Murphy, Andrew R., and Jennifer Miller. "The Enduring Power of the American Jeremiad." In *Religion, Politics, and Religious Identity: New Directions, New Controversies,* edited by David S. Gutterman and Andrew R. Murphy, 49–72. New York: Lexington Books, 2006.

Myers, Julie. "An Interview with Ron Athey." *TheatreForum* 6 (Winter–Spring 1995): 60–65.

Nelson, Robert, and Richard Shiff, eds. *Critical Terms for Art History.* Chicago: University of Chicago Press, 2003.

"Neo-orthodoxy Goes to Kindergarten." *Religion in Life* 20, no. 1 (Winter 1950–51): 3–20.

Nepstad, Sharon Erickson. *Religion and War Resistance in the Plowshares Movement.* Cambridge: Cambridge University Press, 2008.

O'Dell, Kathy. *Contract with the Skin: Masochism, Performance Art, and the 1970s.* Minneapolis: University of Minnesota Press, 1998.

O'Hara, Morgan, and Susan Hewitt. "Formal Records of the Use of Time and Movement through Space: A Conceptual and Visual Series of Artworks." *Leonardo* 16, no. 4 (1983): 265–72.

Orsi, Robert A. *Between Heaven and Earth: The Religious Worlds People Make and the Scholars Who Study Them.* Princeton: Princeton University Press, 2005.

Orsi, Robert A. *The Madonna of 115th Street: Faith and Community in Italian Harlem, 1880–1950.* New Haven: Yale University Press, 1985.

Orsi, Robert A. *Thank You, St. Jude: Women's Devotion to the Patron Saint of Hopeless Causes.* New Haven: Yale University Press, 1996.

Osteroff, Roberta. "The Old Evangelism: Hard-Sell Salvation." *Los Angeles Times,* September 19, 1971, A9.

O'Toole, James M., ed. *Habits of Devotion: Catholic Religious Practice in the United States.* Ithaca: Cornell University Press, 2004.

Parker, Theodore. "Justice and the Conscience." In *Ten Sermons on Religion,* 66–101. Boston: Crosby, Nichols, 1853.

Peralta, Steve. "John Duncan." *Neo-Aztlan,* 2007. http://www.neoaztlan.com/issue-three/art/john-duncan/, accessed September 16, 2008.

Phelan, Peggy, ed. *Live in L.A.: Performance in Southern California.* New York: Routledge, 2012.

Phelan, Peggy. *Unmarked: The Politics of Performance.* New York: Routledge, 1993.

Piehl, Mel, and Peter Maurin. *Breaking Bread: The Catholic Worker and the Origin of Catholic Radicalism in America.* Philadelphia Temple University Press, 1982.

Pilkington, Ed. "Obama Angers Midwest Voters with Guns and Religion Remark." *Guardian,* April 14, 2008.

Pollack, Barbara. "The Elephant in the Room." *ARTnews* 103, no. 8 (September 2004): 118–19.

Pollock, Griselda, ed. *Visual Politics of Psychoanalysis: Art and Image in Posttraumatic Cultures.* London: I. B. Tauris, 2013.

Poloma, Margaret M. *Main Street Mystics: The Toronto Blessing and Reviving Pentecostalism.* New York: Altamira Press, 2003.

Powers, Charles T. "Rev. A. A. Allen: He Shakes, Sways Hallelujah Trail." *Los Angeles Times,* March 8, 1970, A1.

Presbyterian Church in the U.S. General Assembly. *The Confession of Faith of the Presbyterian Church in the United States.* Richmond, VA: Board of Christian Education, 1965.

Princenthal, Nancy. "Whither the Whitney Biennial?" *Art in America* 90, no. 6 (June 2002): 49–53.

Prothero, Stephen. *American Jesus: How the Son of God Became a National Icon.* New York: Farrar, Straus and Giroux, 2003.

Queen, Edward L., II. "Neoorthodoxy." In *Encyclopedia of American Religious History,* edited by Stephen R. Prothero and Gardiner H. Shattuck Jr., 496–99. New York: Facts on File, 2001.

Quinonez, Lora Ann, and Mary Daniel Turner. *The Transformation of American Catholic Sisters.* Philadelphia: Temple University Press, 1992.

Rampling, David. "Ascetic Ideals and Anorexia Nervosa." *Journal of Psychiatric Research* 19, nos. 2–3 (1985): 89–94.

Raskin, David. "Specific Opposition: Judd's Art and Politics." *Art History* 24, no. 5 (November 2001): 682–706.

Reust, Hans Rudolf. "Christian Jankowski: Museum für Gegenwartkunst." *Artforum* 42, no. 7 (Mar 2004): 192–3.

Ricci, Massimo. "John Duncan." *Paris Transatlantic,* January 2005. http://www.paristransatlantic.com/magazine/interviews/duncan.html, accessed July 10, 2009.

Richey, Russell E. "Revivalism: In Search of a Definition." *Wesleyan Theological Journal* 28, nos. 1–2 (Spring–Fall 1993): 165–75.

Robeck, C. M., Jr. "Prophecy, Gift Of." In *The New International Dictionary of Pentecostal and Charismatic Movements,* edited by Stanley M. Burgess and Eduard M. van der Maas, 998–1012. Grand Rapids, MI: Zondervan, 2003.

Roberts, Oral. "Oral Roberts's Life Story." In *Encyclopedia of Religious Revival in America,* edited by Michael McClymond, 298–303. Westport, CT: Greenwood Press, 2007.

Robinson, Hilary. "God! I Love Time: An Interview with Linda Montano." *n.paradoxa* 5 (January 2000): 63–70.

Román, David. "Solo Performance and the Body on Stage." In *Acts of Intervention: Performance, Gay Culture, and AIDS*, 116–53. Bloomington: Indiana University Press, 1998.

Rosenfeld, Kathryn. "S/M Chic and the New Morality." *New Art Examiner* 28, no. 4 (December 2000–January 2001): 27–31.

Rossinow, Douglas C. *The Politics of Authenticity: Liberalism, Christianity, and the New Left in America*. New York: Columbia University Press, 1998.

Roth, Moira. *The Amazing Decade: Women and Performance Art in America*. Los Angeles: Astro Artz, 1983.

Roth, Moira. "Matters of Life and Death: Linda Montano Interviewed by Moira Roth." *High Performance* 1, no. 4 (Winter 1978): 2–7.

Roth, Moira. "Toward a History of California Performance, Part One." *Arts* 52, no. 2 (February 1978): 94–103.

Roth, Moira. "Visions and Re-visions: A Conversation with Suzanne Lacy." *Artforum*, November 1980, 42–45.

Roth, Susan, and Ronald Batson. *Naming the Shadows: A New Approach to Individual and Group Psychotherapy for Adult Survivors of Childhood Incest*. New York: Free Press, 1997.

Roth, Susan, and Leslie Lebowitz. "The Experience of Sexual Trauma." *Journal of Traumatic Stress* 1, no. 1 (1988): 79–107.

Roth, Susan, and Elana Newman. "The Process of Coping with Sexual Trauma." *Journal of Traumatic Stress* 4, no. 2 (1991): 279–97.

Salter, Anna C. *Transforming Trauma: A Guide to Understanding and Treating Adult Survivors of Child Sexual Abuse*. Thousand Oaks, CA: Sage Publications, 1995.

Saukko, Paula. *The Anorexic Self: A Personal, Political Analysis of a Diagnostic Discourse*. Albany: State University of New York Press, 2008.

Scarry, Elaine. *The Body in Pain*. New York: Oxford University Press, 1985.

Schimmel, Paul, ed. *Out of Actions: Between Performance and the Object, 1949–1979*. Los Angeles: Los Angeles Museum of Contemporary Art, 1998.

Schneider, Rebecca. *The Explicit Body in Performance*. New York: Routledge, 1997.

Schneider, Rebecca. *Performing Remains: Art and War in Times of Theatrical Reenactment*. New York: Routledge, 2011.

Scott, Ann. "Trauma, Skin: Memory, Speech." In *Memory in Dispute*, edited by Valerie Sinason, 42–50. London: Karnac Books, 1998.

Selzer, Mark. "Wound Culture: Trauma in the Pathological Public Sphere." *October* 80 (Spring 1997): 3–27.

Shank, Theodore. "'Mitchell's Death': Linda Montano's Autobiographical Performance." *TDR/The Drama Review* 23, no. 1 (March 1979): 43–48.

Sharf, Robert H. "Experience." In *Critical Terms for Religious Studies*, edited by Mark C. Taylor, 94–116. Chicago: University of Chicago Press, 1998.

Shattuck, Gardiner H., Jr. "Presbyterian Church (U.S.A.)." In *Encyclopedia of American Religious History*, edited by Edward L. Queen II, Stephen R. Prothero, and Gardiner H. Shattuck Jr., 571–73. New York: Facts on File, 2001.

Shattuck, Gardiner H., Jr. "The Reformed Tradition." In *Encyclopedia of American Religious History*, edited by Edward L. Queen II, Stephen R. Prothero, and Gardiner H. Shattuck Jr., 598–600. New York: Facts on File, 2001.

Shaw, Gwendolyn DuBois. *Seeing the Unspeakable: The Art of Kara Walker*. Durham: Duke University Press, 2004.

Shulman, George M. *American Prophecy: Race and Redemption in American Political Culture*. Minneapolis: University of Minnesota Press, 2008.

Slosberg, Steven. "Robertson's 20-Year Vigil for Peace." *The Day*, October 5, 2006.

Smith, Gary Scott. *The Seeds of Secularization*. Grand Rapids, MI: Christian University Press, 1985.

Smith, Jonathan Z. "Religion, Religions, Religious." In *Critical Terms for Religious Studies*, edited by Mark C. Taylor, 269–84. Chicago: University of Chicago Press, 1998.

Spencer, Duane E. *Tulip: The Five Points of Calvinism in the Light of Scripture*. Grand Rapids, MI: Baker Books, 1979.

St. Augustine. *Concerning the City of God, against the Pagans*. New York: Penguin Putnam, 2003.

St. Marguerite Marie Alacoque. *The Autobiography of St. Marguerite Marie Alacoque*. Translated by the Sisters of the Visitation. Rockford, IL: Tan Books, 1986.

St. Thérèse of Lisieux. *Story of a Soul: The Autobiography of St. Thérèse of Lisieux, a New Translation from the Original Manuscripts*. Translated by John Clarke. Washington, DC: ICS Publications, 1996.

Steele, Thomas J., and Eugene R. Delay. "Vertigo in History: The Threatening Tactility of 'Sinners in the Hands.'" *Early American Literature* 18, no. 3 (Winter 1983–84): 242–56.

Stefani, Giuliana. "Ideas on 'Blind Date': Interview with John Duncan." Unpublished document, Duncan personal archive, 1997.

Steger, Lawrence. "Lawrence Steger Interviews Ron Athey." *Dialogue* 17, no. 5 (September–October 1994): 8–9.

Stewart, Don. *Only Believe: An Eyewitness Account of the Great Healing Revivals of the 20th Century*. Shippensburg, PA: Revival Press, 1999.

Stiles, Kristine. "Afterword: Quicksilver and Revelations; Performance at the End of the 20th Century." In *Performance Artists Talking in the Eighties*, edited by Linda Montano, 473–92. Berkeley: University of California Press, 2000.

Stiles, Kristine. *AmaLIA perjovschi*. Bucharest: Soros Center of Contemporary Art, 1996.

Stiles, Kristine. "Barbara Turner Smith's Haunting." In *The 21st Century Odyssey, Part II: The Performances of Barbara T. Smith*, edited by Rebecca McGrew and Jennie Klein, 37–50. Claremont, CA: Pomona College Museum of Art, 2005.

Stiles, Kristine. "Burden of Light." In *Chris Burden*, edited by Paul Schimmel, 22–37. Newcastle: Merrel and Locus Plus, 2007.

Stiles, Kristine. "Cloud without Its Shadow: Marina Abramović." In *Marina Abramović*, edited by Marina Abramović, Kristine Stiles, Klaus Biesenbach and Chrissie Iles, 33–94. New York: Phaidon, 2008.

Stiles, Kristine. *Concerning Consequences: Studies in Art, Destruction, and Trauma*. Chicago: University of Chicago Press, 2016.

Stiles, Kristine. "I/Eye/Oculus: Performance, Installation, Video." In *Themes in*

Contemporary Art, edited by Gill Perry and Paul Woods, 183–229. New Haven: Yale University Press, 2004.

Stiles, Kristine. "Never Enough Is Something Else: Feminist Performance Art, Probity, and the Avant-Garde." In *Contours of the Theatrical Avant-Garde: Performance and Textuality*, edited by James M. Harding, 239–89. Madison: University of Wisconsin Press, 2000.

Stiles, Kristine. "Notes on Rudolf Schwartzkogler's Images of Healing." *Whitewalls* 25 (Spring 1990): 10–26.

Stiles, Kristine. "1.1.78–2.2.78: Roberta Breitmore." In *Roberta Breitmore Is Not Lynn Hershman*, 5–14. San Francisco: De Young Memorial Museum, 1978.

Stiles, Kristine. "Performance." In *Critical Terms for Art History*, edited by Robert Nelson and Richard Shiff, 75–97. Chicago: University of Chicago Press, 2003.

Stiles, Kristine. "Performance Art and the Experiential Present: Irregular Ways of Being." In *The Third Mind: American Artists Contemplate Asia*, edited by Alexandra Munroe, 332–75. New York: Guggenheim Museum, 2009.

Stiles, Kristine. *Raphael Montañez Ortiz: Years of the Warrior, Years of the Psyche, 1968–1988*. New York: El Museo del Barrio, 1988.

Stiles, Kristine. "Return to Double: Revisiting Roberta Breitmore." In Kristine Stiles, *Concerning Consequences: Studies in Art, Destruction, and Trauma*. Chicago: University of Chicago Press, 2016.

Stiles, Kristine. "Shaved Heads and Marked Bodies: Representations from Cultures of Trauma." *Strategie II: Peuples Mediterraneens*, nos. 64–65 (July–December 1993): 95–117.

Stiles, Kristine. "Shaved Heads and Marked Bodies: Representations from Cultures of Trauma; Afterword." In *Talking Gender: Public Images, Personal Journeys, and Political Critiques*, edited by Jean O'Barr, Nancy Hewitt, and Nancy Rosebaugh, 36–64. Chapel Hill: University of North Carolina Press, 1996.

Stiles, Kristine. "Teaching a Dead Hand to Draw." In *Kim Jones: A Retrospective*, 45–84. Cambridge: MIT Press, 2007.

Stiles, Kristine. "Uncorrupted Joy: International Art Actions." In *Out of Actions: Between Performance and the Object, 1949–1979*, edited by Paul Schimmel, 226–328. Los Angeles: Los Angeles Museum of Contemporary Art, 1998.

Stiles, Kristine. "Wangechi Mutu's Family Tree." In *Wangechi Mutu: A Fantastic Journey*, edited by Trevor Schoonmaker, 51–79. Durham: Nasher Museum of Art, Duke University, 2013.

Stiles, Kristine, and Peter Selz, eds. *Theories and Documents of Contemporary Art: A Sourcebook of Artists' Writings*. Berkeley: University of California Press, 1996.

Stoever, William K. B. "The Calvinist Theological Tradition." In *Encyclopedia of the American Religious Experience*, edited by Charles Lippy and P. W. Williams, 1039–56. New York Charles Scribner's Sons, 1988.

Synan, Vinson. *The Century of the Holy Spirit: 100 Years of Pentecostal and Charismatic Renewal, 1901–2001*. Nashville: Thomas Nelson, 2001.

Synan, Vinson. *The Holiness-Pentecostal Tradition*. Grand Rapids, MI: William B. Eerdmans, 1997.

Taft, Catherine. "Wolfgang Stoerchle." In *California Video: Artists and Histories*, edited by Glenn Phillips, 214. Los Angeles: Getty Research Institute, 2008.

Taves, Ann. *Fits, Trances, and Visions: Experiencing Religion and Explaining Experience from Wesley to James.* Princeton: Princeton University Press, 1999.

Taylor, Mark C. *After God.* Chicago: University of Chicago Press, 2009.

Taylor, Mark C., ed. *Critical Terms for Religious Studies.* Chicago: University of Chicago Press, 1998.

Taylor, Mark C. *Disfiguring: Art, Architecture, Religion.* Chicago: University of Chicago Press, 1992.

Taylor, Mark C. *Hiding.* Chicago: University of Chicago Press, 1997.

Terr, Lenore. *Unchained Memories: True Stories of Traumatic Memories, Lost and Found.* New York: Basic Books, 1994.

Thrapp, Dan L. "Miss Kuhlman: Preacher Sways Throngs with Healing Service." *Los Angeles Times*, February 16, 1970, A1.

Thurman, Suzanne R. "The Medical Mission Strategy of the Maryknoll Sisters." *Missiology* 30, no. 3 (July 2002): 361–73.

Tipson, Baird. "Calvinist Heritage." In *Encyclopedia of the American Religious Experience*, edited by Charles Lippy and P. W. Williams, 451–66. New York: Charles Scribner's Sons, 1988.

Townsend, Tess. "Christmas Vigil a Show of Solidarity for Peace." *The Day*, December 25, 2014.

Tuchman, Maurice, ed. *The Spiritual in Art: Abstract Painting, 1890–1985.* New York: Abbeville Press, 1986.

Turley, Stephen Richard. "Awakened to the Holy: 'Sinners in the Hands of an Angry God' in Ritualized Context." *Christianity and Literature* 57, no. 4 (Summer 2008): 507–30.

Tweed, Thomas A. *Crossing and Dwelling: A Theory of Religion.* Cambridge: Harvard University Press, 2006.

Tweed, Thomas A. *Our Lady of the Exile: Diasporic Religion at a Cuban Catholic Shrine in Miami.* New York: Oxford University Press, 1997.

Ukeles, Mierle Laderman. "Touch Sanitation." In *Issue: Social Strategies by Women Artists, an Exhibition*, edited by Lucy Lippard, n.p. London: Institute of Contemporary Arts, 1980.

Van Alphen, Ernest. *Caught by History: Holocaust Effects in Contemporary Art, Literature, and Theory.* Stanford: Stanford University Press, 1997.

Van der Kolk, Bessel A., ed. *Post-traumatic Stress Disorder: Psychological and Biological Sequelae.* Washington, DC: American Psychiatric Press, 1984.

Van der Kolk, Bessel A. *Psychological Trauma.* Washington, DC: American Psychiatric Press, 1987.

Van der Kolk, Bessel A., ed. *Traumatic Stress: The Effects of Overwhelming Experience on Mind, Body, and Society.* New York: Guilford Press, 1996.

Van der Kolk, Bessel A., J. Christopher Perry, and Judith Lewis Herman. "Childhood Origins of Self-Destructive Behavior." *American Journal of Psychiatry* 148, no. 12 (December 1991): 1665–71.

Vauchez, André. *Sainthood in the Later Middle Ages.* Translated by Jean Birrell. New York: Cambridge University Press, 1997.

Vergine, Lea. *Body Art and Performance: The Body as Language.* New York: Abbeville Press, 2000.

Voskuil, Dennis N. "Neo-Orthodoxy." In *Encyclopedia of the American Religious*

Experience: Studies of Traditions and Movements, edited by Charles Lippy and P. W. Williams, 1147–57. New York: Charles Scribner's Sons, 1988.

Wacker, Grant A. *Heaven Below: Early Pentecostals and American Culture*. Cambridge: Harvard University Press, 2001.

Wacker, Grant A. "The Pentecostal Tradition." In *Caring and Curing: Health and Medicine in the Western Religious Traditions*, edited by Ronald L. Numbers and Darrel W. Amundsen, 514–38. Baltimore: Johns Hopkins University Press, 1986.

Wacker, Grant A. "Pentecostalism." In *Encyclopedia of the American Religious Experience: Studies of Traditions and Movements*, edited by Charles Lippy and P. W. Williams, 933–45. New York: Charles Scribner's Sons, 1988.

Wacker, Grant A. "Travail of a Broken Family: Radical Evangelical Responses to the Emergence of Pentecostalism in America, 1906–16." In *Pentecostal Currents in American Protestantism*, edited by Edith L. Blumhofer, Russell P. Spittler, and Grant A. Wacker, 23–49. Chicago: University of Illinois Press, 1999.

Wagner, Benjamin. "Bodily Manifestations in Revivals." In *Encyclopedia of Religious Revivals in America*, edited by Michael McClymond, 55–57. Westport, CT: Greenwood Press, 2007.

Wagner, Benjamin. "Fasting and Revivals." In *Encyclopedia of Religious Revivals in America*, edited by Michael McClymond, 166–68. Westport, CT: Greenwood Press, 2007.

Walsh, Fintan. *Male Trouble: Masculinity and the Performance of Crisis*. Basingstoke: Palgrave Macmillan, 2010.

Ward, Frazer. *No Innocent Bystanders: Performance Art and Audience*. Lebanon, NH: Dartmouth College Press, 2012.

Warner, Michael. "Tongues Untied: Memoirs of a Pentecostal Boyhood." In *Curiouser: On the Queerness of Children*, edited by Steven Bruhm and Natasha Hurley, 215–24. Minneapolis: University of Minnesota Press, 2004.

Warner, Wayne E. *Kathryn Kuhlman: The Woman behind the Miracles*. Ann Arbor, MI: Servant Publications, 1993.

Warr, Tracey. *The Artist's Body: Themes and Movements*. London: Phaidon, 2000.

Weber, Max. *'The Protestant Ethic' and the 'Spirit of Capitalism' and Other Writings*. New York: Penguin Classics, 2002.

Weber, Max. *The Sociology of Religion*. Translated by Ephraim Fischoff. Boston: Beacon Press, [1922] 1963.

Weeks, Louis B. "Presbyterianism." In *Encyclopedia of the American Religious Experience*, edited by Charles Lippy and P. W. Williams. 499–510. New York: Charles Scribner's Sons, 1988.

Wells, David F., ed. *Reformed Theology in America*. Grand Rapids, MI: Baker Books, 1997.

West, Cornel, and Christa Buschendorf, eds. *Black Prophetic Fire*. Boston: Beacon Press, 2014.

Wiederman, Michael W. "Women, Sex, and Food: A Review of Research on Eating Disorders and Sexuality." *Journal of Sex Research* 33, no. 4 (1996): 301–11.

Williams, J. R. "Baptism in the Holy Spirit." In *The New International Dictionary of Pentecostal and Charismatic Movements*, edited by Stanley M. Burgess and Eduard M. van der Maas, 354–63. Grand Rapids, MI: Zondervan, 2003.

Williams, J. R. "Laying on of Hands." In *The New International Dictionary of Pentecostal and Charismatic Movements*, edited by Stanley M. Burgess and Eduard M. van der Maas, 834–36. Grand Rapids, MI: Zondervan, 2003.

Williams, Paul. "Twenty-First-Century Jeremiad: Contemporary Hip-Hop and American Tradition." *European Journal of American Culture* 27, no. 2 (2008): 111–32.

Wilmore, Gayraud S. *Black Religion and Black Radicalism: An Interpretation of the Religious History of African Americans*. Maryknoll, NY: Orbis Books, 1998.

Wilson, D. J. "Kulman, Kathryn." In *The New International Dictionary of Pentecostal and Charismatic Movements*, edited by Stanley M. Burgess and Eduard M. van der Maas, 826–27. Grand Rapids, MI: Zondervan, 2003.

Wilson, John P., and Beverley Raphael. *New International Handbook of Traumatic Stress Syndromes*. New York: Plenum Press, 1993.

Wilson-Hartgrove, Jonathan. *New Monasticism: What It Has to Say to Today's Church*. Grand Rapids, MI: Brazos, 2008.

Wilson-Hartgrove, Jonathan. *School(s) for Conversion: 12 Marks of a New Monasticism*. Eugene, OR: Cascade, 2005.

Wlassoff, Boris. "John Duncan." *Revue & Corrigée* 51 (March 2002). Reprinted under "Bio and Press" at the website for John Duncan, http://johnduncan.org/wlassoff.rc1.html, accessed July 10, 2009.

Wuthnow, Robert. *The Restructuring of American Religion: Society and Faith since World War II*. Princeton: Princeton University Press, 1988.

Young, Alison. *Judging the Image: Art, Value, Law*. New York: Routledge, 2005.

Young, James E. *The Texture of Memory: Holocaust Memorials and Meaning*. New Haven: Yale University Press, 1995.

Index

Note: Page numbers in italics refer to figures.